ELI MANNING

ELI MANNING

The Making of a Quarterback

RALPH VACCHIANO

FOREWORD BY ERNIE ACCORSI

SPORTS
PUBLISHING

Visit our website at www.sportspubbooks.com

Library of Congress Cataloging-in-Publication Data
Vacchiano, Ralph.
Eli Manning: The making of a quarterback / by Ralph Vacchiano; foreword by
Ernie Accorsi.—1st ed.
p. cm.
Includes index.
ISBN 978-1-61321-238-7 (alk. paper)
1. Manning, Eli, 1981 2. Football players—New York (State)—Biography.
3. New York Giants (Football team)—Biography. I. Title.
GV939.M2887V33 2008
796.332'092—dc22
[B]
2008022481

10 9 8 7 6 5 4 3 2 1

Printed in the United States of America

For my girls,
Kara and Alexandra

Contents

CONTENTS

Foreword

IT ALL STARTED for me—this doctrine, which would shape my football career, that the quarterback is the most important player in professional sports—without me really knowing it.

It started in 1951, on a black-and-white round screen Motorola television, watching the Cleveland Browns, led by Otto Graham, against the Detroit Lions, led by Bobby Layne. The Browns and Lions were the powers in the early days of televised football. They met in the NFL Championship Game in 1952 and 1953. I was twelve years old in 1953, and I knew then that the Lions won them both because Layne played better than Graham. Maybe not in every game over his career—they are both in the Pro Football Hall of Fame—but Layne played better in those two games. I knew it when Layne hit Jim Doran with a game-winning touchdown pass in the final minutes of the '53 championship game.

And when Eli Manning threw the Super Bowl–winning touchdown pass to Plaxico Burress to win Super Bowl XLII, it was only the third time a touchdown pass in the final minutes ever won a championship: Layne to Doran in 1953, Joe Montana to John Taylor in 1989, and Manning to Burress in 2008.

As the years passed, and as rooting for the Baltimore Colts every Sunday began to dominate my teenage life, I watched Layne continue to beat my team and I understood the fear of having your team facing a great quarterback. Then *my* team got a great one.

In fact, my team—the Colts—got the greatest of all-time: Johnny Unitas.

Rooting for Unitas as a kid, then joining the Baltimore Colts organization at age twenty-eight, laid the foundation for and shaped my core beliefs about professional football: To be a great team, you had to have a great quarterback. You couldn't ever be better as a team than your quarterback. I faced them and I had them, first as a fan and then as an NFL guy. I knew what they meant. I remember when we traded for the supplemental draft pick that enabled the Browns to acquire Bernie Kosar in Cleveland in 1985, and Hank Peters—a dear friend and the president of the Cleveland Indians at that time—asked me, "What's the fuss?" I said, "Hank, how would you like to have Jim Palmer pitch every day?"

In 1970, the first summer of my career in the NFL, the Colts trained in Golden, Colorado for three weeks, preparing to play pre-season games on the West Coast. A short players' strike had delayed the start of training camp in Westminster, Maryland, so I left to advance the club out West (my job) before practice started. I had spent the previous two seasons—1968 and 1969—covering the Philadelphia 76ers for the *Philadelphia Inquirer* and working at Penn State, and I'd seen little of the Colts in person or even on TV.

So as the Colts began their first practices in Golden, I was standing on the field with a man who would become a lifelong close friend, Milt Davis. Milt was a Colts' scout, had a PhD, and was a star defensive corner for the Colts who played in the 1958 and 1959 NFL Championship Games. I was stunned at the diminished power in Unitas's arm. It's now fashionable among some of the uneducated pundits to say he didn't have a laser arm. Nonsense. In his prime he had a rocket for an arm. Sam Huff told me that in the '58 championship game he kept hearing Unitas's passes whistling by his ear.

But something had changed. Two years earlier, in the preseason of '68, he injured his throwing elbow. Many of the fine tendons just gave way from wear and tear—not only the result of thirteen years of passing the football, but from the countless hours of throwing to Raymond Berry long after practices had ended. Everyone knew that. I just hadn't yet seen the results of the injury up close.

I turned to Milt and said, "Milt, he can't throw like he used to. Can we win with him throwing like that?"

Milt, quite fatherly, turned to this brash rookie employee, put his hand on my shoulder and said: "Ernie, listen to me. You evaluate the great quarterbacks on one element alone: Can they take their team down the field, with the championship on the line, and into the end zone? That's how you evaluate a great quarterback."

That, Unitas could still do. We won the Super Bowl that season.

I had learned my first lesson about quarterbacks from a master scout. Those words created a doctrine for me and articulated what I had seen on that little television in 1952 when Graham and Layne battled each other. From there, my philosophy only grew. I said then that my definition of leadership was watching Unitas get on the bus. I knew we always had a chance because he was on our side. When we lost Unitas, we got Bert Jones, who would have a bust in Canton, too, if it weren't for a shoulder injury that was never repaired—and possibly, at least in my opinion, never correctly diagnosed. No one who ever played this game had more talent than Jones or a more fierce desire to win. When he left, I drafted John Elway despite a national protest. When the owner of the Colts traded him away against my wishes, I left my boyhood team.

I went to Cleveland, took one look at their pitching staff, and knew we weren't going anywhere. In 1985, I pulled off a trade—forcing the league to change the rules on trading supplemental draft choices—to acquire Bernie Kosar, who took the Browns to five

straight playoffs, four divisional titles, and three AFC championship games. Kosar would have been in two Super Bowls, and possibly three, with any play from our defense in those title games.

We didn't necessarily have the best talent in the AFC Central
during those five years; but we had the best quarterback.

When I became the general manager of the Giants, I inherited
quarterbacks Danny Kanell and Dave Brown. My first official
transaction as general manager was to waive Brown. I had seen
enough of his play while I was the assistant general manager to
know we weren't going anywhere with him. Kanell had played his
heart out in '97 and won the division. I picked up Kent Graham as
his backup. I loved Danny, but Graham eventually replaced him,
and I knew that this wasn't going to work unless we got someone
under center who could make a difference. That's when I made
another quarterback move that attracted a loud protest—signing
Kerry Collins. Kanell, a great kid, didn't say a thing, but Graham
criticized me in print. My reaction to those remarks: "I've been with
Johnny Unitas, Earl Morrall, Bert Jones, and Bernie Kosar. Do you
think I care what Kent Graham thinks?"

I knew each quarterback move made us better and that Collins
gave us a chance. He played admirably and quarterbacked the
Giants to the Super Bowl. We gave him a chance and he rewarded
us. But after Super Bowl XXXV, I had growing doubts that we
could play for championships consistently unless we reached for
greatness at that position.

Late in the 2002 season, we began to hear rumors that Eli
Manning of the University of Mississippi might declare for the
NFL Draft following his junior season. Our player personnel director and current Giants general manager, Jerry Reese, and I talked
about it. Jerry said, "Ernie, I don't know if he's coming out or not,
but you better go see him in person." So I did. What I saw that

bitterly cold day in Oxford, Mississippi is detailed in the pages of this book. I had to sit outside and almost froze to death. Before the game, I went to the field and watched him throw through the gray cold of November. The power and arm strength were there. Then I took my seat and watched him lead a vastly inferior Mississippi team against powerful Auburn. Manning kept leading his team to scores, staying close, then finally I watched him put his team ahead late in the game. I kept hearing Milt Davis's words: "Ernie, can the quarterback take the team down the field and into the end zone?"

Yes, he could.

Auburn regained the lead and was still up by a touchdown late in the fourth quarter. Now, with time running out, here came Manning again. This time it ended with an interception in the end zone. No one else on his team made it in the NFL. He was trying to do it all by himself, and he tried to force his team into the end zone when he was finally picked off. He was all over the field. Never chastised a teammate or gestured when the player dropped the ball or ran the wrong pattern. I had seen all I needed to see.

There were other quarterbacks in that 2004 draft. We especially liked Ben Roethlisberger, whom we would have drafted had we not been able to make the trade for Manning. But Eli was the one we wanted. And it wasn't any personal obsession of mine. Everyone involved in the Giants' decision making process felt the same way.

I was standing in the New Orleans Saints' indoor practice facility at Eli's workout shortly before the draft. His brother Peyton was there. His father, Archie, wasn't. I asked Peyton, "Where is your dad?" Peyton told me, "He's driving around the parking lot. He's too nervous to watch."

Eli had already wowed his audience of NFL scouts. I said, "Peyton, call him on your cell phone. Tell him it's OK to come in now. Eli's throwing lasers all over this field."

I left New Orleans feeling quite down. I didn't think we were going to be able to get him. I felt it would be a long, uphill battle to pull off that trade. But somehow we did it. I was showered with criticism. It never bothered me at all.

Make a list of the championship quarterbacks since the T formation came into the National Football League. You essentially have the Hall of Fame. Sure, you can bring up the '63 Bears with Billy Wade. But if Y. A. Tittle—a Hall of Famer—isn't injured, the Giants (who lost 14–10) win the game. And furthermore, how many more titles did the Bears win after that? You can bring up the 2000 Ravens with Trent Dilfer. Did they win again? In fact, within a year they got rid of Dilfer.

If you want to be a consistent championship contender, you need a great quarterback. I know what it's like to face one as a fan (Layne, Starr, Namath) and as an NFL employee (Griese, Stabler, Elway). And I know what it's like to have one on my team (Unitas, Jones, Kosar, and Manning). Quarterback ratings—they really aren't quarterback ratings, they're passer ratings—are for people who don't know how to evaluate a quarterback.

I only care about championships.

There never was any doubt in my mind about Eli Manning. And there is no doubt in my mind that he will win many more championships for the Giants franchise.

When I made the trade for Manning, I received a lot of mail that was extremely critical. One of the most significant was from the father of a media friend who was a lifelong Giants fan. "You don't understand the Giants' tradition of defense," he wrote. "We win championships on defense. Not with quarterbacks. This was a big mistake."

I was very respectful in my reply. I wrote: "You won the NFL championship in 1956 because Charlie Conerly was better than Ed

Brown (the Bears quarterback). You won in '86 because Simms had the greatest day a quarterback ever had in an NFL championship game.

"However, in 1958 and 1959, you had the best defense in the NFL. You had Hall of Famers Andy Robustelli, Sam Huff, and Emlen Tunnell on defense. And you also had great players like Rosey Grier, Jim Katcavage, Dick Modzelewski, and Jimmy Patton.

"And, you know what happened? The great quarterback—Unitas—shredded them both times. I rest my case."

That's why we traded for Eli Manning.

—*Ernie Accorsi*
April 2008

ELI MANNING

One: "He did what we drafted him to do"

HE HAD SPENT the last four weeks on a scouting trip of sorts, moving from camp to camp, eyeing every elite athlete he could find, looking for that next golden arm. He watched their arm angles and their deliveries. He tried to gauge the zip on their throws, their accuracy, their field presence. He took mental notes at every stop, watched as many games as he could get to, and in all put almost 5,000 miles on his car.

When the scouting trip was over, Ernie Accorsi drove alone back up Interstate 95 toward his Manhattan home with a cigar in his mouth and baseball on his satellite radio. He had just bounced around the Grapefruit League for a month, sitting in the stands, relaxing, watching nothing but his favorite sport—baseball. Free agency had already opened in the NFL and the draft was less than a month away, but the truth was, he didn't care. His biggest worry was the state of the Yankees pitching staff. The business of the NFL? It was meaningless now.

Still, the former general manager of the New York Giants, a little more than a year into his retirement, couldn't put football completely out of his mind. As he drove home from Florida, alone with his thoughts, he kept drifting back to that magical night in the desert in early February. It seemed like yesterday, though two months had already passed since the night he would always remember as the greatest of his career.

"It's amazing," Accorsi said. "Sometimes I have to tangibly remind myself that it happened. You work for your whole career, not only for a championship, but for a quarterback to win a championship—especially me. And then to win it that way? I can't tell you how many times I fantasized and dreamt that was the way it was going to be."

He was sitting in the stands, fifteen rows off the field, on February 3, 2008, when Eli Manning—his hand-picked successor to the legends of Johnny Unitas and John Elway—made all his dreams come true. The kid led the Giants to one of the most unexpected Super Bowl championships ever, 17–14 over the previously undefeated New England Patriots, and he did it with a last-minute drive taken straight out of Joe Montana's biography. Just the idea that Eli and the Giants would make it to Super Bowl XLII—let alone win it—seemed ridiculous two months earlier when they were being booed out of their own stadium. Even Accorsi walked out on one of Eli's November disasters because it was so bad, so disheartening, he couldn't bear to watch.

Now he was watching history. Imagine that. He was watching his quarterback do the impossible. For nearly four decades, Accorsi was like Captain Ahab chasing his white whale around the ocean of the NFL, coming so close to finding the quarterback of his desires, yet always seeming so far away. He was close friends with the great Unitas, who embodied everything he believed a quarterback should be, and he'd spend his career looking for the next one. He thought he had one in Elway, the quarterback he drafted in 1983 when he was the general manager of the Baltimore Colts, but that lasted only six days before the Colts owner traded Elway away and broke Accorsi's heart. Years later, he'd find another one in Bernie Kosar, who turned out to be pretty good for Accorsi's Cleveland Browns. But that damn Elway kept swatting down their Super Bowl dreams.

Then, on April 24, 2004, Accorsi hooked another with a trade so massive, so controversial, that it would haunt him until his final days in the league and threaten to overshadow everything he had ever done in the NFL. Accorsi went off into retirement at the end of the 2006 season in danger of being known as the man who threw his legacy away by handing the San Diego Chargers Philip Rivers and three draft picks for Eli Manning. And as he began to distance himself from the league he loved, that trade wasn't looking very good at all.

Yet there he was, one year later, with tears streaming down his face, fans screaming all around him, his children at his side, as his football legacy marched down the field looking every bit like Unitas, Elway, and Montana. The kid that was booed mercilessly in New York, the one Accorsi once couldn't bear to watch, was leading a drive that would send him down the Canyon of Heroes, being cheered by a million people in the same place New York had honored soldiers, presidents, astronauts, and kings.

He can still see the amazing, acrobatic catch by David Tyree that bailed the Giants (and Eli) out. He can still picture Plaxico Burress so unbelievably wide open in the end zone with thirty-five seconds left. He can still feel the knot in his stomach when Tom Brady took the field with way too much time remaining, with a chance to do to Accorsi what Elway had done so many times before.

But, for a change, the worst didn't happen. The good guys won. The Patriots' perfect season was gone. Eli had fulfilled the destiny that Accorsi had laid out before him. He pulled off an upset so stunning that John Mara, son of the late icon Wellington Mara and co-owner of a team with six other championships and two other

Super Bowl titles, called it "the greatest victory in the history of this franchise, without question."

It was exactly what they had all imagined and dreamed about exactly three years, nine months, and ten days earlier, when Accorsi made his big, bold, gutsy draft-day deal that set this incredible chain of events in motion: the trade that finally landed him his championship quarterback and brought Eli Manning to New York.

. . .

FOR WEEKS AFTER it was over, people kept coming up to Eli Manning with the exact same story—at least it seemed like the exact same story to him. They just wanted to tell him about the euphoria they had felt when his thirteen-yard pass landed in Plaxico Burress's hands in the end zone. They'd tell him how they held their breath as Brady made them sweat out his three game-ending incompletions, and how they celebrated when the last one finally hit the turf. In every story the theme was the same, even if the details were slightly different. People were jumping up and down, yelling, screaming, hugging each other, hugging anyone they could find, and quite simply going out of their minds. And it wasn't just football fans, either. Everyone seemed to get caught up in the excitement.

"A lot of people said 'My wife has never watched a football game before,'" Eli said. "'And at the end of it she was jumping up and down and screaming and yelling, too.'"

Eli's reaction down on the field at the University of Phoenix Stadium in Glendale, Arizona, on that wonderful night was a lot more reserved—so typical of him. While fans in New York poured into Times Square for an impromptu celebration that caused police to set up barriers and block traffic, people all around the tri-state area honked their horns and flashed their lights on the highways, or ran out onto their lawns like they were escaping a fire, Eli took the final snap, took a knee, and then got up and pumped the football into the air. It was exactly what the world had come to expect of him, keeping his emotions in check on the outside, even though he felt like he was bursting on the inside.

"It is hard to explain what that feeling is," Eli said. "You don't know whether to scream or cry or yell. You don't know what to do."

It was that way, really, for months as he went from a ticker tape parade, to a secluded beach, to Mississippi, to Tennessee, to New Orleans, and eventually back to New York. He'd find Giants fans everywhere, wanting to offer congratulations or a handshake, maybe buy him dinner or a drink, or maybe just wanting to tell him how happy they were. At some point he realized those were many of the same people who had booed him, cursed him, or called up the radio stations saying he should be run out of town. They were happy hypocrites, gladly and blindly hitching themselves to his bandwagon, even though they once tried their best to force it off the road.

"They probably were," Eli said. "But that's OK by me. It really doesn't bother me. I've been a fan before. You can be down on somebody. You can be upset. But in the end, to give them that joy and to give them that experience and that championship that we all won—and when you win a championship, your fans win it and they're just as excited as you are—to give them that joy, I feel like I've done my part and done something special for them."

And make no mistake about this: he did it. No player on the Giants will be more identified with this championship than Eli Manning, which is the way it always is with a quarterback. Right guards don't lead teams to Super Bowl championships and neither do tight ends. Think of Super Bowl III, and Joe Namath comes to mind. Think of the great Steelers teams of the '70s and it's

Terry Bradshaw, even before the Steel Curtain defense. The 49ers of the '80s and it's Joe Montana, before Jerry Rice. The Cowboys of the '90s and it's Troy Aikman first, Emmitt Smith second. Even the 2006 Indianapolis Colts will be remembered as the team that helped Peyton Manning finally win it all.

Maybe that is insulting to everyone else, especially the Giants, who relied on so many different people during their championship drive. But just ask the Giants how they won the Super Bowl. They'll give the credit to Eli, too.

"This team goes nowhere without him," said Michael Strahan, who played fifteen NFL seasons before Eli delivered him his first championship. "This team goes as far as Eli Manning takes us. And Eli Manning has taken us to the Super Bowl. And Eli Manning has won it for us."

That was why Eli was the MVP of Super Bowl XLII—pulling off an amazing double for the Manning family, who celebrated Peyton's MVP performance the previous year in Super Bowl XLI. In truth, it was a game absolutely dominated by the Giants' defense, which put a brutal beating on Tom Brady. If that defense hadn't unleashed the fury of its league-best pass rush on the NFL's top quarterback, Eli would never have gotten the chance to win it in the end. But they did, so he did, putting together a drive for the ages. He got the ball back in his hands deep in his own territory with 2:39 remaining, trailing by four, and marched the Giants to the win—only the second time in history a quarterback has won a Super Bowl with a touchdown pass in the final minute. Along the way he had more help than many people remember. Brandon Jacobs picked up a first down by just inches on a fourth-down run. Rookie wide receiver Steve Smith caught a pass on the sidelines and tiptoed for a first down. The offensive line, with some help from Jacobs, gave Eli just enough room to throw. Tyree made that circus catch that just might be remembered as the most clutch grab in the history of the NFL.

That was Eli's drive, though, and Eli's victory. The credit, the glory and everything—it always goes to the quarterback. From high school, when the quarterback is often the three-sport star, probably even dating the homecoming queen, to college where he's the biggest man on the biggest of campuses, to the NFL where it's the quarterbacks that rake in the $100 million contracts, the radio shows, the TV commercials, and an overwhelming percentage of the postseason awards. The quarterback is at once the conductor and a musician, forced to play a little of every instrument in the band. He's the starting pitcher, with the ball in his hands to start every play, only he's forced to go all nine innings and play every game. And he's the coach, the CEO, the spokesman for the franchise who must stand there every day and face the press, the critics, and either explain what went wrong or go over in painstaking detail what went right.

It's the quarterback that gets to stand up on the podium with the owners and the coach and the general manager as the confetti swirls all around. He's the one that almost always gets his hands on the Vince Lombardi Trophy first.

Of course, after four years of struggle, of up-and-down performances, of psychoanalysis and worries and organizational meetings about what was going wrong with their quarterback of the future, there was nobody inside or outside the Giants organization that ever imagined Eli Manning's fingerprints would be on that trophy so soon.

• • •

WHEN IT WAS all over, when the clock finally said 0:00—and boy, did the final seconds seem to take forever—and the confetti began to swirl and people started hugging him (one fan even tried to kiss him), Accorsi felt so much … so much something. Relief, maybe?

Sure, maybe a little. But mostly he just had a feeling of incredible joy. He was so unbelievably, unexpectedly happy at that moment. And not just for himself, but for Eli, too. The past four years had been hellish at times for the still-only-twenty-seven-year-old quarterback. He was, by most accounts, the most overanalyzed, dissected, discussed, and criticized quarterback New York had ever had—maybe the most beleaguered in the entire history of the league. Given his ties to Accorsi, he was expected to be the next Elway. Because he played for the Giants, he was expected to be the next Phil Simms. And because of his last name, he was expected to be the next Peyton Manning, who might be the greatest quarterback of his generation and is on his way to the Hall of Fame.

Plus, as the first overall pick in the draft he was expected to save a franchise that was searching for its first Super Bowl championship since the 1990 season—a franchise that had been unable to find a quarterback it truly believed it could lean on since painfully cutting ties with Simms in June of 1994. Meanwhile, the quarterback the Giants could have taken in 2004—Ben Roethlisberger—won a Super Bowl in his second season. And, as Eli was often reminded, the San Diego Chargers turned three of the four picks they got from the Giants in the deal they made for Eli on Draft Day 2004 into Pro Bowl players—including a player (Shawne Merriman) who was becoming one of the best linebackers in football and the quarterback (Philip Rivers) the Giants had drafted and traded away.

Put it all together and it was an enormous, unfair—insane, really—cross to bear. Then he had to deal with the constant booing, the weekly discussions about his mechanics, his demeanor, the way he answered questions in his press conferences, the weekly back and forth from fans who believed in his potential one minute and cursed his performance the next. As it was all happening for four long years, seemingly every day, especially during the season, it was impossible for Accorsi not to watch it and think, "I did this. I did this to him."

"It's amazing, I felt a lot of it," Accorsi said. "We were both getting it. But I caused it. If I don't do that trade, he doesn't have to face it. It's the biggest city in the world, you've got the Manning name…"

The bottom line was this: A Super Bowl championship—and an MVP to boot—might not have been Eli's birthright, but it was always the expectation that burdened him, whether it was expressed or not. Maybe it was more than expectation. Maybe it was a demand. And if he didn't demand it himself, it was certainly demanded by everyone around him, from the fans, to the media, to his teammates, to his coaches, and even to the man that gambled his legacy on the talents of a twenty-something kid with a golden arm and famous last name.

Because when it finally happened, when Eli finally fulfilled those ridiculously unreasonable expectations, here's how Accorsi summed up the whole, agonizing, messy, wild, and remarkable Eli experience:

"He did what we drafted him to do."

Two: "Call it magic"

THERE'S SOMETHING ABOUT a cold, damp, raw wind in the Deep South that just sends a shiver up Ernie Accorsi's spine. The temperature doesn't even have to dip below freezing. With the wind it feels like ice is being whipped right through his veins. That's the first thing he remembers about the first time he saw Eli Manning in person.

He had seen him on television and read all about him, and really, who in the NFL wasn't familiar with Peyton Manning's little brother? The youngest of the three Manning boys was having a pretty good career of his own, standing in the shadows of his father, daring to play at Archie Manning's alma mater. He had talent, he had toughness, he definitely had the genes, and like his brother he was destined to be a top ten pick the moment he decided to come out of college.

He was still only a junior, but Jerry Reese, then the Giants' director of player personnel, kept hearing rumors that Eli was going to turn pro. Accorsi watched the kid on TV, saw how much the Ole Miss Rebels were overmatched in the powerful Southeastern Conference, how Eli had no one on his team as talented as he was, and he told Reese, "If that was my son I'd get him the hell out of there." The longer the year went on, the stronger the rumors got. Eventually, Reese said to Accorsi, "You better go see him."

And so he did. On November 2, 2002, he went to see Ole Miss play Auburn, one day before the Giants would host a game against the Jacksonville Jaguars. He was usually given a press box seat at old Vaught-Hemingway Stadium, but on this day his seat was outside, in the auxiliary press section. It was so cold that he half-jokingly asked the sports information director, "Can I just come in every twenty minutes?"

The setting, though, was perfect. What better way to evaluate a quarterback than under adverse conditions, to see how he handles the cold and the wind against a team that clearly has his out-manned? Could he raise the level of his game? Could he make his teammates better? Could he rise above the circumstances? Accorsi started down on the sidelines, where he watched the pre-game warm-ups so he could gauge Eli's arm strength up close. Then he went back up into the stands to watch Eli really put on a show.

The kid, barely into his twenties, went 26 for 46 that day, throwing for 284 yards, three touchdowns, and three interceptions, including an awful one in the end zone with 1:32 left in the game—a killer interception on a play where he probably would have—should have—been able to run for the tying touchdown from the Auburn eight-yard line. But that mistake in what turned into a 31–24 loss wasn't what Accorsi remembered. And he didn't care about the numbers, because he never judges a quarterback by numbers alone.

"He carried this team completely on his own," Accorsi said. "And every time Auburn scored, he came right back. At the end of the game, Auburn goes right down the field and scores, and he's got like a minute and ten seconds, he takes them down the field again. He throws an interception in the end zone. He forces it. That's in my report. But he's trying to win the game and he needs a touchdown to win, not a field goal."

"I was convinced."

Almost as soon as he got back, he sat down and typed out the four-paragraph, 494-word scouting report that would eventually change the fortunes and fate of the Giants organization. He typed it in bold capital letters, too:

WEARS LEFT KNEE BRACE.... DURING PREGAME
WARM-UP, DIDN'T LOOK LIKE HE HAD A ROCKET
ARM.... AS GAME PROGRESSED, I SAW EXCELLENT
ARM STRENGTH UNDER PRESSURE AND THE ABILITY
TO GET VELOCITY ON THE BALL ON MOST THROWS.
GOOD DEEP BALL RANGE. GOOD TOUCH. GOOD
VISION AND POISE.

SEES THE FIELD.... IN A SHOTGUN ON MOST PLAYS
AND HIS ONLY RUNNING OPTION IS A DRAW.... HIS
OFFENSIVE LINE IS POOR. RED-SHIRT FRESHMAN
LEFT TACKLE. ELI DOESN'T TRUST HIS PROTECTION.
CAN'T. NO WAY HE CAN TAKE ANY FORM OF DEEP DROP
AND LOOK DOWNFIELD. WITH NO RUNNING GAME
(10 YARDS RUSHING IN THE FIRST HALF) AND NO
REAL TOP RECEIVERS, HE'S STUCK WITH THREE-STEP
DROPS AND WAITING TIL THE LAST SECOND TO SEE IF
A RECEIVER CAN GET FREE. NO TIGHT END EITHER. NO
FLARING BACK. SO HE'S TAKING SOME BIG HITS. TAK-
ING THEM WELL. CARRIED AN OVERMATCHED TEAM
ENTIRELY ON HIS SHOULDERS. I IMAGINE, EXCEPT
FOR VANDERBILT, HIS TEAM IS OVERMATCHED IN
EVERY SEC GAME.... HE'S BIG, NEVER GETS RATTLED.
RALLIED HIS TEAM FROM A 14–3 HALFTIME DEFICIT
BASICALLY ALL BY HIMSELF. LED THEM ON TWO SUC-
CESSIVE THIRD QUARTER DRIVES TO GO AHEAD 17–
16. THE FIRST TOUCHDOWN, ON A 40-YARD STREAK
DOWN THE LEFT SIDELINE, HE DROPPED THE BALL
OVER THE RECEIVER'S RIGHT SHOULDER. CALLED
THE NEXT TOUCHDOWN PASS HIMSELF, CHECKING
OFF TO A 12-YARD SLANT.... MAKES A LOT OF DECI-
SIONS ON PLAY CALLS AT THE LINE OF SCIMMAGE, BUT
THEY ASK TOO MUCH OF HIM. THEY DON'T LET HIM
JUST PLAY. THIS IS A GUY YOU SHOULD JUST LET PLAY
....WHEN HE'S INACCURATE, HE'S USUALLY HIGH, BUT
RARELY OFF TARGET TO EITHER SIDE.... PLAYS SMART
AND WITH COMPLETE CONFIDENCE. DOESN'T SCOLD
HIS TEAMMATES, BUT LETS THEM KNOW WHEN THEY
LINE UP WRONG OR RUN THE WRONG PATTERN....

THREW THREE INTERCEPTIONS. TWO WERE HIS FAULT. TRYING TO FORCE SOMETHING BOTH TIMES. HE COULD HAVE RUN ON ONE OF THEM, A FOURTH DOWN PLAY. HE HAS A LOT TO LEARN.

SUMMARY: I THINK HE'S THE COMPLETE PACKAGE. HE'S NOT GOING TO BE A FAST RUNNER, BUT A LITTLE LIKE JOE MONTANA, HE HAS ENOUGH ATHLETIC ABILITY TO GET OUT OF TROUBLE. REMEMBER HOW ARCHIE RAN? IN THAT DEPARTMENT, ELI DOESN'T HAVE THE BEST GENES, ALTHOUGH I NEVER TIMED MOM OLIVIA IN THE 40. BUT HE HAS A FEEL FOR THE POCKET. FEELS THE RUSH.

THROWS THE BALL, TAKES THE HIT, GETS RIGHT BACK UP....HAS COURAGE AND POISE. IN MY OPINION, MOST OF ALL, HE HAS THAT QUALITY YOU CAN'T DEFINE. CALL IT MAGIC. AS [former Colts defensive back] BOBBY BOYD TOLD ME ONCE ABOUT UNITAS, 'TWO THINGS SET HIM APART: HIS LEFT TESTICLE AND HIS RIGHT TESTICLE.' .... PEYTON HAD MUCH BETTER TALENT AROUND HIM AT TENNESSEE. BUT I HONESTLY GIVE THIS GUY A CHANCE TO BE BETTER THAN HIS BROTHER. ELI DOESN'T GET MUCH HELP FROM THE COACHING STAFF. IF HE COMES OUT EARLY, WE SHOULD MOVE UP TO TAKE HIM. THESE GUYS ARE RARE, YOU KNOW.

Talk about pressure. In those four paragraphs, Accorsi compared Eli to Unitas, Montana, and Peyton Manning. More specifically he said Eli had a chance to be better than Peyton. Sure, the definition of his most important quality—"magic"—was vague. But coming from Accorsi that was the highest praise he could give a quarterback. Unitas had magic. Elway had magic. All the great ones did. Maybe he couldn't put it into words—at least not specific, detailed words—but he knew magic when he saw it.

Those were the expectations that Eli would be saddled with forever. Accorsi made it crystal clear to anyone who read the report that this wasn't just any old draft prospect he was scouting. This was a kid he believed could change a franchise, maybe even carry the whole thing on his back.

Of course, Eli didn't come out of college after his junior season, which gave Accorsi more time to scout him, more time to watch tape, and more time to fall in love. At the end of the 2003 season, after countless more hours of studying his future star, Accorsi and Reese sat down to discuss making a trade for Eli. Someone pulled out Accorsi's original scouting report.

"I'm not changing a word," he said.

• • •

IT WAS PROBABLY no coincidence that one of Accorsi's closest friends in football and in life turned out to be Johnny Unitas. Their friendship started not long after Accorsi began to work for the Baltimore Colts in 1970, and they became so close that, years later, Unitas gave Accorsi his jersey from his final NFL game rather than send it to the Hall of Fame. So it was hardly surprising that when Accorsi returned to the Colts as their assistant general manager in 1977, after a couple of years working in the league office, finding the next Unitas was the first thing on his list. Over the years, especially after he got the chance to really see what Unitas could do up close, quarterback had become an almost mystical position to him. Sports were Accorsi's life and he knew the ins and outs of most of them. He had the ultimate respect for the way a baseball pitcher had control of a game literally in his hands. But that was nothing, Accorsi thought, compared to the kind of control a quarterback had. There was, quite simply, no position like it in any game, anywhere.

"I think it's the most important position in sports," Accorsi said. "He has more to do with the outcome of a game than a starting pitcher. In the seventh inning, he can't come out. Mariano Rivera can't come in and close the game. The quarterback has got to finish the game. He can't say 'Well, I'll give you three good quarters, coach.' And the quarterback pitches every game. There's no three days rest. So he's pitching every day, he's got to pitch a complete game, and really somebody else can't bail him out with ten runs."

Watching Unitas lead the Colts all those years was enough to shape that philosophy, and his friendship and countless conversations with Unitas after that were more than enough to cement it. And nothing could change his mind, not even the advice of a man he calls one of his idols in the business: Jim Finks. That came after the 1979 season, Accorsi's third in the Colts' front office, when Finks was still the general manager of the Chicago Bears. In 1978 and 1979 the Colts had combined to win only ten games, mostly because their quarterback, Bert Jones, was only healthy enough to start seven of them.

"Jim said to me, 'Don't depend on a quarterback, because if you don't have him, look what happens to your team,'" Accorsi recalled. "He said, 'That's why I never thought the quarterback was that important.' He took the opposite approach."

Instead of listening, though, Accorsi used the struggles of those Colts teams to form his second theory, which was this: "The second most important player on your team is the backup quarterback." He had seen what Morrall did for the Colts when Unitas got hurt, and later for the Miami Dolphins when Bob Griese got hurt, and what not having a good enough backup quarterback had done to the Colts in '78 and '79. He remained absolutely resolute that for an NFL team to win a championship it needed a top-flight quarterback.

And just in case the first one got hurt you better be sure to have two.

So it should have come as no surprise to anyone that when Accorsi became the general manager of the Colts in 1982, he made finding a quarterback his first order of business. They hadn't had a winning season in five years when he took over, and in his first season—a strike-shortened mess—the Colts bottomed out at 0–8–1. The upside of that miserable record was that Accorsi would have the first pick of the 1983 draft, which everyone knew was rich with quarterback talent. Best of all, there was the next Unitas sitting right atop the draft board in the form of Stanford quarterback John Elway.

One problem: the coach that Accorsi inherited in Baltimore, Frank Kush, was a former college coach at Arizona State and wasn't well-liked. One man who seemed to particularly despise him was Jack Elway, father of John, and the head coach at San Jose State. That was the real reason John Elway insisted he'd never play in Baltimore, though Accorsi wouldn't learn the truth for another fourteen years. ("Why didn't you tell me that?" Accorsi told Elway's agent years later. "I didn't hire Kush anyway.") At the time, the Elways used geography as an excuse. John said he wanted to play out West. And he wasn't kidding, he insisted. He even had the appearance of a little leverage because he had signed a minor league baseball contract with the New York Yankees two years earlier. Not that Accorsi was buying any of it. Even though an angry town and a nervous owner in Robert Irsay seemed to want no part of the petulant quarterback, Accorsi knew better than to do what the Pittsburgh Steelers had done in 1955 when they made the mistake of a lifetime and let a great quarterback get away. They cut a rookie named Unitas that year before the season even began.

As the draft got closer, Irsay was trying to trade the pick right out from under Accorsi's nose. In fact, he nearly sent it to the New England Patriots for John Hannah, a thirty-two-year-old guard on his way to the Hall of Fame, and two first-round draft picks. Accorsi got wind of the deal and immediately put his foot down.

"Mr. Irsay," Accorsi told him, "it probably doesn't matter to you, but if you make this trade there are going to be two press conferences. You announce the trade and I will announce my resignation."

Accorsi—who had assured Irsay that Elway would relent, though it would likely cost the Colts an unheard of sum of $5 million over five years—appeared to win the battle, and the second the draft clock started on April 26, 1983, he selected Elway. He had his quarterback. He was about to bring the next Unitas to Baltimore.

Or so it seemed.

"I came back upstairs and my secretary held her hand out, as if to say 'Don't come in the office,'" Accorsi recalled. "And I heard the attorney, Michael Chernoff, whining, 'What are we going to do? We don't have the money.' Irsay said, 'Mike, let him have his day. When we leave here we'll go do what we want.'"

Six days later, Accorsi was watching the NBA playoffs on television when they interrupted the game and cut to an empty table with microphones on it. Then he watched Dan Reeves, the coach of the Denver Broncos, and their owner, Edgar Kaiser, walk into the room and he knew immediately what they were about to announce. So he picked up the phone and called Kush.

"Are you watching the NBA playoffs?" Accorsi said.

"No," Kush said.

"Well you better turn it on," Accorsi replied. "Because they just traded our quarterback."

Sure enough, Irsay had traded Elway to Denver for quarterback Mark Herrmann, tackle Chris Hinton, a first-round pick in the '84 draft, and the promise of a couple of preseason games that would be worth about $400,000 each.

Accorsi would resign at the end of the season, ending his chance to fulfill a boyhood dream and bring a championship—and a championship quarterback—back to his beloved Colts, who were about to pack up their trucks and sneak out of town to Indianapolis in the middle of the night anyway. Accorsi eventually resurfaced in Cleveland, where he served as the Browns' general manager from 1985–92. He got them a pretty good quarterback as soon as he arrived, too, stealing Bernie Kosar out of the University of Miami by convincing the Youngstown, Ohio native to skip the 1985 draft and wait for the supplemental draft instead. Of course, Accorsi had traded four draft picks to the Buffalo Bills for the first pick in that supplemental draft, and he teamed with Kosar for a heck of a power play that made both their dreams come true.

Almost, anyway. Kosar helped get Accorsi's Browns to the AFC championship game three times. Three times, though, they lost. Each time the losses came at the hands of Elway, the quarterback that got away.

. . .

IT WAS NO wonder that everyone thought Accorsi was obsessed—a word he despised—as the 2004 draft got closer. The Giants had the fourth overall pick and the worst kept secret on the planet was that Accorsi was trying to trade up for number one. It was as if he was trying to right a wrong from twenty-one years earlier. The next Unitas got away once. He wasn't going to let that happen again.

"We're not obsessed with this at all," Accorsi said in a press conference nine days before that draft. "It's come out that way, but that's not the way it is. There are other players up there that, believe me, if we end up with them we're all going to be very pleased.

"But without any disrespect to anybody that's played in the last five Super Bowls, just answer me one question: In his prime, would any of these coaches have said 'Yes, I'll take Elway'? That's all I ask. How many of them are going to say 'No'?"

OK, so maybe "obsessed" was harsh. But there was no doubt to anyone that Accorsi had become single-minded from the first day he saw Eli in Oxford, Mississippi. The Giants had already begun having concerns about Kerry Collins, even though the strong-armed quarterback had rescued them from the Dave Brown/Kent Graham/

Danny Kanell era and led them to Super Bowl XXXV. But his performance in that ugly, 34–7 loss at the end of the 2000 season had many worried about his mettle. No one doubted Collins's arm strength or his physical toughness. But he looked scared that night. Or at least lost. And, truth be told, they felt he often looked that way when he was under pressure. The feeling in some corners of the Giants organization was that he was physically strong but mentally weak and he wasn't likely to get much better.

Collins, in other words, wasn't ever going to be Unitas. But Eli had a chance. After all, the kid followed his father to Ole Miss—a daring choice, considering how much of a legend Archie was in Oxford. And Eli rarely flinched behind a porous Rebels offensive line. He never complained, never looked scared. Heck, it never even looked like it bothered him. He just kept getting up, brushing himself off, and calmly coming back for more.

There were other quarterbacks coming out in 2004 as well. Ben Roethlisberger, from Miami of Ohio, had wowed the scouts—even Accorsi—at the GMAC Bowl against Louisville. Philip Rivers had a funky delivery, but was lighting it up for North Carolina State and would become the star of the Senior Bowl. And though most people didn't include him in the Big Three, Accorsi had developed a liking for Virginia quarterback Matt Schaub.

But there's only one Unitas, and there was only one Eli, and there was no point in trying to convince Accorsi of anything else.

"I pulled out his first scouting report on Eli Manning when he was a junior and Ernie and I laughed about it," Giants co-owner John Mara said a few years later. "I don't think a day went by between the end of Eli's junior year and the day we drafted him that we didn't have at least one conversation about the guy."

The kid had it. Accorsi had no doubt about that. He had seen it before, and he was determined not to let it get away again.

Three: "To me, they were just out there playing ball"

THE GAMES WERE always much more fun when it rained, and it rained a lot in New Orleans. As soon as it did, if Dad was home, the boys knew what was coming. So did some of the other kids in their upscale neighborhood. They'd line up in the front yard and one of the most famous men in New Orleans would stand up on the porch of his large, two-story, pre–Civil War home and signal them to go. One by one they'd take off and he'd throw each of them a perfect spiral, always just a little bit out of reach.

"My dad had this great knack for throwing the ball just perfectly out in front of you," said Peyton Manning. "He'd throw it where you had to dive for it and make a one-handed catch."

And if they had to dive through the mud, all the better, and all the more fun. After all, that's what it was all about to Archie Manning. He wasn't barking instructions or orders. There would be no review of the film so the boys could study their technique. It was just him, his boys, the mud, a made-up game called "Amazing Catches," and plenty of smiles to go around.

That's what it was like in the Manning household back in the 1980s, which in hindsight isn't exactly what anyone would expect considering Archie and his two sons, Eli and Peyton, would eventually become three of the most famous quarterbacks in NFL history, making up the the First Family of the NFL. Back then, though, there was not even a hint of pretentiousness. They were just a bunch of kids covered in mud.

And that was fine, because Archie never wanted his boys to play in the NFL, and he certainly never wanted to push them in that direction. "I still kind of don't quite understand how I got two sons playing pro football," Archie said. "That was never part of the plan when we set out to raise kids."

The plan that Archie and his college sweetheart, Olivia, had was to raise good Southern gentlemen with good manners who were free to follow their dreams. If they wanted to play football, fine. Archie would be there for them every step of the way, anytime they wanted, with as much help as they needed. But just because he was a former NFL star didn't mean Cooper, Peyton, or Eli had to be football players—or even athletes—too.

"I think my parents did a great job of not putting expectations on us," Eli said. "They wanted us to be ourselves and do whatever we loved to do. If we wanted to be in a band or be in a play or do anything, they were supportive of us. We loved playing sports. They didn't force it on us. My dad never said, 'You're going to be a football player.' Growing up, we played every sport. Whatever season it was in, we were outside. We weren't into computers, Nintendo, or that kind of stuff. We wanted to be outside."

And so they were, all the time, for those games of Amazing Catches or another one they made up called "The Kickoff Team," where the object was to run the kickoff back for a touchdown or be forced to kickoff again. They played actual football games, too—Eli was usually the center, while Peyton and Cooper were the quarterback and receiver. They played baseball when they could. Basketball too. Whatever sport or activity they could find.

. . .

Cooper was born to Olivia and Archie in 1974. Peyton followed two years later on March 24, 1976. Then there would be a five-year gap before Elisha Nelson Manning came on January 3, 1981. He was given the middle name of his father, whose full name was Archibald Elisha Manning III. But as he grew up, he was much closer to his mother. "I'd say I was a momma's boy," Eli admitted. "And I'm not ashamed of it."

There was little choice, really. He wasn't even two yet when his father, near the end of his stellar fourteen-year NFL career—a career some say would've landed him in the Hall of Fame if only he hadn't been stuck on the woeful Saints for most of it—was traded to the Houston Oilers. A year later, Archie was traded even farther away, to the Minnesota Vikings. That kept him somewhat removed from Eli's life until his youngest son was nearly four. The fact that Cooper and Peyton were seven and five years older and inseparable pushed young Eli even closer to his mother. He was the classic little brother, always wanting to hang out with the older boys, yet never really sure if he was invited to come along.

"Yeah, I'd say I was the tagalong," Eli said. "Growing up I always thought Cooper and Peyton liked being around me. There would be weekends where they were at home and my parents were out, and they'd sit and watch me with my buddies. I assumed they liked being around. Later I found out they were being grounded and they had to stay home."

He was different than his brothers, too. Cooper was loud and demonstrative—"the comedian of the family," Eli said. Peyton was an imposing presence even then. Focused. Competitive. Driven. Incredibly sure of himself, whether it was on the football field or in a school play. Eli described himself as "the shy one." He took after Mom, the former Ole Miss homecoming queen, who was the most reserved member of the Manning clan. Dinner conversations when

Eli was a young boy were dominated by Cooper, Peyton, and Dad. Eli and his mother just sat back, ate, and took it all in.

It didn't help Eli's shyness either that, at first, he struggled in school, unable to read as well as the rest of the kids his age. It was so bad, his first-grade teacher at Isidore Newman—the private pre-kindergarten through twelfth grade school all the Manning boys attended—suggested he needed to be left back. Instead, Archie and Olivia transferred Eli to another school, where he stayed until he asked to go back to Newman when he entered seventh grade.

By then, his brothers were Newman legends. Peyton had become a star quarterback in high school, and Cooper had been his top receiver after a failed attempt to make it at his father's old position. When he was a senior and Peyton was a sophomore, Cooper caught 76 passes for 1,250 yards. Peyton threw to Cooper so often, in fact, that Archie joked that after games he had to hide from the parents of the other receivers. They were so good and had so much fun playing together that Peyton had set his mind to following Cooper to Ole Miss, so they could follow in their father's footsteps together.

But during Cooper's senior year at Newman, he began experiencing numbness in the fingers on his right hand, which caused him to drop what used to be easy catches. He found himself unable to shoot as well as he used to in basketball, too. He went to Ole Miss anyway, because that was the plan, but the numbness followed him there, too. Unsure what was wrong, he went to the Mayo Clinic and the Baylor Medical Clinic and any doctor he could find before he was finally diagnosed with spinal stenosis—a narrowing of the spinal canal.

Just like that, his football career was done.

Peyton's continued, of course. He became the best high school quarterback in the land, and though he eventually decided against Ole Miss he went on to star at Tennessee. He became legendary for his preparation and his determination, as if he had been preparing to be an NFL quarterback all his life. Of course, unlike Eli, in some ways he had.

• • •

COOPER AND PEYTON's earliest days were spent in the shadows of the NFL. Teammates of Archie's would visit the family at their home in New Orleans' Garden District. On Sundays when the Saints were home, they'd head down to the Superdome and watch—and occasionally boo—Dad and his team. When the games were over, they went to the locker room to hang around the usually beaten players. Then they'd have the run of the place, scampering all over the Superdome, replaying the games, just the two of them together on Dad's field.

Peyton admitted that influenced his life and his choice of a career. How could it not? But Eli didn't grow up like that. He was too young to remember any of his father's NFL seasons. He only knew the stories. And the stories were larger than life.

Archie Manning was born in Drew, Mississippi, which only made it more special to football fans in his home state when he decided to go to Ole Miss. He spent three years as the Rebels' starting quarterback, throwing for 4,753 yards and 56 touchdowns while running for 823 yards. He was fourth in the Heisman voting in 1969 and third in 1970. He became such a legend that not only did the school retire his number, 18, but the speed limit on the campus is still eighteen miles per hour in his honor.

In 1971, Archie was the second overall pick in the NFL draft by the New Orleans Saints, and he would suffer with them through eleven miserable seasons. When his fourteen-year career ended, he had thrown for 23,911 yards and 125 touchdowns (with 173 interceptions)—outstanding numbers for that run-first era. He might have been remembered as one of the all-time greats, but for the losing record. His Saints teams—the 'Aints, as they were called by fans that showed up to watch with bags over their heads—didn't make the playoffs. Not even once.

But the losing didn't matter when it came to the legend of Archie Manning because there was no bigger football star anywhere in the South. They never forgot how the old redhead had brought some pride back to the Mississippi Delta during a time when his home state was a powder keg over civil rights. There was even a song written about him: "The Ballad of Archie Who." He wasn't just a football player, he was a folk hero. And his legend followed him right down the Mighty Mississippi to New Orleans.

That was a lot to live up to. The whole Manning legend was too much, really. A brother on his way to being one of the NFL's greatest quarterbacks? A father who was immortalized in song? When Eli started to show that he was pretty good at football, too, it was hardly a surprise. Football, after all, was wired into the Manning boys' genes. And though Archie may not have forced his sons in that direction, greatness was still expected by everyone else. That was especially true for Eli, who had to follow in two pairs of shoes—a tough task, even for a kid who was nicknamed "Easy" for his laid-back, unaffected approach to life.

It probably didn't help that his family didn't completely shy away from the expectations heaped on Eli, either. Even in his own senior yearbook at Isidore Newman, Peyton had a message about Eli printed under his picture:

"Watch out world, he's the best one."

He was a Manning, after all.

• • •

"TO ME, THEY WERE JUST OUT THERE PLAYING BALL"

IMAGINE WHAT IT must have been like for Archie Manning, fresh off an NFL career filled with loss and disappointment, looking out into his yard and knowing he'd been given two more chances for the NFL glory that had eluded him. "How about having a one year old and a six year old and looking at them and saying 'You're going to win back-to-back Super Bowls,'" Accorsi said. "I don't care what your bloodlines are. It's not like, 'Just because your father is a quarterback …'"

Of course, it was never like that at all. Archie was remarkably oblivious to the depth of the talent his young boys possessed. His friends would tell him how good they were, and on some level he knew. But that was never his focus. It was if he was purposefully stopping himself from seeing what was right in front of his eyes.

"I didn't admit it until Peyton was a junior in high school and was getting letters from every school in the country," Archie insisted. "I didn't admit until then that he might have a chance to play college football. I didn't know and I didn't try to know. I was always scared of that stuff. I let other people talk about that. I never tried to make any kind of judgment of where they were or what stage they were.

"To me they were just out there playing ball because it was fun and it was what they wanted to do."

Of course, he was there. He was always there for a little football instruction whenever his boys needed it. But he never volunteered it. It only came when they asked.

"He was there to help us, but he never forced anything upon us," Eli said. "It's not about trying to live up to any expectations. It's just about being yourself, having fun, and trying to do the best you can do."

Four: "It's my little brother"

THE FIRST MANNING Bowl was played on the night of September 10, 2006, at Giants Stadium, and it was won—not surprisingly—by Peyton. Weren't these games always won by the older brother? And while it was the first time Peyton and Eli had faced each other in a game that counted, it wasn't the first time they faced each other in a game that truly mattered to them. They've never forgotten those countless backyard battles, those times they faced off against each other in any number of games and sports.

On almost every occasion—proudly proclaimed by Peyton and reluctantly admitted by Eli—Peyton's little brother came out on the short end. It didn't matter whether it was Amazing Catches, backyard football, pickup basketball, or anything else. Peyton was the mountain that Eli seemed to be forever trying to climb. And Eli chased him around for most of his life, first around the house, the yard, and the playgrounds of New Orleans, then to high school, the Southeastern Conference, and finally to the top of the NFL draft and into the pros. There, Peyton was first to the Pro Bowl, to the playoffs, to 4,000 yards, to the record books, to the Super Bowl, to the MVP. Peyton was *always* first.

There was a day, though, when he wasn't, and the memory still brings a smile to Eli's face. It was far from the glare of the media and the fans, far removed from the money and the fame. They both say the details aren't important (though the slight sparkle in

Eli's eye suggests he remembers every single one), but there was a day where Eli rose up and climbed over Peyton for his moment of triumph and revenge.

It was the day Eli finally beat Peyton in a pickup basketball game.

They were playing in their driveway—first to ten points wins, and you've got to win by two. Eli was up 9–8. Peyton turned up the pressure and, with Eli standing at the top of the key, the older brother went for an ill-advised steal.

"It didn't work," Eli recalled, and the little brother added an exclamation to the insult with what he remembered as a thunderous dunk.

"It's one thing to lose to your little brother," Eli said, "but to get dunked on, on the last play...."

And if you don't think that ranks as one of Eli's all-time greatest victories ... well, think again.

"You beat your big brother in anything—and that was the first thing I ever beat him in besides ping pong and pool," Eli said, still eager to gloat after all these years, "it was a big step. He always had the advantage, but to get that one win ..."

Eli paused for just a second. "I know it hurt him," he said.

He wasn't sorry, either.

· · ·

IGNORE THE HELMETS and the uniforms and, from afar, they are the same man. Eli is 6-foot-4, 225 pounds. Peyton is 6-foot-5, 230 (or so their teams say). They both have the same long Manning face. They both have a calm look about them as they approach the line of scrimmage. They both gesture and point as they bark signals (some real, some fake), though the more experienced Peyton is slightly more demonstrative. They have a similar stance as they drop back to pass. There's a similar look they share. Maybe Peyton is a little more confident, especially when it comes to standing in the pocket as the rush descends upon him, a little less frantic as he slides out of trouble (he's always been a little more mobile than most people think).

It's the personality that's different. The presence. Peyton is commanding. He didn't need a Super Bowl MVP to earn a starring role in one of the most memorable athlete-driven commercials in the last decade—the MasterCard commercial where he acts like a fan toward regular people, and memorably serenades a deli worker with chants of "Cut that meat!" It's an outward confidence that's apparent the moment anyone meets him. Where Eli comes across as shy, reserved, introverted even, Peyton is as a natural leader, ready to take over a room.

"I think Eli has always been a little quieter than Peyton, maybe a little more laid-back," Archie said. "I would say that Peyton has always kind of been a real take-charge guy and Peyton never blinks at anything. That's kind of the way he is. Eli competes in a real quiet way. He works real hard. Eli never gives anybody any trouble. He doesn't have a big ego. They call him 'Easy.' He is pretty easy to get along with."

Easy to get along with, but difficult to figure out. That's what Jim Finn thought in 2002 when he was a teammate of Peyton's, a fullback for the Indianapolis Colts, and Eli—then a junior at Ole Miss—came to visit. They went out to dinner with a group of people and for most of the night, Eli didn't say much at all. Peyton was with his wife and at the end of the night he decided to turn in early. Finn was single and wasn't ready for the night to end.

Eli had a reputation for enjoying the nightlife in college. In fact, in January of his freshman year at Ole Miss he had been arrested outside of a fraternity party and jailed briefly for public drunkenness and disorderly conduct—an incident he'd later call the turning point of his career. He never got into any public trouble again, though he still managed to get the full college experience. He was known to hit the dance floor pretty hard and, as one former teammate said, "Get a couple of pops in him and he heads right for the karaoke machine." So not surprisingly, given a chance to ditch big brother and hit the town with another single guy, Eli perked up—at least for a moment—as soon as Peyton started to leave.

"I'm going to stay with Finn," he said.

Amazingly, those were the first words Finn recalled hearing him say.

They went out to a bar for a couple of drinks and a mostly one-sided conversation. "I was trying to pull info out and have a conversation with him as much as I could," said Finn, who would later become Eli's teammate on the Giants. "At first when you meet him, he's quiet. Then he slowly opens up."

He never opens up as much as Peyton does, though—on or off the field. "Peyton, you'll know right away if he's happy, sad, angry, whatever," Finn said. "Eli, he's so laid-back, you have no idea. You can't tell if Eli's thrown an interception or a touchdown. Peyton, you'll know."

The late Wellington Mara once described Eli as "not a guy who jumps out at you." He even said you could walk right past him in the dining hall and not know he was there. He didn't mean that as an insult, either. It was a quiet dignity that Mara could appreciate. It was just the way Eli was.

A psychologist would probably say that's the natural result of being the little brother to two aggressive, outgoing older siblings. Peyton gleefully recalls the days when he used to jump on his brother and keep punching him until he could name all the teams in the Southeastern Conference. Peyton had an encyclopedic knowledge of everything about college football. Eli couldn't have cared less. And even with Peyton sitting on top of him, flailing away, he wasn't in a hurry to learn.

Eventually he did, but then Peyton would just beat on him for something else. Maybe NFL teams, maybe brands of cars—any excuse to take advantage of his little brother. And that wasn't just his older brother beating him up, either. It was the world's next great athlete, the man everyone would expect Eli to be. On top of everything else, he was burdened with expectations so outrageous and unreal so early in life, it made sense that he'd turn inward and become shy.

Then again, shy isn't really the right word. Maybe that describes his personality, but it's not like he shied away from Peyton's sport … or his high school team … or the conference he dominated … or even the college where his dad was the biggest legend of them all. He didn't choose to focus on basketball, where the Manning name meant nothing, even though they each had considerable skill. Nor did he choose to go play football out West, far away from the glare of the spotlight and the family name. He would never, ever say as much, but the path he chose suggested a mission: A mission to prove he was worthy of his name. A mission to prove he could fill those larger-than-life shoes.

"I think there's something in him that he'd like to show his big brother that 'I'm as big as you are,' or 'I can compete at your level,'" said Kevin Gilbride, Eli's offensive coordinator (and former quarterbacks coach) with the Giants. "As all of us are within our families, you want to show you belong and that you're just as good."

. . .

IN THE DAYS before Eli arrived in Albany, New York, for his first NFL training camp, here's the big advice Peyton gave him: Carry your own Sharpie. It'll make signing autographs a less demanding and time-consuming task. If you're waiting for a fan to give you one, you'll be there forever while he's fumbling with the cap or borrowing it from the guy standing next to him. So bring your own. It'll make life easier.

"Those are the tips I get from Peyton," Eli said. "Nothing on the Cover 2."

It's a natural assumption—and one that would follow them both throughout the early stages of Eli's career—that the two brothers talk nothing but football, that they share advice, tips, and insights on opposing defenses. Before his first camp, his first game, his first start, his first full season, even later after his first trip to the White House after his first championship season, Eli was always asked the same question: "Did you get any advice from Peyton?"

Almost every time he'd say "No," or "Not much," and no one would believe him. But it always turned out to be true. Sure, Eli would occasionally ask Peyton for advice, and Peyton was always glad to offer some insight. But it didn't happen often. And advice wasn't always something Peyton wanted to volunteer.

"It's just like with any older brother," Peyton said. "Just like I ask my older brother Cooper plenty of questions and I still go to him for advice. Cooper's always there for me when I need him. I try to be there for Eli as well.

"But only when he asks."

Peyton is a believer that "experience is your best teacher," and Eli agrees. That's why, Eli said, "We don't break down film together." Besides, Eli said, that would be pointless. They're running different offenses, different game plans. They have different coaches with different techniques.

But still, they share a bond that's impossible for most others to grasp. Not only do they know each other better than anyone on the planet, but they share a career and a passion that few others could understand.

"To get pulled out of a game, or certainly get booed by the fans, or get criticized, nobody knows what it's like besides other quarterbacks," Peyton said. "It doesn't matter who the commentator is in that game or who the beat writer is covering that game. Nobody knows what it's like besides another quarterback, especially a current quarterback that's playing right then and just had a game three hours before and knows what it's like when things just start going right."

Even Eli admitted that having a brother as accomplished as Peyton was an invaluable resource that he couldn't afford to waste.

"It's great that you have a brother and a best friend and a guy who's also the NFL MVP on your side who you can just talk to," Eli said. "You can talk about certain things and he knows exactly what you're talking about and sometimes he doesn't have to give advice, it just gives you someone to listen to."

And sometimes, they just talk, because what they strive for most in their lives is normalcy. Beneath everything, they are brothers, not so unlike any set of brothers in the world—minus the fame, fortune, commercial success, incredible athletic ability, Super Bowl rings, MVP trophies, the legendary father, the … OK, so maybe normal is a relative term. But, as Eli said, it's not as if they spend their free time breaking down Cover 2 defenses, working on their three-step drops, or discussing the best way to beat a Bill Belichick defense.

"Obviously football stories come up," Eli said. "But we don't talk Xs and Os. We were brothers and had known each other a long time before football was even a factor for us. We have tons of old stories. We do movie quotes. We just talk about whatever is happening in each other's lives. Sometimes that's football, but there are a lot of other things also."

And sometimes they do what two brothers have done ever since the first ball was invented. They go outside and just play catch.

"It doesn't happen very often," Peyton said. "But any chance we get to get out there and go play catch ... to play catch with your brother whether he's an NFL quarterback or not, it's just fun to throw the football back and forth."

• • •

NFL QUARTERBACKS ARE like the world's most exclusive fraternity. They operate in their own social circles, live in their own financial stratosphere, and spend hours studying film far from their teammates who are already out with their friends or home with their families. They golf together, help charities together, even have dinner together more often than most people think. "It's kind of a unique fraternity," Peyton said. "Whether it's Donovan McNabb or Tom Brady or Drew Brees or Eli, quarterbacks for the most part really kind of pull for each other."

They feel each other's pain, console each other when things go wrong, cringe at their injuries. And while they're understandably jealous of each other's successes, they have a unique ability to be happy for each other, too. They also bristle when they hear a member of their fraternity being ripped apart in the press.

"I think quarterbacks generally are pretty defensive of other quarterbacks," Peyton said. "Add the fact that he's your little brother and I'm a little more defensive."

Peyton obviously wasn't thrilled when the fans and media in New York immediately began dissecting and overanalyzing his little brother. But this wasn't just family pride. Peyton was a fan. He followed Eli and knew the whole city was badly overreacting. Every week he'd know where and when Eli was playing, who he was facing, and what challenges were in front of him. Take the Colts jersey off his back and put a Giants cap on his head, and Peyton wasn't much different from any other loyal fan.

"As soon as I get in the locker room after my game, I always check the sheet to see if the Giants won, or I'm asking somebody what the score of the Giants game is," Peyton said. "I've been known in the second or third quarter of my game to kind of check the scoreboard. Once I know the score of our game, I check on the Giants game."

And remember, one of the most memorable sights of Super Bowl XLII was of Peyton, standing up in a luxury box at University of Phoenix Stadium, pumping his fist and screaming like he was born and bred in New York and had lived and died with the Giants all of his life. He looked more excited that night than he had appeared one year earlier, when he won a championship—and a Super Bowl MVP trophy—for himself.

Who could blame him? That was his little brother down there on the field, the one he used to beat up until he remembered that Vanderbilt is the Commodores. The one he forced to play center so he could throw passes to Cooper. The one who once beat him with that thunderous dunk—or so Eli says—and still smiles when he remembers the pain on Peyton's face.

Competition is one thing. Blood is something else.

"People always ask me who my favorite player is," Peyton said. "I always say, 'It's my little brother.'"

That will never change.

Five: "You just have to feel it"

HOW DO YOU define magic?

Maybe the problem is this: you can't. It's the quality Ernie Accorsi looked for in a quarterback. It's the thing that makes a quarterback special. It's the immeasurable feature that told him whether the quarterback would be good or great. But even Accorsi admits it's indefinable, and if he tried to define it, he'd get a different definition from every scout in his room. Some people see greatness in a quarterback in their arm strength. Others look to his leadership qualities. Others rely on more tangible, measurable attributes like size and production at the collegiate level.

Then there are some, like Accorsi, who never really see it at all.

"The fact is that you can look at all the measurables you want, but sooner or later you have to feel it," Accorsi said. "Don Klosterman, who was my first general manager with the Colts, told me, 'Don't ever evaluate a quarterback the way you evaluate the twenty-one other positions because they're playing a different sport.' You know, it was how I felt, not only when I had Unitas, but how I felt as a fan when my teams were playing a Bobby Layne [the Detroit Lions' quarterback in the '50s]. He did not have great athletic ability. He did not throw a spiral. But I was terrified of him. It was how I felt with Elway when I was a professional, that you knew how important that guy was. You just have to feel it and believe it."

That, of course, is the problem that scouts and general managers all face in the months before a draft. What, exactly, does that mean? It's relatively easy to draft some positions. You don't want an offensive lineman nowadays who weighs much less than 300 pounds. The best receivers seem to separate themselves by a fraction of a second in the forty-yard dash. Body type and production can often define a defensive tackle. And just by watching film, scouts can usually tell whether a linebacker can play.

But a quarterback? Sure, there are some guidelines, but nothing definitive. Most general managers prefer their quarterback tall so he can see over the offensive line. Then again, Doug Flutie once made the Pro Bowl despite being generously listed at 5-foot-10. And arm strength would seem to be a necessity, but Jeff George had a cannon. Unfortunately, he didn't have the head to match. After being selected number one overall by the Colts in 1990, he ended up kicking around with seven different teams in his lackluster fourteen-year NFL career.

Statistics can be a pretty useless measure of a quarterback, too. A quarterback's completion percentage could easily be skewed by butterfingered receivers, a porous offensive line that forces him to throw on the run, or being smart enough to throw the ball away rather than take a sack—a positive trait that produces negative stats. Yards can be diminished by a run-first offense or by receivers who can't break tackles downfield. Touchdowns can be irrelevant, too, depending on the quality of opponents. A Division I quarterback could throw for six touchdowns against a Division II team, but what could he do if his team played one of the toughest defenses in the SEC?

Then there's the passer rating, the most widely used and widely scorned measurement for the quarterback position. It was developed in 1973 by a special committee led by Don Smith, the retired vice president of the Pro Football Hall of Fame. It factors completion percentage, yards per attempt, touchdowns per attempt, and interceptions per attempt into a formula so complicated it would give a calculus major a headache.

Accorsi recalled being at the first league meeting after the NFL decided to make passer rating an official statistic. Everyone was handed a list of the best single-season quarterback performances of all-time and Accorsi said he went "berserk" when he saw the name at the top of the list was Cleveland Browns quarterback Milt Plum.

Plum topped the list based on the 110.4 rating he would have had in the 1960 season. Never mind that the Browns had only the sixth-best passing offense that season, or that at 8–3–1 they missed the postseason by finishing second in the NFL's Eastern Division. Accorsi couldn't get over the fact that Plum, of all people, topped a list that didn't include the likes of Johnny Unitas or Joe Namath anywhere in the top ten. Sure, Plum had a good season in '60—he completed 60.4 percent of his passes and was only picked off five times.

But he was talking about two Hall of Famers. And Milt Plum.

"Unitas and Namath, they threw so many interceptions because they tried to carry their team," Accorsi said. "If you mention Milt Plum to the Brown family, they'll go through the roof because they had two Hall of Fame backs at two different times—Jim Brown and Bobby Mitchell, and then Brown and Leroy Kelly. And they didn't win. Because of Plum."

• • •

IT ALL STARTS with the film, which theoretically should be enough, but with scouts and general managers it never is. They want to see more than what a kid can do on the field. They want to poke him, prod him, try to trick him so they can see whether he can think on his feet. They want to see him throw every route they can think of, up close, so they can find the flaws that weren't evident on film. Is the ball he throws really a spiral? Is he really throwing hard? Which passes can he make? Are there times when his ball floats?

That deconstruction process starts at the scouting combine in Indianapolis, where most of the top prospects have an on-field audition, followed by a medical exam, followed by interviews with team after team. They also take the Wonderlic exam—a fifty-question quiz that's partially a test of intelligence and partially a test of quick decision-making skills. That would seem to be two things all quarterbacks should have, but it's a test that has proven to be remarkably meaningless over the years. Tom Brady got a 33 on his Wonderlic in 2000, yet he was still drafted in the sixth round after Tee Martin, who scored an 11. Ryan Leaf, arguably the biggest draft bust of all time and a player who couldn't handle the NFL pressure, scored a respectable 27. Drew Henson, a remarkable athlete, scored an impressive 42 yet spent only two years on an NFL roster. And three Hall of Famers—Terry Bradshaw, Jim Kelly and Dan Marino—each reportedly scored only a 15.

Still, they all take it, for whatever it's worth, and then some of them take it again. They do everything two or three times or more, in fact—first at their college Pro Days, where packs of scouts attend, and later maybe even at a private workout or two. And a single bad day in all of that could send a quarterback spiraling down the draft, which is not exactly fair considering quarterbacks are forced to perform at those workouts in a very un-game-like setting, often throwing to receivers they have never met before.

"Their timing is way off," said Kevin Colbert, the Steelers' director of football operations. "When a kid looks good at the combine it's probably a bonus. The majority of them don't, only because they can't even anticipate who their receiver is going to be because it happens so quick. He doesn't know how fast he is, where he's going to break things off.

"You've got to be real careful about the quarterbacks in these drills. You look for footwork first, quick release, arm strength. Then the accuracy."

Not everyone agrees. Mike Martz—the former head coach of the St. Louis Rams who found value in an eighth-round pick named Trent Green, a sixth-round pick named Marc Bulger, and an undrafted Arena League player named Kurt Warner—said of quarterbacks, "Accuracy is number one. The whole premise is if you throw the ball from Point A to Point B that you can do it consistently and hit that spot, no matter how hard you throw it or how far that ball goes. If you're spraying it around there, you're making it hard for us."

Most scouts agree that accuracy can't usually be taught. A quarterback either has it, or he doesn't. So what good is a rocket arm if the rocket never hits its mark?

"People think a quarterback's ball has to be more like John Elway's ball, and I think that might be the least important thing," added former Vikings and Cardinals head coach Dennis Green. "It's not about the ball, it's about whether it gets there or not."

Of course, there are different ways to get the ball there—including having the quarterback carry it himself. And that's a factor that has made evaluating the position more complicated than ever. Over the last decade or so there has been an explosion of so-called "running quarterbacks," who are equally dangerous with their arm and their feet (sometimes their feet are their most dangerous weapon). There was a time when ultra-mobile quarterbacks like Steve Young and Randall Cunningham were a novelty.

Nowadays, everyone is looking for the next Michael Vick, the number one overall pick in the 2001 draft. Before he became infamous for his dog-fighting escapades, Vick was thought to be the prototype for the quarterback of the twenty-first century. He was the first quarterback ever to rush for 1,000 yards in a season, and Vick was so athletic and had such a cannon for an arm, he seemed to have the potential of throwing for 300 yards and rushing for 100 yards in the same game.

As more and more defensive coordinators stayed up nights trying to figure out how to defend against the pass and the run simultaneously, head coaches began dreaming of having a Vick for themselves.

"Vince Young [who was drafted third overall by the Tennessee Titans in 2006] is a special, special guy," said Indianapolis Colts head coach Tony Dungy. "And if you're willing to tailor your offense to what he can do well, people are going to have to defend things they've never had to defend before—even with Michael Vick. But you have to be willing to utilize the talents he has. Vick and Young revolutionize the position only if you're willing to do what they do and you put the right person in the right situation. Steve Young went to Tampa and it wasn't the right situation. Not many people envisioned him being special at that point in time. He went to San Francisco and it was the right situation."

The problem, as enticing as that all-around talent can be, is that not many coaches are willing to overhaul their entire offense to accommodate it. And even if they were willing to do it, not all of them can. Not all offensive linemen can block for a quarterback who makes most of his throws outside the pocket. Not all receivers are good enough to adjust their routes on the fly. It's great to have a quarterback that can improvise and make something out of nothing. But football is so structured and choreographed, like an eleven-man ballet, that having Baryshnikov at quarterback is useless if everyone else is tripping over their two left feet.

"I don't think the qualities that teams are looking for have changed all that much," said Drew Bledsoe, a pure pocket passer who was drafted first overall by New England in 1993. "You keep hearing it's kind of been in vogue to get a more mobile quarterback. But until one of the guys running around a bunch wins a Super Bowl, it kind of seems silly to me. Donovan [McNabb] is having great success now with the Eagles, but that's because he is sitting in there, throwing it, and distributing it to his guys. You go back as far as Steve Young, he was a guy who was a running quarterback but really had his best success when he decided to sit in the pocket and throw it around a little bit. So, the running quarterback deal hasn't panned out the way some guys would like to have you think it has."

Of course, evaluating pure pocket passers like Bledsoe isn't easy, either, especially based on what they did (or didn't do) in college. Take the curious case of Alex Smith, the first overall pick of the 2005 draft. He seemed to have it all. Good size (6-foot-4), intelligence (got his degree in economics in just two years and scored a 40 on the Wonderlic), a winning pedigree (Utah went 12–0 during his final season), and he completed 66.3 percent of his collegiate passes while throwing forty-seven touchdowns and eight interceptions. He even ran a little too, picking up 1,083 yards and fifteen rushing touchdowns in two years as a starter for the Utes.

So what's not to like? Only the fact that he played for Urban Meyer, who employed the "spread option" offense. It was a scheme designed to strain the defense, forcing them to defend the run and pass simultaneously. And defending the pass was at times impossible with the quarterback lined up almost exclusively in the shotgun with four or five receivers spread wide. It was a great system and Smith ran it to perfection.

But it was unlike any system Smith was likely to see in the NFL.

"It's a process," said Scott McCloughan, the 49ers general manager, who was the team's vice president of player personnel when they drafted Smith. "You've got to get him comfortable underneath the center. You've got to get him used to the technique that's needed. A lot of times the shotgun quarterback is not reading the defense. The ball is snapped, they have one, two or three reads and they're throwing the ball. They don't care what the defense is in. It can be a 3–4, 4–3, it can be a nickel or dime package, but they're just worried about getting the ball out quick."

. . .

SO LET'S MAKE it easy: Let's say a team has found a college quarterback playing a pro-style offense, who is coached by someone with roots in the NFL. He's a typical drop-back passer, maybe with some mobility as a bonus, good size, a good-enough arm, and he's had success against good competition on the college level. Your team has a chance to take him at the top of the NFL draft.

Is he Peyton Manning or Ryan Leaf? Drew Bledsoe or Rick Mirer? Those were the top two picks in the 1998 and 1993 drafts. And they were close. Real close. In both of those years you could find just as many scouts that preferred one as you could that preferred the other. In both years the top two spots were considered a toss-up. But while Manning went on to what will surely be a Hall of Fame career, Leaf was a head-case who became the poster child for draft disasters. Bledsoe played fourteen years and threw for more than 44,000 yards. Mirer lasted only three and a half seasons as a full-time starter before becoming the ultimate journeyman, kicking around a total of seven teams with little success.

How could two players in the same draft class rated so closely by most NFL talent evaluators go on to have such vastly different careers? It comes back down to those indefinable intangibles: magic, leadership, charisma, grace under pressure ... maybe all of the above.

"I think, number one, does he look like he can lead the team?" Green said. "Does he have leadership qualities? I think all of the things you look for, Tom Brady had those. I think Joe Montana, who was a third-round pick, he had those, too. I think you want a quarterback who shows he can get the team in the end zone, he can lead the team, that the team has a lot of confidence in."

Of course, Brady was a sixth-round pick, almost a complete afterthought in the 2000 draft (a byproduct of having to split time with Henson as a senior at Michigan). Montana, like Green said, went in the third round in 1979. Unitas was a ninth-rounder who was then cut by his first NFL team, his hometown Steelers. All of those quarterbacks had what Green considered ideal qualities, but obviously for the majority of NFL scouts those qualites proved awfully difficult to see.

Then again, maybe those qualities aren't so tough to see. One problem with evaluating quarterbacks is that because the position is so important, the process is much more intense. A team might overlook a flaw in a linebacker or take a chance on a corner without ideal size if they fall in love with the player. If they're wrong, they're wrong. Life goes on. But it's hard to make a commitment to a quarterback because he becomes the centerpiece of the team and the franchise. As a result, during the long months leading up to the draft it's easy for the evaluators to focus on the flaws.

"When we looked at Marc Bulger, I'll never forget this, I was told, 'There's a terrific quarterback down in West Virginia I want you to look at,'" Martz recalled. "'He had a bad senior year. His

47

junior year was phenomenal, but he got hurt his senior year, he didn't play well and he threw a lot of interceptions. But I want you to think about him.' We put a pretty good grade on him, and the first chance that we had we went and snatched him away."

The Rams actually passed on Bulger five times in the 2000 draft before he was eventually selected in the sixth round by the New Orleans Saints. It was a year later, after he was cut by both the Saints and the Falcons, that Martz and the Rams finally snatched him and watched him become a two-time Pro Bowler.

"My point in all that is we tried not to let that bad senior year affect us," Martz said. "You just get distracted on so many things that aren't important. You've got to believe what you see. Then you'll have a better chance."

. . .

EYES CAN BE deceiving, though, a lesson Accorsi learned the day he saw Johnny Unitas up close and in person for the very first time. It was back in 1970, Accorsi's first year in the NFL, at the Colorado School of Mines, of all places. He had just joined the Colts as the public relations director after a few years as a sportswriter and as the assistant sports publicity director at Penn State. Unitas, his boyhood hero, looked like a shell of himself as he labored through training camp drills that summer. He had torn tendons in his elbow and Accorsi was worried that his thirty-seven-year-old hero was done.

He was so worried, in fact, that he approached Milt Davis, a former all-pro defensive back and then a Colts scout, and dared to question whether the Colts could still win with Unitas at the helm.

"Ernie, listen to me," Davis said. "You evaluate the great quarterbacks on one element alone: Can they take their team down the field, with the championship on the line, and into the end zone?"

That was a line that would follow Accorsi throughout his career, especially when he saw what happened in the 1970 season. It was hardly one of Unitas's finer statistical seasons. His completion percentage (51.7), yards (2,213), and touchdown-to-interception ration (14 to 18) were well below his career averages. But he somehow managed to lead the Baltimore Colts all the way to Super Bowl V.

Accorsi couldn't see that possibility when he watched those practices in Golden, Colorado. But Davis could. He could feel it, too.

Not surprisingly, that experience with Unitas was on Accorsi's mind when he scouted Eli Manning at Ole Miss in 2002, especially since what he saw in that game against Auburn could have been interpreted two ways. Eli had given a brilliant performance and kept leading his overmatched team back against a superior opponent, carrying them on his back all the way. That's what Accorsi saw. On the other hand, Eli didn't win. And in the end he made a critical mistake and threw a terrible interception when he had a chance to win it.

Was it good, or was it bad? Was he a star in the making or someone who couldn't hack it in the clutch?

It all depends on what you feel.

"I've always felt that there are givens that are obvious and they're physical," Accorsi explained. "You like the big guy who can throw, has a quick release and decent feet. But ultimately it's got to be an instinct that he has and you have for him that he's got. You can call it anything you want—intangible, magic. But he's got to have some quality that you feel. And it's different than other positions because the quarterback position is so different. Athleticism is important, there's no question about it, but the magic to me is more important. I drafted Kosar. He's almost a reject as far as an athlete. But he had something about him and he was very successful.

ELI MANNING

"There's a lot of people that do not know how to evaluate quarterbacks. When I start hearing people say 'Here's what I like about him: He's got a big strong arm, he's got good size, he's had good success …' then I know they're on a trail, but I'm on a different road. We're on two different tracks."

Six: "You can't overpay DiMaggio"

THERE WEREN'T MANY times in the months and weeks leading up to the 2004 draft that Ernie Accorsi truly believed he had a shot at making a trade for Eli Manning. Even with a week to go he thought his chances were less than 50–50. But at least there was a chance, which is why the week before the draft he and the Giants' brain trust got together for a few days of meetings to determine just how far they were willing to go. It was their first serious, crunch-time discussion about the parameters of what their final offer would be and how to approach their talks with the Chargers. It was the first real sign that things were about to heat up.

There weren't many arguments during the meetings. Nobody spoke out against their desire to make the deal. "There was really no dispute in this," Accorsi recalled. "It was not divided in any way by anybody, either by which quarterback to go after or whether to do it."

But as the hours ticked away and the discussions dragged on, Accorsi couldn't help but notice that Wellington Mara, the wise, old patriarch of the franchise, wasn't saying much.

That wasn't a good sign.

"With Well, things would bother him, but he never erupted," Accorsi said. "That's not the way he was. He'd ponder things and think things over. There were a lot of times when he didn't say much at three or four in the afternoon, but he'd go home, ponder it and take up a stronger position the next morning. He was the opposite of someone who was impulsive."

Accorsi remembered thinking that Wellington was "cool" to the whole idea of trading for Eli. It wasn't until the next morning, though, that Accorsi realized how cool he really was.

It was a Sunday morning, just six days before the draft, and Accorsi and the rest of the top executives had all taken the day off to clear their heads. It was a beautiful day, too, so he decided to spend the morning with an old friend, strolling through Gramercy Park in Manhattan, trying to keep his mind as far from football and Eli as he could. But his tranquility was interrupted by the ring of his cell phone and his heart stopped for moment when he looked down and saw that the call was from his eighty-seven-year-old boss.

Wellington had gone home on Saturday night and pondered, just as Accorsi suspected, and decided he wasn't happy with what he had heard. Wellington was a fiercely loyal man, who had developed a soft spot for quarterback Kerry Collins, and believed the Giants' quarterback situation was just fine. He didn't see a need for them to trade for Eli, and told Accorsi as much in their short, to-the-point conversation. Wellington didn't tell him not to make the deal—that wasn't his style—but he voiced his displeasure using what Accorsi called "his classic phrase."

"You all do what you want," Wellington said, "but I'm not going to be very happy."

Talk about a shot right to the heart. Accorsi was crushed. He figured what little chance he had of actually making the deal was now officially dead. And his relaxing walk in the park was ruined, too. So he excused himself from his friend and found a quiet spot, alone, and immediately called Wellington's son, John, interrupting his Sunday afternoon with his family.

"John," Accorsi said. "I think I've got a real problem on my hands."

John knew immediately what the problem was. It had nothing to do with Eli, and everything to do with the quarterback he'd be replacing—a quarterback and a man who had turned his own life and the Giants' fortunes around. When Accorsi signed Collins on February 19, 1999, Collins was in an alcohol rehabilitation clinic. He was also known more for an incident in which he used a racial slur toward a Carolina Panthers teammate than he was for his powerful right arm. His football career had been shattered. His life, at the time, was a mess.

But five years later, Collins had turned the Giants into contenders and even led them to Super Bowl XXXV. And he had battled back his own demons to become a good man who spent his free time not in bars, but visiting sick children in hospitals and buying groceries for poor families in his community. He helped save the Giants and the Giants helped save him. That had earned Wellington's loyalty, admiration, and respect.

"That was the one thing that really, I thought, was holding my father back from giving his final approval on the trade," John Mara said. "He didn't want to give up on Kerry at the time."

Wellington, of course, wasn't just another NFL owner. He was a league and team icon who, in many ways, *was* the Giants. He had seen every minute of the team's history since it was founded in 1925. He had scouted more players, acquired more players, and watched more practices than anyone in his organization. He was revered and respected by everyone who knew him. Anything he said—no matter how softly—was like a commandment, even though he would never issue an actual commandment. He had too much respect for the structure of his organization and the people he hired to work for the club.

So he was never going to step in and tell Accorsi who to draft or how to run the Giants. But just a hint of displeasure in Wellington's voice was enough to momentarily stop Accorsi in his tracks.

John told Accorsi to relax, to enjoy his day, and not to worry about Wellington. He said they'd talk about it again in the office the next morning, and that they would move forward with the trade.

"Look," John told him, "We're all for it. I'll talk to him and he'll go along with it, too."

Accorsi still thought the deal was dead.

Over the next few days, whenever the possibility of a deal was discussed, Accorsi would approach Wellington and ask, "Are you OK, Mr. Mara?" Wellington always answered with a quick "Yes," insisting he was fine. "But he wasn't," Accorsi said. "He wasn't happy." John remained Accorsi's lead counsel on the matter, assuring him his father would come around and that their pursuit of their new franchise quarterback should continue.

If at any point John had sided with his father, that would've been the end of the deal.

John never did, but Accorsi was still wary of Wellington's unhappiness. He noticed Wellington was quiet again on the day of the draft as they all sat in the general manager's office. "I was looking at him every step of the way," Accorsi recalled. Even when the talks were coming down to the wire with the Giants on the clock, the unhappy look on Wellington's face was making Accorsi uncomfortable. So with time running out, Accorsi gave him one final chance to veto the deal.

"Mr. Mara," Accorsi said, "if you don't want me to make this trade, we're not going to make it."

"No, no, no ..." was Wellington's reply.

"He had a way of letting you know he wasn't happy about something," John said. "And you never want to really do anything if you felt that he was going to be that unhappy about it.

54

"But I think the more we got into it, the more he listened to Tom Coughlin and Jerry Reese and the scouts, I think he kind of came around. He still wasn't thrilled with it. And it wasn't because of any doubts about Eli. He loved the Manning family. But it was just the affect that it was going to have on Kerry."

When did Wellington Mara stop being unhappy about the trade? The minute Eli, along with his father, Archie, and mother, Olivia, walked in the front door of Giants Stadium a few hours after the deal was made. When they arrived, Wellington made sure he was the first one out in the lobby, ready to greet them. He wanted them to know they were welcomed with open arms.

"It changed instantly," Accorsi said. "That's the specialness about Wellington. The minute that Eli walked in the lobby, the door opened, Wellington greeted his mother and father and everything was fine.

"It was all about being a Giant. That's what it was all about. Before the trade, Eli wasn't and Kerry was. But the minute Eli walked through those doors, he was a Giant. From that instant on, there was never any blinking of Wellington's eyes."

• • •

TEAMS WERE GIVEN fifteen minutes to make their picks in the first round of the draft at the time, and when the Giants were on the clock that afternoon, each tick was like the beat of a bass drum. As time passed—and it moved agonizingly slow and a little too fast at the same time—each beat reverberated throughout the team's offices inside Giants Stadium.

They had their fates and futures—not to mention those of the franchise—in their hands. And out of their hands, too. On the table in front of them was their quarterback of the future. He wasn't their first choice, but Ben Roethlisberger was still going to make them fairly happy. Even better, the Cleveland Browns had just called and offered a sweetheart deal. The Giants could trade down a few spots in the 2004 draft, still get Roethlisberger (and save a little money, by the way, by drafting him lower), and pick up an extra second-round pick. "A steal," was how Accorsi described it.

But there was a little voice in the back of Accorsi's head telling him to wait just a little bit longer. He had spent a year and a half lusting over Eli Manning—the real object of the Giants' desire—and Accorsi was still holding out a slim hope that he could get him. The night before the draft he had gotten a phone call from a member of the media with some interesting news. It didn't come from one of his friends. If it had this all would've been a little easier. But he thought the reporter was sincere in relaying what he heard.

He outlined a scenario for Accorsi in which A. J. Smith, the general manager of the San Diego Chargers, was going to select Eli with the first overall pick. Then, the reporter said, Smith was going to wait until it was the Giants' turn to pick fourth, and until they had seven or eight minutes left on their fifteen-minute clock. Then he was going to call and offer Accorsi a deal. There was no telling what the offer would be, of course, but Smith's intention was to make a trade.

So there he sat, with a great deal from Cleveland sitting on the table and a top flight quarterback well within his reach. But he was stuck, unsure of what to do, based solely on a phone conversation he wasn't sure he could believe. The Cleveland offer wouldn't be good forever. He also worried the Browns might screw him in the end by dealing with the Chargers themselves. He wasn't sure if he could trust Smith. He wasn't even sure if Smith was going to call. He was stalled at the crossroads of a lifetime and a career.

There were now eight minutes left before he'd have to make his choice, and that damn clock was still tick, tick, ticking away.

By then, of course, Accorsi knew exactly who needed a quarterback and who didn't. The general managers of those teams all felt like they were riding a tour bus together that off-season, going from workout to workout to see the top quarterbacks perform. They all schlepped out to Oxford, Ohio to watch Ben Roethlisberger throw, and then down to Raleigh, North Carolina for Philip Rivers. A couple of them even made it to Virginia to check out Matt Schaub.

The feature attraction, of course, was Eli Manning, who had dazzled everyone with his poise and professionalism at the combine (where, by the way, he scored a 39 on the Wonderlic—11 points higher than his celebrated brother). At his workout for scouts in New Orleans, he was joined by J. P. Losman of Tulane, and nearly every team sent a representative. Some teams, in fact, came armed with a half-dozen scouts and executives because they all wanted to see the future star for themselves.

That, Accorsi said, was one of his lowest moments during the whole Eli pursuit. He wanted to keep that secret all to himself. By then he had made up his mind that he was going to select a quarterback in the 2004 draft. The Giants were three years removed from a disastrous performance in Super Bowl, XXXV, which had raised all sorts of questions about Collins and his ability to win a championship. It wasn't just that Super Bowl, either. Two years later, a red-hot Giants team went to San Francisco for a first-round playoff game and blew a 38–14 second-half lead and ended up losing 39–38. The second-biggest collapse in NFL postseason history wasn't all Collins' fault (hell, he went 29 for 43 for 342 yards and four touchdowns). But the way the offense shut down late when one lousy field goal could have put the game out of reach bothered everyone back in New York. It didn't help that he then struggled in

2003 before an ankle injury landed him on injured reserve, where he watched the Giants fall apart down the stretch of Jim Fassel's final season and finish a miserable 4–12.

The Giants weren't going to get rid of Collins anytime soon, especially since they felt their window of opportunity would soon be closing on several of their veteran players, but given the amount of talented quarterbacks in the draft and the fact that the Giants were going to pick fourth convinced Accorsi the time to pick Collins's successor was now. And after having a laser-like focus on Eli for more than a year, he decided that since he was sitting so close to the top of the draft, he might as well take his shot at the best player on the board.

Of course, by then the entire league was onto Eli, including the Chargers, who held the first overall pick. To that point, Accorsi had only had one very short conversation about that pick with Smith, their general manager, who had begun his NFL career as a part-time scout for the Giants in 1977. He was only a year into his new job in San Diego, which he inherited after his predecessor, John Butler, died of lung cancer in April 2003. Accorsi knew who Smith was but didn't know him well, which would make any negotiation tricky—assuming Smith wanted to negotiate at all. There was another problem, too: Smith's relationship with his coach, Marty Schottenheimer, was strained. And Schottenheimer just happened to be Accorsi's best friend in the league.

So, in late February, after the scouting combine and before the annual NFL owners meetings, Accorsi called his old buddy, Schottenheimer, his old coach from his Cleveland days, and told him, "You and I have to make a pact that we're not going to speak until the draft is over." No dinners at the league meetings. Nothing more than a casual hello. The last thing Accorsi wanted to do was tick Smith off by appearing to go behind his back.

"It wasn't a fake," Accorsi said. "We never spoke about it again."

But he wasn't speaking to Smith about it much, either. In fact, another month went by before Accorsi talked to Smith again, on March 30, 2004, at the league meetings in Palm Beach, Florida.

"Are you interested in trading that pick?" Accorsi said.

"I might be," Smith replied.

"Well, as time goes on, let's talk later," Accorsi said.

And that was it.

There were twenty-five days to go before the draft, and at that point Accorsi was still struggling to feel Smith out, trying to get a handle on his adversary's style, how he operated, what kind of games he was going to play before making a trade. The truth was that Accorsi had "no clue. I just don't know this guy," he said.

Right around that time, though, Accorsi got the break of a lifetime—the perfect revenge for what had happened to him back in 1983. Eli, through his father and his agent (Tom Condon)—both of whom clearly seemed to be pulling the strings—began to let Smith know Eli had no interest in playing for the Chargers. They were a woeful franchise with a history of losing, and Archie was worried that Eli would suffer the same career-long fate he once suffered in New Orleans. Their reasons didn't matter to Accorsi, who loved the irony. It was, after all, exactly what Elway had done to Accorsi's Baltimore Colts twenty-one years earlier. Eli had no leverage, no contract from the Yankees waiting in the wings, but he and his camp seemed determined. They all wanted the Chargers to trade the number one pick.

And yes, they told Smith, ideally they preferred a trade to New York.

Word of that power play didn't hit the press until two days before the draft, but everyone around the league was aware of it—even if it was only a rumor to most—and it loomed over the trade talks the entire time. Actually, trade "talks" is an exaggeration, since Accorsi and Smith only spoke four or five times, and most of those conversations were brief. Like the one on April 6, with less than three weeks to go, when Accorsi called Smith to restate his interest. "It never went anywhere," Accorsi said.

Meanwhile, Smith was playing an odd public game. The day after he talked to Accorsi, he divulged that conversation to reporters in San Diego—a move that didn't sit well with the Giants' front office. The Giants' interest in Eli was already the worst-kept secret in the world by then, but Accorsi didn't want it to be confirmed. He was too afraid of losing leverage or finding someone else trying to jump ahead of him. When reporters started calling to tell him Smith admitted they were talking, Accorsi was pissed. But Smith didn't stop there. Eight days later, he went public with a call he supposedly got from Redskins owner Dan Snyder about the same thing. The next day, the Redskins issued a statement ripping Smith for "trying to use the Redskins as they've used the New York Giants, to generate interest in a trade."

At that point, it appeared that only the Giants and Browns really wanted the top pick, and clearly the Giants seemed to want it the most. Eventually, on Monday, April 19, with just five days to go before the draft, Smith finally set some parameters for a possible deal, basing it on what the Chargers got in 2001 when they traded away the top pick (and the rights to quarterback Michael Vick) to the Atlanta Falcons: the fifth overall pick, a third-rounder, a future second-rounder, and receiver/returner Tim Dwight. This time, the player Smith requested was defensive end Osi Umenyiora, a twenty-two-year-old pass rusher with one career sack and unlimited potential.

Since Accorsi describes his team-building philosophy as "quarterbacks and pass rushers," the deal started to look like it was dead.

"Just so you know, that's a deal-breaker," Accorsi told Smith. "That's not a negotiating point. It's not going to happen."

That wasn't the only problem with the Chargers' demands, either. Their entire asking price seemed way too high to the Giants, who had decided they'd be willing to part with a future first-round pick instead of a player, but they didn't intend to give up a second-round pick, too. Still, Accorsi kept the door open and Smith set a Friday deadline for the talks—hardly unreasonable since the draft would begin Saturday at noon. The next day, Accorsi went on WFAN, New York's biggest all-sports talk radio station, and sounded positively depressed when he said, "If you asked me to put my two dollars down, I'd say they're going to keep it and make the pick. In the final analysis I think they won't [make a trade], but I think they want to see what they can get."

Actually, what Accorsi sensed was that the Chargers were unsure what to do because of Eli's threat not to sign with them. They seemed to want Eli, but they were ticked off by his petulant demands. Who did that spoiled brat think he was? How dare he say the Chargers—and beautiful, sunny San Diego—weren't good enough for him? They were torn between wanting to call his bluff and wanting nothing to do with him. They were being pulled between a desire for a player and a desire to avoid the headaches that would surely follow if they took a player who didn't want to play for them.

"His back was really up against it because of this threat by the player," Accorsi said. "I said, 'Hey A. J., if you want to call his bluff, more power to you. I was in the same situation you were in and I did it. And not because I was trying to prove something. I thought Elway was the best player and I was going to pick him. And I would've stuck it out, too. So if that's what you want to do, I'll applaud you. You just tell me and I'll back out of this so I don't make it harder for you.'"

Accorsi decided it would be best to leave Smith alone for a few days and let him sort it all out for himself. Meanwhile, as he was baring his soul to WFAN, Archie Manning was out in San Diego having a private meeting with Schottenheimer, who was trying to convince him that the Chargers, who had only four winning seasons in the last twenty-one years, weren't the modern day 'Aints. Archie wasn't convinced and the meeting went nowhere. The next day, hours after Archie boarded his flight to New Orleans, Condon called Smith to reiterate the Mannings' desire for Eli to be traded to New York. Now it was beginning to sound more like a demand.

Clearly Smith was feeling the pressure, and a few hours later, Accorsi's phone rang. "Are you still interested?" Smith said. That began what Accorsi called "our first real talk" about the deal. The Chargers wanted the Giants' first-, second-, and third-round picks in the 2004 draft, plus their first-rounder in 2005. They also wanted Umenyiora.

Once again, the conversation ended before the negotiations began.

As far as Accorsi knew, that was it. The deal, not that there really ever was one, was off. He was mentally preparing himself to accept that Eli was gone and he'd have to learn to like Roethlisberger. That wasn't so bad, really. Big Ben was a different quarterback than Eli. So different, in fact, that when some of his scouts ranked the quarterbacks they put them in two separate categories. Roethlisberger was more of a gunslinger and definitely less polished. He hadn't really been tested against NFL-ready competition. When the Giants' draft board was finalized, Eli was at the top, Iowa left tackle Robert Gallery was second, and Roethlisberger was third. There was nothing, really, that the Giants liked about Philip Rivers—certainly not picking that high in the draft, anyway. And the truth is they never had any intention of picking Rivers, even if they traded down. His arm strength didn't match the others and he had a funky windup. Accorsi's third choice for a quarterback actually would have been Schaub, but the consensus was that Schaub wasn't worthy of a pick that high.

So the plan was to watch Eli go and then sweat out the next two picks. There was a chance that the Oakland Raiders, picking second, were going to pick Roethlisberger or trade the pick to someone who would. Then the Giants were going to have a tough decision. They needed a quarterback and they knew it. They needed a left tackle, too. And Accorsi loved the acrobatic ability of Pittsburgh receiver Larry Fitzgerald, but he called himself the "lone wolf" in the draft room on that front (everyone else was worried about Fitzgerald's lack of speed). So the debate inside the war room was raging: What if the two quarterbacks and Gallery were gone? Would everyone else give in and let Accorsi take Fitzgerald? Or would Rivers be forced back into their thinking?

No, their research told them Roethlisberger was going to be available. So Roethlisberger it was. Accorsi was prepared for that, right up until his phone rang on Friday night.

"It was a member of the national media who I was not particularly close to, but I had no reason to question his credibility," Accorsi said. "He said, 'A. J. is picking Manning tomorrow and he's going to call you with about seven minutes to go when you're on the clock.' I don't know if that's going to happen or not, but we're ready to pick Roethlisberger."

That night, John Mara was at a school function for one of his children, but he spent most of the time on the phone with Accorsi, going over the possibilities. "We were still pretty far apart on what it was going to take to make the deal," Mara said. "We didn't know whether they even wanted to make the deal or not.

A. J. was being pretty coy about it. I give A. J. credit. He played it pretty cool."

That night, Smith's deadline passed. He didn't call Accorsi, and Accorsi didn't call him.

· · ·

By the morning of the draft, Eli Manning had gone from all-American hero to poster child for spoiled, rich athletes everywhere. He had arrived in New York a few days early for the draft and was sitting in his hotel room watching television that Thursday night when he suddenly saw himself being blasted for trying to force his way out of San Diego. It had been a few weeks since the Chargers first learned Eli didn't want to play for them and a few days since his agent made it official. But only now had word of the demand mysteriously and suddenly been leaked to the press, and Smith had no problem confirming it for the record. Eli sat there, stunned.

If the Mannings were surprised, Condon was furious, though he later conceded that the whole maneuver made sense to him. A lot of people suspected the Chargers wanted Rivers right from the beginning. He was the MVP of the Senior Bowl where, by the way, Schottenheimer had been the coach. In fact, after the draft Schottenheimer compared Rivers favorably to Bernie Kosar—an Accorsi favorite—which probably says it all about who he wanted all along. Now that the Chargers had leaked Eli's demands, they could calm the Eli hysteria in their town by telling everyone the big baby didn't want to play for them, and if they did trade him they'd be the heroes, getting a bushel of draft picks and a player happy to call San Diego home.

Once all that was out, Eli was an easy target all across the country. So was Archie, for seemingly being an overprotective, nightmarish Little League Dad. Eli swears it was all his decision—"My dad did not even want to get involved," he said. Still, it sure seemed like Archie's and Condon's fingerprints were all over the maneuver from the start. Archie wanted his son to experience winning, which hadn't happened often in San Diego. And Condon knew what a huge star Peyton had become in the relative isolation of Indianapolis. He was dying to have a star quarterback—a Manning—in New York.

Making matters worse, Eli seemed to be flaunting the fact that he was holding up the Chargers and trying to grab control of the draft. He filmed a commercial for Reebok that showed him first with a Chargers hat on, then holding a Chargers and Giants cap in his hands. He even had a Redskins hat on at one point during the ad, which ended with him on screen holding a handful of hats and asking, "What happened to the Chargers?"

It was funny, but to a lot of people it wasn't a joke. They were furious out in San Diego, and even in New York—the place he wanted to play—the Manning name was being dragged through the mud. There was already talk that if the Chargers picked him he'd refuse to come out on stage to shake NFL commissioner Paul Tagliabue's hand, or at the very least that he wouldn't hold up the Chargers' jersey or wear a Chargers hat.

When the draft began, Eli was sitting in the back room with the other top draft picks at a table with Condon and both of his parents. They were just waiting for a phone call, hoping he'd be traded. But after a few minutes, his father turned to him and said "Well, they're going to draft you."

"What do I do?" Eli said.

"Go out there and be happy you've been selected to go into the NFL," Archie told him. "The first pick in the draft, that's a great honor."

When Tagliabue called his name, that's exactly what Eli did. He went out on stage and acted happy. Or at least he tried. He shook Tagliabue's hand and held up a blue Chargers jersey with the number 1 on it with a forced smile and pained look on his face, like he was on his way to root canal. The Chargers hat never touched his head. And, not surprisingly, the crowd of mostly Giants and Jets fans packed into the Theater at Madison Square Garden showered him with boos and chants of "Eli sucks!" Meanwhile, rumors surfaced that a plane was waiting to whisk Eli off to San Diego. It appeared, by all accounts, that Smith had decided to call Eli's bluff.

A few miles away, in the Giants' offices at the Meadowlands, Accorsi took a deep breath and began again to accept his expected fate. Then he watched as the Oakland Raiders took Gallery and the Arizona Cardinals took Fitzgerald, leaving Roethlisberger sitting there in Accorsi's hands.

. . .

THE PARTY LINE that came out of the Giants organization for years was that the decision to trade for Eli was unanimous. No one outside ever knew Wellington Mara was against it. As far as the world was concerned, the front office would be portrayed as if they were the Harlem Boys Choir singing Handel's Messiah—one beautiful voice, loud and strong in their praise, banded together to make some beautiful music.

Of course, there was a moment when the music stopped. The Giants' brain trust had left the "war room" for the quiet of Accorsi's office. There they all sat—Accorsi, Wellington, John and his two brothers, Frank and Chris, along with co-owner Bob Tisch and Jerry Reese. They had decided Roethlisberger was their guy and they had all but given up on any trade with the Chargers, who still hadn't called.

Then, not long after their clock began, Accorsi's secretary told him he had a call from the Browns.

"Here's that fateful moment," Accorsi said. "The Browns call and they offer me a great deal. We're fourth and they're seventh. The clock is ticking now. They offer me a swap of firsts for a second. A great trade. I conclude we're still going to get Roethlisberger at seven. I came *that close* to making that deal."

Accorsi told the Browns he wanted to wait until there were seven minutes left on his clock. In the back of his mind was the call he got the night before from that reporter. He was determined to at least find out if the reporter had told him the truth.

It was an agonizing wait, but with Wellington reluctantly on board, Accorsi had the green light to wait as long as he wanted. With about eight minutes to go, though, the Browns called back and again Accorsi nearly said yes. That's when he got cold feet, or at least a cold splash of reality. He began to wonder why Smith hadn't called him yet. All that pre-draft talk of a trade, then nothing on the day of the draft? What if Smith had called the Browns instead? What if the Browns wanted the fourth pick to trade to San Diego so they could swipe Eli out from right under Accorsi's nose?

All the press reports said that the Browns had their eyes on Gallery before the draft, but now Gallery was long gone to Oakland at the number two pick. So it was thought they were trying to make a preemptive strike for Miami tight end Kellen Winslow Jr.—the player they would end up drafting after trading up to the sixth spot. But Accorsi had been hearing from his sources for months that the Browns were secretly in love with Eli. Yes, he thought, "We all hear eight billion rumors," but this was one he couldn't shake. He kept asking the Browns, "What are you doing this for?" They kept avoiding the question, which made him even more nervous than he was before.

"My concern was if I make a deal—even though that's a great deal and we'd end up with Roethlisberger—and they make the trade with the Chargers that I would've been happy to make, I have to live with this the rest of my life," Accorsi said. "I thought, 'They're going to end up making the deal and that'll drive me crazy.'"

So Accorsi backed out on the Browns just in the nick of time. And almost as soon as he hung up the phone, his secretary buzzed in with the five words he'd been waiting to hear.

"A. J. is on the phone."

Smith proposed a new deal. He wanted the Giants to select Rivers for San Diego—a technically illegal maneuver by NFL rules, though no one in the Giants' organization was worried about that—and then send Rivers, their third-round pick, a fifth-round pick in 2005, and Umenyiora to the Chargers in exchange for Eli. Smith had dropped the demand for a second-round pick, but still wanted Umenyiora. The clock was ticking fast, but the executives in Accorsi's office were running out of patience even faster. The fifth-round pick was a new wrinkle in the deal. John Mara's initial reaction was "Enough is enough."

"Then my brother Frank said to me, 'We're not going to lose this guy for a fifth-round draft pick now,'" John recalled. "'Let's just give it to him.'"

But there was still one more seemingly insurmountable problem: the Chargers' insistence on getting Osi Umenyiora.

"Osi is a deal-breaker and that's it," Accorsi told Smith. "We're not even going to discuss it."

"OK," said Smith. "Would you give me next year's number one instead?"

"We've got a deal," Accorsi said.

And so they did. The Giants would take Rivers and eventually send him, their third-round pick, and their first- and fifth-rounders in 2005 to San Diego in return for the quarterback Accorsi wanted all along. Everyone in the office was elated and relieved—everyone, it seemed, except for Accorsi, who knew there was still some worrying to be done. Remember, he didn't know Smith and wasn't completely sure he could trust him. And technically the trade was against league rules. Once a player is selected a team can't trade him for draft picks, and teams also aren't allowed to select players for other teams. There was a chance, however slight, that the Chargers could back out of the deal and stick the Giants with Rivers, whom they never, ever wanted. And if that happened, the Giants couldn't ask the league to enforce a deal they weren't really allowed to make.

"If I would've gone to the league, they would've said, 'Tough luck,'" Accorsi said. "Now, I'm not saying we would've been shooting ourselves over it, but ..."

Accorsi was so nervous that he thought about having Chargers president Dean Spanos promise the trade directly to Wellington Mara because no one could lie, he thought, to such a distinguished and honorable man. But that damn clock was ticking and there just wasn't time. So he made the deal himself and held his breath.

A few minutes later, Smith made it official by sending word of the trade to NFL officials in New York, where they announced it to a suddenly pro-Eli crowd.

Said Accorsi: "Thank God he kept his word."

. . .

THERE WERE SMILES everywhere in the building when the deal was announced, and Accorsi and Tom Coughlin looked positively giddy as they made their way into the pressroom one floor below. If their plan was to temper expectations and not add to the pressure already mounted on the kid … well, they did a poor job of it. Neither was able to face the press and maintain a poker face.

Coughlin called Eli "a very special football player." Accorsi called him "a classic prospect" and said, "I think he's got a chance to be a great quarterback."

The move was huge news in New York and Accorsi was lauded for his boldness, but it didn't take long for people to begin questioning the price. Rivers and three picks for Eli when Roethlisberger was sitting right there in front of him? And when it was learned that he could have moved down and picked up an extra pick and still gotten Roethlisberger, the king's ransom he paid for Eli seemed borderline insane. Yes, Accorsi was bold and brave and daring, but maybe he was also just a little foolish. He was also again being portrayed as a man completely and blindly obsessed.

OK, so maybe he was. But he had his quarterback and he didn't care about how it was perceived.

"I just believe that you can get by if you have to, but if you have a chance to pick what you think is a quarterback for the ages, you have to go after him because you're not going to get that many opportunities in your life," Accorsi said. "It's not any big, cryptic mystery why I feel that way. I've been around great ones. I know what they mean."

That was the conversation, in fact, that Packers head coach Mike Sherman and Accorsi had months earlier after Schaub's workout in Charlottesville, Virginia, while they were waiting out a travel delay. Sitting at the airport, they began talking about the impact great quarterbacks can have on a team. Sherman told him that "when Brett Favre walks into the locker room, you know you have a chance." It was the same way Accorsi felt with Unitas, Bert Jones, and Kosar.

And when Unitas or Jones or Kosar or Favre is staring you in the face, you don't flinch. Accorsi had no interest in playing Russian roulette with a low-round draft choice, hoping he'd get lucky and find another Tom Brady waiting for him in the sixth round.

"I know there's all this business now that you don't have to have a first-round pick at quarterback," he said. "Look at Bradshaw, Griese, and Elway right there. There's three number ones in our lifetime. Twelve Super Bowls. I mean, for the most part they're going to bring you into the Super Bowl.

"And Brady … let's review that draft. What pick do you think he'd be? The fact that everybody misevaluated him is our fault. But what pick do you think he'd be? Do you think people would say, 'I know how good Brady is, but let's see if we can get a quarterback later'? He'd be the first pick in the draft. So the point is you can get by if you have to. But if you have a chance to pick one of the great ones, you don't say, 'Oh well, we'll just hope to get lucky later.'

"I've said this a million times: When 67,000 people left Yankee Stadium on December 28, 1958, they weren't talking about getting beat by the safety. That's all I'll say."

That was the famous day when Alan Ameche barreled up the middle and into the end zone to give the Baltimore Colts a 23–17 overtime win over the New York Giants in the most famous NFL Championship Game of all. Of course, Ameche wouldn't have gotten the chance to be the hero if Unitas, with three broken ribs, hadn't led the Colts to a game-tying field goal in the final seconds of regulation. And it was Unitas who led the Colts on a thirteen-play, eighty-yard march toward Ameche's historic touchdown at the end.

You need that kind of quarterback, that kind of star, if you want to win championships, Accorsi believed. He thought he found his once. Now he found him again. And as far as he was concerned, it was worth whatever it cost him. No price was too high.

"You can't give up too much for Elway," Accorsi said. "You can't overpay DiMaggio."

Seven: "It's just a bad situation"

MICHAEL STRAHAN HAD already played eleven seasons in the NFL by 2004 and was well on his way to the Hall of Fame, but when he looked back on his career he didn't see much success. He played on only five winning teams. He was in the playoffs only three times. And the only time he won a playoff game was in 2000 when the Giants were the best team in the NFC and rolled all the way to Super Bowl XXXV. The crowning moment of that season was an unbelievable 41–0 win over the Minnesota Vikings in the NFC championship game. His quarterback that day was Kerry Collins.

As far as he was concerned that was the only quarterback he'd ever need.

So he was understandably a bit grumpy two days before the 2004 draft when it seemed clear to everyone on the planet that the Giants were preparing to take a quarterback, and pretty obvious that they were ready to make a move to get Eli Manning with the number one pick. Strahan was thirty-two years old then. Who knew how much longer his career was going to last? The Giants were in enough trouble coming off a 4–12 season, trying to adjust to a new coach that blindsided them with a long list of unbreakable rules. Turmoil already surrounded him.

The last thing he wanted to do, he said, was break in a new quarterback, too.

"At this point in my career I'd prefer to have Kerry Collins playing for us, to be honest with you," Strahan said. "I don't have the luxury of time, of sitting for two or three years until someone figures it out. And I think [Eli] is a great quarterback, a phenomenal talent, just like his brother. But it took his brother a few years to figure it out before he became the best in the game.

"I personally don't have time for that."

If it was just Strahan who felt that way, those words would have been easy to ignore. For one thing, he didn't play offense. For another, unhappiness seemed to be his default position back then, especially now that new coach Tom Coughlin—a disciplinarian brought in to replace the laid-back Jim Fassel—had hit the Giants' locker room like a hurricane and Strahan was busy trying to stare him down.

But it wasn't just Strahan, and that was the problem. Collins had rescued the Giants from the unsettling era of Dave Brown, Kent Graham, and Danny Kanell. He reminded the organization, the team, and the entire city what a real quarterback looked like, what could be done with a cannon of an arm. He brought the Giants to the Super Bowl for the first time in a decade, and the only time in most of his teammates' careers. They loved him for that throughout the organization, from Wellington Mara on down. There was loyalty to Collins in every corner of the locker room.

They knew Collins's days were probably numbered, and they didn't want him to be quietly ushered out of town.

"Kerry's the man," said left tackle Luke Petitgout. "He's the guy that's led us to success in the past. For him not to be here would be a great loss."

"I think Kerry's definitely the best quarterback I've ever played with," said receiver Amani Toomer.

And added guard Rich Seubert, "I wouldn't want anyone else on my team."

There was more—a lot more when the cameras and tape recorders were turned off—and the whole time, Collins was just taking it all in. He heard or read every word said about him, and couldn't have been more pleased.

"We've gone through a lot together, good and bad. That's why I think they feel that way," Collins said. "I think they see me as a reliable quarterback who gives them a chance to win on Sunday. I don't know why you would ask for more."

•   •   •

ELI SHOULD HAVE known, really. Maybe he did know. His brother never had to deal with this because he replaced Jim Harbaugh and Paul Justin and Kelly Holcomb and … well, the Colts were awful and Peyton was welcomed with wide-open arms. Archie didn't have those worries either because no one was going to miss Billy Kilmer or Ed Hargett, who helped the Saints go 2–11–1 in 1970.

Collins, though, was different. Yes, he had his detractors, but getting the Giants to the Super Bowl had earned him a lot of leeway in New York. If nothing else, his teammates and fans knew the Giants could win with him. Why throw him away and start from scratch?

"Well, I can understand that," Archie Manning said right after Eli was traded to New York. "Obviously, he is respected by teammates, has friends there. That is always a tough deal. Do I worry about it? No. I think maybe if Eli was a little different guy than he is, or if he was the type of person that was going to go in and rub people the wrong way, that could magnify the deal. I know how it works. Some guys are going to sit over there and they're just going to watch him a little. They're going to watch his actions, watch how he deals with this, how he does that. If he asks me about this, I'm going to tell him that you have to be yourself. You roll up your sleeves, you go to work and you just deal with it."

None of this was really new or unique, of course. Unless their teams are a mess and the situation is dire, there are few veterans who want to endure the struggles of a rookie quarterback—and almost all of them struggle. If a rookie guard or defensive tackle has a rough first year, they can easily be helped or hidden. Or they can be replaced with few repercussions to the rest of the team. But the struggles of a rookie quarterback could derail an entire offense, or an entire season. And they can't be yanked in and out of the lineup like a yo-yo. That doesn't help the rookie, the veteran he's replacing, or anyone else on the team.

Ben Roethlisberger would soon face the same worries and bad feelings in Pittsburgh, too. In late September of 2004, after Tommy Maddox got hurt and Roethlisberger was forced to prepare for his debut sooner than expected, veteran guard Alan Faneca was asked if the entrance of their quarterback of the future was exciting.

"Exciting?" Faneca said. "No, it's not exciting. Do you want to go work with some little young kid who's just out of college?"

Roethlisberger, of course, didn't take long to win over his teammates. All he had to do was win his first fifteen games and lead the Steelers to the AFC championship game. It was easier for him, too, because he was replacing an injured starter and the Steelers had no choice but to throw him into the fire. With Eli, some veteran Giants were upset simply that the kid had been anointed the quarterback of the future while Collins was still there. It didn't help that Collins was bitter about the whole affair, too.

Not at first, though. At least, not publicly. On the day of the Eli trade, Collins agreed to do a conference call with the New York media in which he said absolutely all the right things. He said he understood why the Giants made the move for a kid he called "a great talent," and he vowed, "I'll do whatever I can to help him this year. This is a situation where I'm not going to be bitter. I'm not going to hold it against Eli. I'm not going to hold it against the Giants. I'm going to do everything I can for this team to help them win. I've had a great experience here and I think I owe that to them."

The Giants had told Collins they planned to keep him and start him in 2004—at least at the beginning. And they were serious. Accorsi didn't believe throwing a rookie quarterback into the fire in week one would do anyone any good. The general manager was thrilled to hear Collins was open to staying and playing out the final year of his contract. He said having Collins around to start and to mentor Eli "would be the best of all worlds."

Two days later, the worlds collided in a fiery mess when Collins stormed into Giants Stadium, went straight up to Accorsi's office, and made it clear he had dramatically changed his tune, not to mention his tone. Coughlin had called Collins after the draft to let him know the Giants wanted to keep him, but Accorsi and Collins didn't speak until Monday morning when Collins called and said he wanted to talk.

"He got very upset," Accorsi recalled. "He barely was able to restrain himself. He said, 'I want out of here.' I said, 'You're probably going to be the quarterback this year.' He said, 'Well, I want out of here.' I said, 'Well, if you really want out of here, for all you've done for us I'll accommodate you. But I don't want to.'

"I was trying to be real nice to him and he looked at me and said, 'Today.'"

That ticked Accorsi off and even though he knew it was Collins' pride talking, the conversation went downhill fast. Accorsi promised him he wouldn't string things out, but the GM told him, "I'll decide when. Don't tell me when to do it." He wanted to see if there were any willing trade partners before he just dumped a valuable asset. Meanwhile, Collins went public with his demands to be released and even said the Giants only wanted to keep him if he agreed to a cut in pay (the Giants denied that claim, insisting they only wanted to restructure his contract). He said his presence "would've made things very awkward for Eli," and that upon further review he had no interest in being a mentor to anyone. After all, he was only thirty-one. He preferred to take his chance with a team that actually wanted him for his arm, not just for his experience. Within days, he had won his release. Not long after that, he hitched his desperate wagon to the woeful Oakland Raiders.

Of course, he couldn't resist turning up the heat on his replacement as he walked out the door.

"They feel Eli is going to be a special, special player," Collins said. "Ernie even said to me he felt he's one of the three or four best college prospects that he's seen come out in the last twenty years. He mentioned guys like Elway and Marino. Hey, if they feel that strongly about him, I don't blame them for doing what they did."

• • •

WITH COLLINS GONE, the Giants began scouring the market for another veteran backup—one who might be willing to accept a temporary role. They focused first on former Steeler and Jet Neil O'Donnell, but they couldn't lure him out of retirement. Then Kurt Warner fell into their lap when his agent called Accorsi and surprisingly said Warner was willing to come to New York for just one year. The Giants were looking for a bridge to the future. Warner, recently released by St. Louis, was looking for a temporary platform to prove to the league he could still play. It was a perfect match, and it stood to reason that it was a move that would go over well in a skeptical locker room. Yes, they were losing Collins and soon they would have to endure Eli's struggles. But they were going to get a chance to prove they could win with a former NFL and Super Bowl MVP first.

Still, bitter feelings remained and Collins left behind friends everywhere in the Meadowlands. More importantly, when he walked out the door there were many, many people that felt he took the Giants' best chance to win a Super Bowl with him.

"I was worried a little bit, to the extent that I didn't want the players to think we were packing it in for the next year or two," John Mara said. "We had some veterans on the team and I didn't want them to think we weren't going to have a chance to win."

The Maras, of course, were never going to let their feelings for Collins become a distraction. That's not how things worked. And for the most part, their players weren't going let their loyalty to him affect them for long, either. But there were a few skeptical exceptions that were clearly unhappy with what had happened to Collins. Most of them kept their thoughts private, or at least off the record. But the day after Collins was officially released, Strahan—the most vocal presence in the locker room—made his feelings clear to the press again.

"It's just a bad situation for a guy who has done a lot and done well for this organization, everything they've asked him to do, a guy who's been out there getting banged up behind a makeshift line with no protection," Strahan said. "But I guess when you're a quarterback you get blamed for all those things.

"I'm just a little surprised by some of the things that have happened. It definitely changes the scope of what I kind of expected coming into the season. I'm not saying we're not going to be competitive. I know we're going to be competitive. I think it'll be a good year for us. I'm not giving up on it because we have a rookie quarterback. It was just a big surprise for me the way this whole thing turned out."

Strahan tried to make it clear the target of his ire wasn't Eli. "It's management that brought him in," he said, "and management that has him in the starting lineup from day one." He'd soon learn that wasn't the case, that they didn't intend to start Eli right away.

But at that moment the prospect of playing any part of the 2004 season with Eli at the helm clearly didn't thrill one of the Giants' biggest stars.

"Everybody looks back on what rookie quarterbacks have done in the history of this league and it hasn't always been positive," he said. "You just hope your guy is the one guy that changes all of that. But as an older guy in this league and on this team, you just hope that it's not a situation where we sit back and wait for somebody two, three, four years down the road to develop. Because by the time it happens I very seriously doubt I'll be here to enjoy it."

· · ·

EVERY WORD OUT of Strahan's mouth, every one of the grumbles out of the locker room both before and after the draft, made it upstairs to the front office lightning quick. They knew what they were dealing with. They weren't blindsided. They knew it had the potential to be rough. And they knew, if Eli was forced into the lineup and didn't immediately succeed, there was at least some potential for locker room unrest.

It's not that they didn't know. It's not that they didn't care. It's just that they weren't worried.

"You know, you can't let that dictate your decision," Mara said. "If you have a chance to get a guy you think is a franchise player then you have to make a move and worry about everybody's feelings later."

"It was locker-room loyalty," Accorsi said. "That never bothered me. They were loyal to Kerry. Kerry was a warrior out there. You want that, for crying out loud. But I tell you what, players did come up to me afterwards and said they were excited about that trade. Even prior to the draft a couple of players came up to me and asked, 'Do we really have a chance to get this guy?'"

Eight: "Excellent huddle command"

IMAGINE IT'S YOUR first day of work. You are twenty-three years old and only a few days ago you were still just a kid in college. Yet here you are, you've barely had time to look around an unfamiliar city and get acquainted with your new office and co-workers, and now your boss is barking orders in your direction. Moments ago, you were given the office instruction manual. Now you're expected to do the work. Fast. And right.

And imagine you've heard that some of your new co-workers haven't exactly welcomed you with open arms. You're replacing someone they loved working with, someone they knew could do your job well. They've made it known they don't have time or the patience to let you learn on the fly. They won't have much tolerance for your mistakes.

And imagine your boss is relentless. You're being yelled at for every misstep. And there's no going back. You make one mistake, he moves on to the next project before you even have time to think. "The overload principle," he calls it, and you are definitely overloaded and overwhelmed. Pretty soon, you're numb to your surroundings. Your eyes are glazed over. One of those new co-workers who barked at your arrival told others you had "a little deer in the headlights" look.

Now imagine going home later that night and watching it all unfold on the evening news. And not just some tiny little cable channel, either. On the national news. On ESPN.

· · ·

IT WAS MAY 7, 2004 and clearly, there wasn't much else going on in New York that day. The Mets were home that night, too, but they were uninteresting and on their way to irrelevant. The Yankees were way out on the West Coast. The three local hockey teams were long gone from the playoffs. The Knicks were a mercifully distant memory, too. And the Nets were playing the Eastern Conference semifinals, but few really cared (and the Nets were in Detroit that night anyway). Eli Manning had the New York stage pretty much to himself.

So the local media—all of them, it seemed—packed themselves into a small blue box Tom Coughlin had painted on the side of the Giants' practice field, which he designated the "Media Area." It was farther from the field than you'd think, and large football players standing on the sideline often blocked the view.

But on this day, the view was good enough. Just thirteen days earlier, the Giants had made the blockbuster move to grab Eli, and now the city—and more than a few writers and TV types from across the nation—wanted to see what all the fuss was about. It was the Giants' first mini-camp under new coach Coughlin. More significantly, it was Eli's debut.

For Eli, it couldn't have been worse. All rookies struggle at the start, but given the expectations and the high profile of his position, his struggles were magnified. He looked like a high school quarterback—and not a good one, either. He was over-throwing and under-throwing almost everyone, except the tackling dummies in the middle of the field and the couple of defensive backs who picked off errant passes. He was dropping snaps. His head was swiveling so fast as he searched for the right place to throw, it hurt to watch him. He looked tentative. He looked scared.

Strahan was the one who said he had that "little deer in the headlights" look in his eyes. The most damning comment, though, came from Coughlin when he was asked after practice if there were any positives from Manning's performance.

"He had excellent huddle command," Coughlin said.

There it was—the punch line to what seemed like a bad joke. The Giants had traded all those picks and would soon commit all that money and this is what they got? A lost-looking kid who has "excellent huddle command"? For this they jettisoned Kerry Collins, the quarterback who led them to Super Bowl XXXV?

Actually, Coughlin also commended Manning's poise, his knowledge, and his ability to retain what he had taught. He meant all that sincerely, too. Coughlin knew what many were choosing to ignore, that Eli had met with his new coaches and teammates for only about an hour before he was tossed onto the field. "He didn't even know the cadence yet," Coughlin said. The next day, when he saw all the poor reviews, Coughlin thought to himself, "Let's be a little smarter than that about understanding where the young guy's coming from."

But when the world is watching the Next Great Thing, it's not big on understanding or patience, and everyone expects a little more than an ability to "notice when people are lined up well," as Coughlin said.

Years earlier, at Peyton Manning's first mini-camp practice in 1998, the reports said he had displayed "zip and accuracy" on his throws. Teammates described him using words like "confident" and "composed." Some called him "a leader."

As if anyone needed to be reminded that Eli was no Peyton, yet.

Not that Eli cared. When he called Peyton that night, he told his older brother that his first practice went well. He swore he didn't look at the papers or watch himself on the news. He was too busy studying the playbook so that day two would be better. And it was. That's one of the side effects of the "overload principle" that Coughlin was trying to use. The more you throw at someone, the tougher it is as at first. But eventually, it all begins to sink in.

"Looking at some articles, you all were writing how he was playing bad and throwing the ball bad," tight end Jeremy Shockey said after Eli's second practice. "I get in the huddle with him and I feel for him, because he has to learn fifteen different words when he calls the play. He does a great job doing that, and I'm thinking in my head, 'If I was in his position, I couldn't even finish half the play-calling.'"

You think he's kidding? On the first day of rookie mini-camp, players are handed a binder with several hundred pages in it, with all sorts of unfamiliar diagrams and descriptions printed on both sides. The quarterback has to learn an offensive numbering system (which number represents which position), names of personnel groupings, terms for sides of the field, code words for alignments for every position, motion calls, and shift packages. And that's just the offense. The quarterback also needs to know the words they'll be using to describe defenses, coverages, and blitz packages. And all that is before he even gets to the pages with the diagrams of a single play. It was as if he had to learn a new language in the morning and was forced to use it in a conversation later in the day.

And the detail a quarterback needs to know is mind-numbingly thorough. The two-inch thick playbook used by John Hufnagel, then the Giants' offensive coordinator, contained about twenty-five pages of just what he called "basic information." How basic? One full page was devoted to getting in and out of the huddle—and believe it or not it was a ten-step process.... Step 5: The QB does the talking. All others listen! The QB must talk straight out—not up in the air or down at the ground. See all of your men.... Step 6: After giving the snap count, the QB will say, "Ready." Then pause. All clap hands, which is the signal to break the huddle. Jog away from the huddle. Never loaf.... Step 8: All linemen turn to the inside when running to offensive position. Halfback always crosses behind fullback.

In hindsight, it's amazing that Eli's huddle command was even close to excellent that day. Everything in the playbook is that detailed. It's the same way in the separate binders designed for each mini-camp. Absolutely nothing is left to chance.

"It's such an overwhelming amount of information. It can overload you," said Jim Miller, who played in the NFL from 1994–2005 with seven different teams, and spent the last two and a half months of his career as Eli's would-be backup in the spring of 2005. "It's just like anything else, if you're thinking too much your ability is not going to shine. But the quarterback position commands it. You have to know it or you are not going to survive."

It didn't help that the Giants' offense—which was part Hufnagel, part Coughlin, part Kevin Gilbride—employed what Miller called a "streak-read principle." It wasn't enough that Eli would have to know the play call, the protection call, and the motion call—and together, all that could be ridiculously long, like "Zero Strong 72 Streak Y Shallow" (that's one of the shorter ones, by the way)— along with the snap count, all his reads, what each player was doing, what the defense was doing, what audibles he could make, and how to change calls in case the defense changes formation. But a "streak-read" offense allows for sight adjustments, meaning every play has multiple variations. His receiver on the outside could run several different routes for each specific play, all depending on what the man covering him is doing.

In other words, Eli would have to know everything and see what his receivers were seeing, too. If the corner dropped back after the snap, the receiver might stop his route after ten yards. If the corner moved up, the receiver might take off down the sidelines. If he went halfway … well, the receiver would have a choice to make. And Eli would have to hope they were interpreting the defense the same way.

"They ask him to do as much as you can ask a quarterback to do," said Tim Hasselbeck, who backed up Eli in 2005–06. "Bar none."

Is it any wonder, then, that on day one he looked so incredibly lost?

"I'm sure he was absolutely lost," Miller said. "It's a lot of thinking and I think you just see a lot of quarterbacks get buried by it. We talk about it taking three to four years. That's really about the time where it's really sinking into you and the position starts to become pretty easy."

Only three to four years? Well, at least things were bound to get better.

"It's early," Shockey said back then. "That's what I keep telling him. It's only May, so he's got plenty of time. He can go home and work with his brother."

• • •

BY THE TIME training camp arrived in July, the Giants had signed Warner as the mentor and a bridge to the Eli era. And though Coughlin refused to just publicly hand Warner the job—he even declared their competition "even" as they approached the preseason opener—the plan was always to start Warner on opening day. Accorsi had seen Bert Jones, the second overall pick in the 1973 draft, start opening day for the Baltimore Colts that year and complete just six of his twenty-two passes for 56 yards. Jones started for another four weeks, too, but took a physical and emotional beating and didn't appear to make much progress. Accorsi wasn't going to let that happen to Eli.

Still, the perception of competition allowed Eli to keep his head in the game and his spirits up, at least until August 29, when Coughlin officially gave Warner the starting job. And though it was telegraphed from the start, the decision wasn't controversy-free. Never mind what once had happened to Bert Jones, Eli wanted to start from day one, just like Peyton had in Indianapolis. There are many quarterbacks who believe that nothing can be learned from standing on the sidelines, like former Steeler Terry Bradshaw, who stopped by training camp in Eli's first season and announced, "I never have been a believer that you learn by watching. You've still got to go out and play." That, he said, is the only way to truly experience the NFL and grow as a player and leader—for better or for worse.

After all, that's what Peyton had done. He jumped right into the fray at home against the Miami Dolphins on September 6, 1998. He threw for 302 yards, too, though he also tossed three interceptions in a 24–15 loss. And Archie recalled starting his first game, too, on September 19, 1971, for the woeful Saints at home. He was thrown in against a Rams defense with Deacon Jones and Merlin Olsen and he still managed to lead the Saints to an improbable 24–20 win with a touchdown pass on the Saints' final play.

"It was really quite a way to start a professional career," Archie said. "I am kind of sad to say that it never got a whole lot better."

But was he better for starting right away? Would he have been better in the long run if he began the season on the bench? "That's really hard to say," Archie said. "That just depends." It's a question with no easy answer. Twenty-one years earlier, the Broncos threw Elway into the fire on opening day and he bombed so spectacularly he was on the bench by week six. In his first five games he had one touchdown and five interceptions and only thirty-eight completed passes.

Years later, then-Broncos coach Dan Reeves conceded it was a mistake to start Elway so soon. "I should've probably waited," Reeves said. "He wasn't able to get a comfortable feeling in there. I should've waited until he was more comfortable in there. But I don't know that I could've known that. It was a learning experience for me, also."

· · ·

IN THE END, Eli made Coughlin's choice easy by bombing in the Giants' third preseason game—the biggest tune-up before the regular season. In a 17–10 loss to the Jets, he was 4 of 14 for 20 yards with two interceptions. Warner blew him away with a 9 of 11, 104-yard performance. And after the game, Coughlin's words said it all.

"Day to day on the practice field he's been so sharp, so with it," Coughlin said. "The term that everyone has been using is 'unflappable.' He is a young man and he is a human being. This was not a good night for him."

Two days later, Warner had the job and Eli wasn't surprised. His teammates were pleased, to say the least. Warner, they felt, gave them an actual chance to win. "You just feel a veteran presence out of him," Tiki Barber said.

That veteran presence paid off in an impressive and surprising 5–2 start in which Warner was outstanding—131 of 202 (64.9 percent), 1,539 yards, four touchdowns, and two interceptions. The only action Eli saw during the first nine games was in mop-up duty in the opener, a 31–17 loss in Philadelphia on September 12.

His numbers weren't any good that day—he completed just three of nine passes for sixty-six yards—but that debut was still memorable. His first NFL play was a seventy-two-yard touchdown. Of course, all he did was hand the ball to Barber, who took off on a long run. On his second and final drive, he got the Giants all the way to the Eagles' fourteen-yard line before time ran out.

The moment to remember, though, was the final play of the game, when Eli dropped back and drifted a little too far up towards the right and into the path of an oncoming freight train named Jerome McDougle. The 6–2, 264-pound defensive end barreled into Eli from his blindside, swinging his forearm like a hammer. Eli never saw or felt it coming. The next thing he knew he was on the ground on all fours, searching for his mouthpiece.

"Oh, he was out," McDougle said. "I don't really think he knew what was going on."

Coughlin's reaction to the hit? "Welcome to the NFL, son."

Archie Manning's reaction? "I thought he was dead."

"I've never seen anybody get hit that hard," Archie added. "I was glad he got up. I was real glad he got up."

Eli gained a measure of respect from his teammates with the way he handled that hit. It was bone-crunching enough that there was audible gasp inside Lincoln Financial Field. Yet he got up relatively quickly, didn't even have to get checked out by the trainers, showed no pain on his face and never complained.

"No pain, no bruising," Eli said a few days later. "I've seen the play. It was a good hit. I've taken big hits before, had the wind knocked out of me. My sophomore year in college against Alabama I spun around and a guy hit me head-on. You can't have a fear of being hit. You've got to feel the rush."

• • •

IT WOULD BE a while before Eli would get a chance to be hit again, thanks to Warner's hot start. But the seeds were being planted even then. Warner was sacked fifteen times in the first five games. But after the bye week, things started to get worse. He got sacked six times against the Lions, five times against the Vikings, seven times against the Bears, and six times in Arizona. That's twenty-four sacks in a four-game span, and there was a lot of private grumbling by his offensive linemen that it wasn't all their fault.

Publicly, Coughlin supported Warner. After the 17–14 loss in Arizona that dropped the Giants to 5–4, he insisted Warner made no poor decisions and even defended him by saying, "It's very difficult to be the quarterback when you hardly ever get your back foot set." Receivers weren't getting open and the line wasn't offering protection. Those were the public reasons being offered for the Giants' sudden decline.

Behind the scenes, though, the coaches and the front office had been studying the tapes hard with an eye on all the sacks for the last four weeks, and they kept coming back to the same conclusion: It really was Warner's fault. Known for a quick release and an ability to make lightning-quick decisions in the fast-paced "Greatest Show on Turf" offense he used to run in St. Louis, the now thirty-three-year-old was slowing down. On almost every pass he'd hold the ball for at least 3.5 seconds—an eternity that left him a sitting duck in the pocket. Sometimes his snap-to-sack time would be 6.5 seconds or more.

There aren't many offensive linemen that can block that long. It's no wonder he had been sacked twenty-four times in four weeks.

"I promise you, of those twenty-four sacks, more than half of them could have been avoided by the quarterback," said former Redskins quarterback and *Monday Night Football* analyst Joe Theismann. "Everybody says, 'Oh, what a lousy job the offensive line is doing.' No. If you're back there scrambling around and holding onto the football, then it's all on you. It's not those guys up front."

Theismann said Warner was holding the ball "like he thinks it's a seven-on-seven drill"—a camp staple with the quarterback and receivers going up against the linebackers and the secondary, with no pass rush or offensive line. Accorsi, Coughlin, and the rest of the staff agreed. The game tape they viewed week after week showed Warner ignoring open receivers, while waiting for others to get open. It showed linemen making their blocks and holding them … holding them … until they just couldn't hold them anymore.

The Giants were 5–4 and in great position for a playoff run, but the staff just kept coming back to the same conclusion. Their house of cards was collapsing and Warner was looking older and slower every game. Meanwhile, Eli wasn't quite ready for prime time but he had younger legs, much more mobility, and his most impressive trait—especially for someone that young with so much being thrown at him—an ability to make quick decisions. They weren't always the right ones, but he was usually decisive.

So pick your poison. Stick with the veteran who's more capable of running the offense but can't get the ball out of his hands in time, or go with the rookie who'll release the ball, even though it might end up going in the wrong direction. And, not that this was foremost on Coughlin's mind, but what would the rest of the team think if he turned the stretch run over to a not-ready-for-primetime rookie? They had made it clear when he was drafted that they didn't have the patience or inclination to suffer through his struggles. What makes him think they'd be willing to do it now, with a playoff berth in their sights?

Nine: "What the hell have I gotten myself into?"

BOOMER ESIASON WASN'T ready. He knew it, too. It was a dreary, rainy day in Cincinnati, the Houston Oilers were in town, and there was a little buzz in the air since he had been the first quarterback selected in the 1984 draft (second round, thirty-eighth overall)—one year after six went in the first round in the fabled Quarterback Class of '83.

He was twenty-three years old and very, very green.

As he remembers it, his coach, Sam Wyche, drew up about thirty plays for the game plan and every one of them was scrawled on a cheat sheet attached to Esiason's wrist. "The coach would hold up one finger and say, 'Run 1 … and don't screw it up,'" he recalled. "And still, I was like, 'Oh my God, what are they doing?' At times it looked like there were fifteen guys out there."

Troy Aikman was absolutely sure he was ready. He was the golden boy, the first overall pick coming off a storied career at UCLA and he barely broke a sweat during the preseason. The Cowboys, America's Team, went 3–1 in those exhibitions. Their rookie leader didn't throw a single interception. And as he began to prepare for his first regular-season game, he was actually thinking, "Wow, I don't know why everybody makes such a big deal about this NFL stuff."

Then came game day at the loud New Orleans Superdome and the defenses suddenly were more complicated. There were things he had never seen or expected. Everything was faster. Nothing was easy anymore.

"It was unlike anything," Aikman recalled. "I couldn't have prepared myself. Preseason did not prepare me for it. And I don't know that anything could have."

John Elway thought he was ready, too, even though he had injured his elbow one week earlier in the final preseason game. Like Aikman, he was a number one pick, only the spotlight on him was even brighter after he forced his way out of Baltimore and all the way out to Denver. He'd have to return to Baltimore in week two—talk about swift justice for the betrayed fans of the Colts—but that was something to worry about later.

On opening day in Pittsburgh, Elway was confident that he was ready. His coaches thought he was ready. But he obviously wasn't. He went out and completed one of his eight passes for fourteen yards, threw an interception, lost a fumble, and was even called for intentional grounding—one of the worst debuts for a quarterback in the history of the NFL.

"I wanted to click my heels together and say, 'Auntie Em, bring me home,'" Elway recalled. "'You can have your signing bonus back. I don't want to stare at Jack Lambert spitting and drooling at me anymore. What the hell have I gotten myself into?'"

• • •

IT'S HARD TO know for sure what was going through Tom Coughlin's mind on the four-hour flight back from Arizona on November 14, 2004, just as it's hard to pinpoint the exact moment he made his mind up and decided to make the quarterback switch. In a makeshift press tent just outside Sun Devil Stadium in Tempe, Arizona a few hours earlier, he said, "I expect Kurt will start" the following week against Atlanta. Was he lying, just so he could tell the players his decision first—something he seemed to insinuate the next day? Had he just not given it much thought? Did he really believe that then, only to change his mind later?

Coughlin—a difficult man for the media to deal with, especially during his first year with the Giants—certainly had no interest in reliving the details for the press.

"Is that important, really?" he said the day he announced the decision, the morning after the loss in Arizona, just a few hours after the Giants' charter flight landed. "Maybe it was on the couch at three a.m. this morning. Maybe. Maybe that was it."

He told his two quarterbacks the news early the next morning in separate meetings, as soon as they reported to Giants Stadium. Warner, for his part, was stunned. He said Coughlin "told me he felt like he had to do it." He even hinted at pressure from higher up in the organization to get their new bonus baby on the field.

"I think there is a bigger picture here," Warner said. "There are more things that are trying to be accomplished here."

Beyond that, the classy Warner took his demotion as well as could be expected. He even went to Eli that morning, shortly after Coughlin told him of the decision, and said, "Congratulations. Anything you need from me, I'm here."

Warner said Coughlin didn't go into specific reasons for the move and, as you might imagine, he had little interest in going into specifics publicly, either. He praised Warner, insisted Eli was ready and refused to blame his offensive line. He acted, somewhat defiantly, like it was no different than if he had just made a change at left guard or strong-side linebacker.

Of course, it was.

There might be no more difficult decision in sports than figuring out the exact right moment for a quarterback switch. A coach can change left tackles or bench a receiver and it might be nothing but a sidebar in the newspaper, unnoticed on the evening news. But the two most inflammatory words in pro football are "quarterback controversy." It's a platform for a caucus, with everyone choosing sides—some publicly, some behind the scenes. It can be as much political as performance-based, too.

And when the switch involves a green, young quarterback, there are other factors to consider. Though Coughlin swore he never felt direct pressure from above, there was undoubtedly indirect pressure knowing the commitment the Giants had made to Eli—the six-year, $45 million contract he signed as a rookie that could swell to $54 million; the draft picks; all the talk about greatness and about him being the franchise's quarterback of the future.

Maybe in an earlier era teams could wait to see if their young princes could fulfill a prophecy of greatness, but not in an era where a twenty-three-year-old had a contract worth $33 million more than his head coach.

And even if he was successfully able to factor that out, Coughlin needed to figure out if Eli really was ready. Could he handle the pressure he was about to face? Veterans drool at the thought of facing rookies, but this would be no one-on-one battle. It would be eleven defensive players, a defensive coordinator, and an entire defensive coaching staff all focused on one goal: Rattling the rookie.

"You go into the game and try to confuse them, try to disguise coverages," said veteran safety Brent Alexander, a teammate of Eli's in 2004. "Then the second part is the pressure aspect. You try to get him rattled early and get pressure in his face. It's not always getting sacks. It's making him keep his feet moving, making it hard for him to set his feet and make accurate throws, keeping him uncomfortable."

Aikman felt that pressure back in 1989, when he debuted with a 17-for-35, two-interception performance in a 28–0 loss. It was the start of what would become a 1–15 season for the Dallas Cowboys. Aikman lost all eleven of his rookie season starts.

"Maybe if I'd have sat and watched nine games I would've been able to at least assimilate some of the speed of it from having been on the sidelines," Aikman said. "But I wasn't afforded that."

Coughlin seemed unconcerned about Eli feeling any pressure—odd, since the Giants were staring at a relative murderers' row of defenses over the next five weeks. The Falcons, Eagles, Redskins, Ravens, and Steelers were all ranked among the NFL leaders in either sacks or overall defense. If Eli was going to fall, Coughlin's timing guaranteed the landing wouldn't be soft.

"I'll tell you one thing," Accorsi said. "For the next two weeks, he doesn't have Duke and Vanderbilt."

Of course, at 5–4, Coughlin had another problem. The Giants had a shot at their first playoff berth in two seasons. Yes, after two straight losses the season was starting to slide away, but with seven games left their chance hadn't completely disappeared. And despite appearances, Coughlin maintained winning was still his primary objective.

That turned up the pressure on Eli even more, and it made things dicey for the unpopular coach. He had nothing but internal problems in his rookie season with the Giants. Almost as soon as he arrived, nearly a dozen players went crying to the NFL Association to complain that his stringent off-season workout program was violating league rules. On the first day he dumped a rule book on his players thicker than his playbook, with everything from how they should sit in meetings to what color socks they needed to wear and how high they should be. He set all the clocks at Giants Stadium back five minutes to guarantee everyone would always be on time. Every meeting he held started earlier than scheduled. If a player wasn't inside when Coughlin started, he was locked out. He would also be fined.

Throw in the fact that none of the veterans were too pleased back in April when Collins was essentially dumped for Eli, and now Coughlin was running the risk of losing them all by throwing a rare playoff chance away. Publicly, Eli's teammates offered nothing but support. But privately, at the very least, they cast a skeptical eye.

Now, one year into a four-year contract, Coughlin wasn't worried about his own long-term future, but he had to know the move had potential to terminally undermine his career, too. Make the wrong call or have bad timing with a switch of safeties and who cares? Correct it and move on. But be wrong about a quarterback and you might never get a chance to make it right.

"We all want to win immediately," said former Buffalo Bills coach and general manager Marv Levy. "But when you say you're building for the future that's an incomplete sentence. You're building for the future coach and general manager is what you're doing."

That cautionary statement belongs on page one of the general manager's handbook, according to Accorsi. Still, the best way to make a mistake is to make it full speed, looking straight ahead, with no turning back. If Eli was the quarterback of the future, the Giants had to give him time to fulfill his promise. Reversing the decision a few games down the road could easily ruin him. It also wouldn't do any good for the team.

"When you make a decision to go with a guy, you have to stick with it, especially at this position," Warner said. "It's too hard and we're too much of a leader, too much of a focal point to bounce back and forth and to present that kind of image to your team. You rally around the guy and you do what you can do. You've just got to battle with him.

"WHAT THE HELL HAVE I GOTTEN MYSELF INTO?"

"This guy, Eli, is the New York Giants' future. And basically, the decision in my mind is, 'The future starts now.'"

• • •

THIS IS HOW excited Eli was about earning his first start in the NFL: He never bothered to tell his father. Archie found out about the news when reporters started calling to ask him about it. He had to call his youngest son himself to confirm. And even then, Eli didn't bring it up until Archie did first.

Eli did eventually call Peyton and shared the news, but only because they talked to each other all the time. The conversation, they both said, wasn't exactly football-related. And Peyton, then six and a half years into his NFL career, wasn't dispensing any sage advice.

"His only piece of advice was, 'If they call out the offense before the game, don't trip running out,'" Eli said. "That was really the only thing he said."

According to Peyton, he didn't even bother congratulating his little brother for winning the job because, "It's not an award. It's not a time to say, 'Congratulations.' It's a time to call and say, 'Good luck'—especially with the five defenses he's about to have to face."

So the Manning family was keeping a lid on its excitement, but nobody else was. After Eli's first start, teammates would talk about the unusual buzz they felt in Giants Stadium. It had begun building throughout the entire city the moment word began to leak that Coughlin had made his stunning announcement. The expectations for Eli were enormous, even inside the Giants' locker room.

Asked what he hoped the Giants would see from Manning in his first start, Tiki Barber brought up what would be a sore subject for years around the Giants. "We hope we get Roethlisberger," he said.

Ben Roethlisberger, at the moment, was already 7–0 in the NFL.

"That doesn't put any pressure on me," Eli insisted. "Obviously other people might look at it as pressure on me to compete with him, but we're in two different situations with two different teams. I just have to go out there and play my game."

Everyone who knows Eli insisted he was serious, that he was oblivious to the pressure, unconcerned with the expectations, and completely, totally focused on his job. He was too busy studying the Atlanta Falcons' sack-happy defense to worry about anything else.

Of course, not everyone was buying into that.

"I would imagine he'll be sick to his stomach," former NFL quarterback and ESPN analyst Sean Salisbury said before Eli's first start. "We never want to admit it. We have to tell everybody that we're relaxed. But there's a combination of 'I can't eat much because I'm a little nervous,' and then again 'I can eat, because I feel great. What an opportunity. This is my team now.'"

• • •

THE FIRST SIGN of hope that Eli would someday really be king came in the second half of his first start on November 21, 2004. For the first thirty minutes, he was a nightmare—5 for 14 for 46 yards and a terrible interception at the end of the first half. Michael Vick, himself a former number one overall pick (2001), was ripping the Giants apart, though mostly with his legs (10 rushes for 91 yards in the first half). Eli was down 14–0, admittedly felt "rushed" and left the field at halftime at Giants Stadium to a chorus of surprisingly quick boos.

And it was obvious what was going on. The game was happening just a little too fast for him. He looked jittery as he swiveled his head searching for an open receiver. By the time he thought he found one, the opening was closed.

"I call it 'The Ghost Syndrome,'" Esiason said. "It's when you think you saw something that didn't happen. You think there's a player standing in a certain spot, then when you look at the film the next day you say, 'Damn, I thought … well, I guess not.' It's all of that indecision and anxiety wrapped into one."

When Eli came out for the second half, though, he showed very little indecision or anxiety. It had appeared as if he had found his groove. He quickly went 6 of 10 for 62 yards on the opening drive and threw his first career touchdown pass to Jeremy Shockey. Two drives later, he got the Giants to the Atlanta eight-yard line for a field goal that pulled them within 14–10. He even had the ball in his hands in Atlanta territory and a chance to win in the final minutes. But he couldn't connect on a fourth-down throw to Shockey, leaving the score where it stood.

The numbers weren't great—17 for 37, 162 yards, one touchdown, two interceptions—but the reviews were all positive. The way he calmly shook off his jitters and the first-half adversity impressed everyone, including his teammates. After the game, Barber said, "I think he showed he can do well this year. Not five years from now. He can do well this year."

Maybe that was a bit premature, because things would get much worse before they got better. One week later, he was battered and rattled by the blitz-crazy Philadelphia Eagles, completing just 6 of 21 passes for 148 yards and two interceptions while being sacked five times. That dropped the Giants to 5–6 and sent them spiraling to the outer edge of the NFC playoff picture. One week later, a 31–7 loss in Washington—in which Eli went 12 of 25 for 113 yards—pretty much sealed their playoff-less fate.

Coughlin would often call Eli's early experience "painful but priceless." The bad things Eli was experiencing now would only help him later on.

"That was the whole idea," Coughlin said. "The whole key was to get him on the field, to fight his way through the experiences, to face the tough defenses, to pick himself off the floor when things didn't go well, to allow him to play himself through those things, to have those real delicate post-game conversations with him, to work your way through it, to have him again re-commit himself to the kind of football player he knew he could be. They were great learning experiences. There are things that are priceless. You can't pay for that kind of experience that he had to go through."

"The only way that he's going to get better is by going through the process, making the mistakes, looking at himself on film and saying, 'OK, I should've thrown it here,'" Joe Theismann said. "Because he's the only one that can see what's in front of him. Kurt could stand there and explain it to him, but it wouldn't do him any good unless he does it. It's truly a baptism under fire and an education as well."

"When this year's over he'll come back and say, 'You know what? As a rookie, I had no clue,'" Salisbury added. "Because you really don't."

When Eli looked back on his rookie season, he didn't disagree. "You can get overrun sometimes," he admitted. "You have so much going on, your mind is kind of overwhelmed. Everything is being thrown at you and there are days where you can't think anymore."

Overall, Eli's eventual evaluation of his rookie year was simple and to the point: "It was tough," he said.

It was about to get much tougher.

Ten: "I can't watch this"

THE NIGHT BEFORE the worst game of Eli Manning's career, his father couldn't get to sleep. There's an instinct that kicks in for parents when they know their children are in trouble, and something deep down in his gut was kicking away. He had planned out his day weeks earlier. He was going to sit down on his couch at his home in New Orleans, and spend the day watching football, just like a regular guy—as regular as a guy could be watching his two sons play quarterback in the NFL on the same day.

By now, though, that was normal for Archie. For most of the season he had spent his weekends on the road, sometimes watching Peyton play in Indianapolis, sometimes watching Eli play in New York. He was always in the stands, usually with a hat tucked down low on his head, so maybe—just for a few minutes, anyway—he could watch his boys in peace.

On December 12, 2004, though, neither the Colts nor the Giants were home. Peyton was in Houston. Eli was in Baltimore. So Archie and Olivia planned to be in New Orleans, on the couch.

But the night before, Archie lay there with his eyes wide open and the wheels in his mind turning a mile a minute. He knew a bad situation when he saw one, and he certainly saw one in New York, where Eli was struggling more than anyone thought he would. It seemed like half the Giants were injured. Their offensive line was leaky. So was the defense. And each week Eli seemed to be getting worse. Now he was headed on the road to face a Baltimore Ravens defense known for terrorizing quarterbacks. Archie feared Eli would be a chew toy for a pack of wild dogs.

When he finally gave up on sleep early that morning, Archie had a knot in his stomach the size of a football, and he had changed his plans for his normal day at home before he even got out of bed.

"I can't watch this," he said to Olivia. "I'm going to Houston to watch Peyton. Call me if there's anything good in Eli's game."

Archie got up, got dressed, and made the four-and-a-half-hour drive to Houston.

Olivia never called.

. . .

RAY LEWIS WAS like a shark circling chum that day. The powerful Ravens linebacker, at the time the most feared defender in the game, made a living by intimidating quarterbacks. Sometimes he did it with his body. Sometimes he did it with his mind. He was the master of the chess match. He'd orchestrate the eleven men on the Ravens defense like a ballet. He'd move the cornerback to the line of scrimmage, then back ... two linebackers toward the middle, one then drops a step back ... a defensive end stands up, then goes back down ... the safeties switch sides ... one takes a step forward ... now the cornerback moves inside ... all the while, Lewis is barking trash talk mixed in with indecipherable directions and commands.

The whole time, really, Lewis was just stalking his prey. He'd look across the field into Eli's eyes, and he knew from the beginning of the game that he was already deep inside his head.

So what did Lewis see when he looked inside? "A lot of confusion," Lewis said. "You could tell we were really getting to him."

That was a polite way to put it. Eli was tortured by the Ravens' defense. He never knew if the blitz was coming, or where it might be coming from. He had no read on their coverages. He had no read on anything at all. His first two pass attempts were nearly intercepted. His third pass attempt actually was. When the horror show was over—for him, anyway—he had completed just 4 of 18 passes for 27 yards and threw two interceptions.

That's a hard-to-believe quarterback rating of 0.0, which somehow still doesn't tell the full story of how bad Eli was that day. He had the classic deer-in-the-headlights look for most of the afternoon. He was dazed. He was confused.

Eventually, he was benched.

That nearly happened for the first time late in the third quarter when Eli fumbled a handoff, immediately prompting Coughlin to tell Warner to start warming up. The oddly patient coach, though, decided to give the kid a little more time. But Eli rewarded his patience with three more incompletions and no first downs in the next three series.

Mercifully, that was enough.

After a 1-for-7, 6-yard second-half performance, Coughlin fired the starting pistol on an apparent quarterback controversy by sending in the man who had lost his job to Eli five weeks earlier. And, to make matters worse for Eli, Warner—still playing against the Ravens' first-team defense—came in with 6:07 left and completed 6 of 9 passes for 127 yards and led the Giants to their first offensive touchdown in thirteen quarters.

The whole time, Eli's expression on the sideline was difficult to read as he stood watching the rest of the 37–14 loss. It wasn't anger. It wasn't frustration. It wasn't disappointment.

It was … blank.

"I gave him every opportunity to work his way through it," Coughlin said after the game. "It was obvious at one point it wasn't going to happen."

Worse, perhaps, was that the game put the first cracks in Eli's steely exterior. He allowed a very brief look inside his soul and displayed a fading confidence. Actually, what he showed was something more concerning—a fear that his teammates were losing confidence in him.

"I've got to get my teammates back trusting me," he said. "I don't know if I've lost it or not. I haven't proved anything to them."

None of them ever said anything to Eli directly, but he kept looking over his shoulder anyway, listening for clues in their words or tone. He said that outwardly his teammates were "helpful. They just told me to keep my head up." But he admitted he couldn't help but wonder, "Are they going to quit on you? What are they saying?"

"You try not to think about those things," Eli said.

• • •

HIS TOTALS IN his first four starts were just hideous. Eli had completed only 38.6 percent of his passes (39 of 101). His passer rating was 31.4. His record was 0–4. He might have just played the worst game any Giants quarterback had ever played. And though he was new to New York, he wasn't stupid. He knew what was coming. After Warner came in and showed him how it was supposed to be done, he figured the fans and media would immediately begin calling for him to be benched.

What he didn't expect was to read that teammates were calling for that, too. "We need to go back to Kurt," one Giant told the New York *Daily News* after that Baltimore disaster. "I'm sure guys feel that way. Eli is just shell-shocked. If you're going to develop a young quarterback, then you stick with him. But guys who are fighting their butts off, they want to win now. Guys want the best chance to win now."

Coughlin had wanted to head off comments and even thoughts like that, so moments after the game he closed the door to the cramped visitors' locker room and gathered his players around him. He walked to the center of the room, commanded the attention of every one of his players and pointed out the obvious—how poorly they had all just played.

Then he took a few steps towards Eli's locker and looked the twenty-three-year-old rookie square in the eye.

"Eli is our starter," Coughlin told his players.

As far as the coach was concerned, that would be the final word about that.

"I don't think sitting him is the answer," Coughlin later said. "I think the players are in agreement with it."

One who definitely agreed—or so he said—was Warner. The veteran wasn't happy when he lost his job to Eli, but now he wanted no part of getting it back. At least not like this, and not at Eli's expense.

"This is Eli's team," Warner said. "Eli has to understand the confidence that this team has in him, and this team has to understand the confidence that this whole organization has in Eli. That's why it's important that he's the guy. Nobody said it was going to be easy. Nobody said it was going to be the best situation in every single game. Five weeks ago everybody wanted me out of there. That's just the way the tide turns and that's the way the business goes. But the bottom line is that this is Eli's team, period. No question about it. No doubt about it. This is Eli's team from this point on, probably until he retires. That's all there is to say about it."

Well, not quite. The fact was that Eli was lost, struggling, and facing a critical turning point in his career. He could crumble under the weight of what just happened and chalk up his rookie year as a lost season, or he could somehow dig his way out and salvage something out of the last two games.

Unfortunately, to some in the Giants' organization, he looked ready to crumble.

"I was worried, no question" admitted then quarterbacks coach Kevin Gilbride. "Because you've seen some guys that just can't recover from that. He never gave any indication that he couldn't deal with it, but it's a challenge. It's tough. You've got to be a very, very determined, and maybe an inwardly confident person to be able to withstand all that negativity and lack of success.

"It was an ugly feeling after that game. That was about as low as you could go. I don't think I had any question about his ability or what his future potential was, but I did worry about what was going to happen to him psychologically, emotionally, spiritually."

So, after seeing the blank look on Eli's face on the sidelines, noticing the glazed-over pain in his eyes, and after hearing his fears expressed in the post-game press conference, Gilbride just needed to be sure. It was fortunate then, that the Giants preferred to travel by train to road games in Washington and Baltimore. It was a more relaxed trip. Players could spread out. And Gilbride would have extra time to make his point.

Early in the three-hour trip home, he saw Eli sitting alone. So he walked up the aisle and sat down, uninvited, in the empty seat beside him.

"That was the nice thing about the train: You could find everyone," Gilbride said. "Everybody had enough seats, so he was by himself. He was pretty low at that point. Discouraged. But he's a fighter. Sometimes it's not easy to discern the competitiveness of a guy if they're quiet. And he is very quiet about it. But inside he wants to succeed, he wants to excel, he wants to do well. So he was sitting there, beating himself up a little bit about the way the game had gone."

They talked for what seemed like forever about a game that Eli called "disastrous … probably the worst game I've ever played in any sport." But it wasn't just a pep talk. It wasn't a review of what went wrong, or a technical discussion on mechanics. It was about the larger picture of what it takes to be a quarterback in the NFL. It was about leadership and controlling your own destiny. It was about standing up, realizing it was OK for a quarterback to speak his mind.

In a lot of ways, it was about a boy becoming a man.

"It's time for you to say, 'Hey, this is what I can do. This is what I want to do,' and to be a little more assertive," Gilbride told Eli during the ride home. "Because we're only going to go as far as you can take us. We know what we want to do, but the bottom line is if you're not feeling comfortable about those things, then you need to step up and speak your mind."

"He's such a terrific young man and he's so respectful, I'm not sure he felt he ought to say it," Gilbride recalled. He told Eli, "That doesn't mean you say 'Hey, I'm not doing this.' But we need to know what your thoughts are, where you're at. You need to say 'This is what I know I can do.' And then you've got to be willing to go out and back it up."

The next day, back at Giants Stadium, Coughlin summoned Eli to his office to take his shot at rebuilding the confidence of his broken-down young quarterback. But Eli surprised him by taking the lead in the discussion, by being the aggressor, armed with suggestions and ideas. It was a risky move. Imagine the gall of a twenty-three-year-old quarterback who just went 4-for-18, marching upstairs and asking the coach to make some changes. And not just any coach, but a coach who was legendary for his rigidness and his unwavering belief that his way was the right way, no matter what.

But Coughlin has always had more patience than he's been given credit for, and he also had a knack for seeing the big picture. He knew it wasn't all Eli's fault in Baltimore. The Giants had six turnovers that day—"repugnant," was the word Coughlin used to describe that sloppiness. And oh, by the way, the defense allowed Kyle Boller, of all quarterbacks, to throw four touchdown passes.

He also knew that Eli had faced a hellish string of opponents to start his career. He opened against a Falcons defense that at the time ranked first in the NFL in sacks. Next up were the blitz-happy Eagles, followed by the Redskins and their number two–ranked defense. Then came Baltimore. And next up were the Pittsburgh Steelers, who were headed to Giants Stadium not only with Roethlisberger having a successful rookie season, but also with the number one defense in the league.

"A former player told me, 'I've never seen anybody have to start in a tougher situation than Eli has,'" Archie said. "And he's been watching football for thirty years."

Given all that, Coughlin was willing to give Eli some slack. And he understood when Eli looked across his big desk and looked him in the eye and said, "Coach, I want to be good."

"He made up his mind that he was frustrated, too," Coughlin said. "He knows the quality that he can play and he wanted very much to unveil the real him."

What they talked about over the next half hour was partially a pep talk, partially a mechanical analysis, and partially a lecture on leadership—something that, for the first time in his eight months in the NFL, it appeared that Eli was beginning to show. Eli's own evaluation of the Baltimore disaster was simple and on the mark: "It was bad," he said. "They were confusing me. Even the simple

Eli Manning, holding up his new Giants jersey on draft day, 2004, was the quarterback Ernie Accorsi had been searching for his entire career. (*Courtesy of Jerry Pinkus*)

It was a rough start for Eli, who was under pressure right from the moment he made his first start against the Falcons on Nov. 21, 2004. (*Courtesy of William Hauser*)

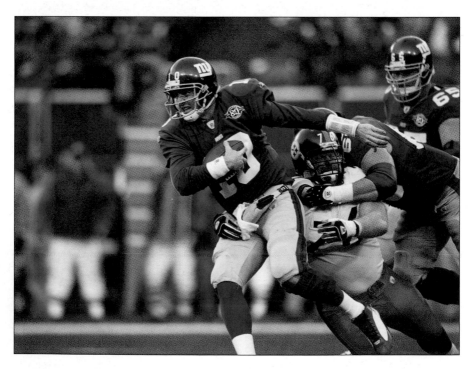

Things got a little better later in his rookie year, when he nearly led the Giants to a victory over the Pittsburgh Steelers' top-ranked defense and their quarterback, Ben Roethlisberger. (*Courtesy of William Hauser*)

Once the Giants gave Eli the starting job, they never looked back. He's started every game for them since. (*Courtesy of William Hauser*)

There were some rough moments, too, like his first four-interception game against the Vikings on Nov. 13, 2005. (*Courtesy of William Hauser*)

And there were some brilliant early moments, like his come-from-behind, last-second win over the Broncos on Oct. 23, 2005. (*Courtesy of William Hauser*)

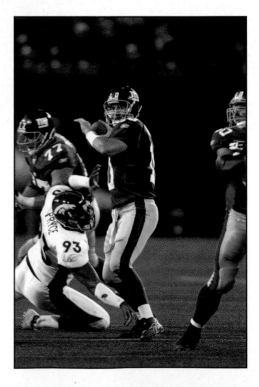

Eli was always in the shadow of his older brother, Peyton, whom he played against in "The Manning Bowl" on Sept. 10, 2006. (*Courtesy of Jerry Pinkus*)

Father Archie, a legend in the South, was a looming presence over both of his sons. (*Courtesy of Jerry Pinkus*)

In his first three years, Eli struggled under the direction of unpopular offensive coordinator John Hufnagel. (*Courtesy of William Hauser*)

Things began to turn around for Eli when quarterbacks coach Chris Palmer was hired in 2007. (*Courtesy of Jerry Pinkus*)

Few could understand the pressure Eli was under in New York, but Jets quarterback Chad Pennington had at least some idea. (*Courtesy of William Hauser*)

Eli was supposed to lead the next generation of quarterbacks. That couldn't happen, though, until he helped end the career of the great Brett Favre. (*Courtesy of William Hauser*)

Eli became the first quarterback to win a regular-season game overseas when the Giants beat the Dolphins in London on Oct. 28, 2007. (*Courtesy of William Hauser*)

The magical 2007 season had plenty of rough spots, including two losses to Dallas that gave the Cowboys the NFC East title. (*Courtesy of William Hauser*)

Things began to turn around near the end of the season, and in the playoffs—starting in Tampa—Eli began to take off. (*Courtesy of William Hauser*)

By the time the Giants got to Dallas in the second round, Eli's teammates—like Antonio Pierce—were fully behind him. (*Courtesy of William Hauser*)

Beating Dallas brought a smile to the face of co-owner John Mara, who never lost faith in his beleaguered quarterback. (*Courtesy of William Hauser*)

In the frozen tundra of Lambeau Field, Eli braved the elements for one of the finest days of his career. (*Courtesy of William Hauser*)

Eli kept warm when the temperature was below zero, and warmed the hearts of Giants fans with an unexpected win in the NFC championship game. (*Courtesy of William Hauser*)

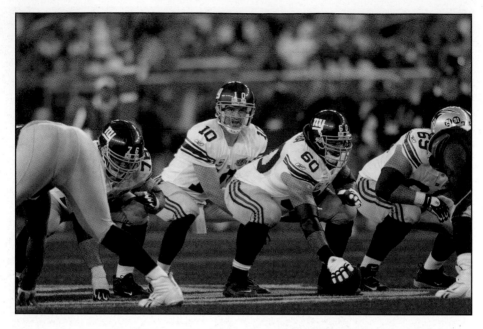

Against all odds, Eli was taking snaps in Super Bowl XLII, just one year after Peyton had done the same. (*Courtesy of William Hauser*)

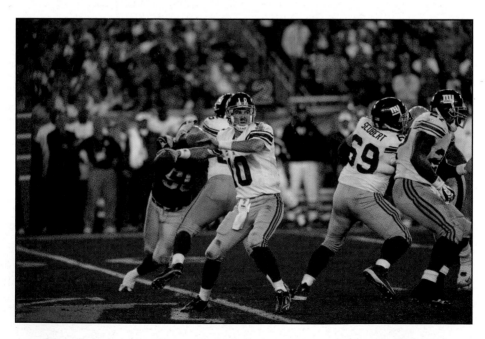

Eli settled in early in Super Bowl XLII, directing an efficient, methodical Giants attack. (*Courtesy of William Hauser*)

Eli consulted with his top receiver, Plaxico Burress, and offensive coordinator Kevin Gilbride. They'd eventually team up on the play that won the game. (*Courtesy of Jerry Pinkus*)

Late in the game, Eli had reason to celebrate as he led the Giants to two fourth-quarter touchdowns against the Patriots. (*Courtesy of William Hauser*)

On one magical play, Eli escaped a certain sack and somehow found David Tyree down the field for a miraculous, game-saving catch. (*Courtesy of William Hauser*)

When it was over, Eli Manning stood in a place many never thought he'd be—on the podium, holding the Vince Lombardi Trophy, and being named a Super Bowl MVP. (*Courtesy of William Hauser*)

throws I was missing. They were moving around and doing things and I was just kind of …

"I hate saying it, but I was just kind of lost."

His solution was to simplify things, so he wouldn't be so lost anymore. And he had come prepared, too. He wrote down a list of plays from the Giants' playbook that he liked or, more importantly, felt comfortable running. Most of them were plays he remembered from training camp, when he was getting a lot of work with the first team offense without the burden of trying to game plan against an opponent. In the summer he was free to study the playbook and the plays, without having to worry about the opposing defense. But everything changed when the season began. First, he was getting limited reps as the backup. Then, when he got the starting job, his focus was always on the next game.

There just wasn't time for him to get comfortable in the offense. So he wanted to take things back to a time when he was.

"I just said, 'We have put in so many new plays from week to week that I don't feel comfortable,'" Eli recalled. "'And if we see a new defense or new blitz, I'm not exactly sure where to go. I think we need to run plays that I know what we're doing, that I'm familiar with, and where I can get the ball out of my hands and make quick decisions.'

"Obviously you just can't run those plays. You've got to put new things in. But I want to be comfortable out there."

Surprisingly, Coughlin agreed. They had tried throwing the kitchen sink at Eli, and all it did was smack him in the head. They wanted a versatile offense with multiple sets and formations and lots of motion, so they could keep defenses guessing all the time. Instead, the one guessing was the one calling the signals. They thought the best way to teach Eli the offense was to force-feed it to him without giving him any real time to digest.

Soon enough, Coughlin realized they were wrong.

"There are times when we need to forget about all of that crap and get up there and snap the ball," Coughlin said. "Let the kid play."

. . .

ONE WEEK AFTER the worst game of his life, Eli had the best game of his rookie season. Standing across the field from Roethlisberger, who was on his way to a remarkable 13–0 regular-season record—a constant reminder of what the Giants could have had—Eli completed nearly 70 percent of his passes against the Steelers top-ranked defense. He was 16 of 23 for 182 yards with two touchdowns and only one interception. His passer rating was a gaudy 103.9.

The Giants lost 33–30, but there was a feeling that day that a star was born.

The next week, on the day after Christmas, he nearly beat the Bengals in Cincinnati. Playing on the coldest day he would experience in the regular season in the first four years of his career, Eli was 19 of 37 for a career-high 201 yards with an interception. Not great, but not terrible, and only good enough for a close call—a 23–22 loss, his sixth, and the Giants' eighth in a row.

One week later, though, everything finally came together. He had his first three-touchdown game, his completion percentage was back near 70 (18 for 27, 66.7 percent), and he was only picked off once in the season finale at home against the Cowboys. Best of all, trailing 24–21 in the final minutes, he led a late fourth-quarter comeback drive. And on the final play, he made a gutsy "reverse audible" out of an ill-fated pass play into a Barber touchdown run that gave the Giants a dramatic 28–24 win. It was an audible call that four weeks earlier he undoubtedly wouldn't have had the composure or the guts to make.

After that comeback and the three-game rally by Eli, there was a bubbling sense of excitement in the Giants' organization—much more than you'd usually find after an otherwise miserable 6–10 season. Eli wasn't brilliant during that three-game stretch, but he was pretty good. And given his age, what he'd been through, and the way he had smashed hard into rock bottom, the Giants would gladly take the numbers he posted—53 of 87 (60.9 percent) for 527 yards, five touchdowns, three interceptions (a rating of 82.9)—on the way back up.

It wasn't much, but it was a start.

"It gives us great hope," Coughlin said. "We look at the price we had to pay for that and see rewards are on the way."

"There was never any time that anyone in this organization was shaken by the confidence that we had in him," Accorsi added. "We saw enough when we made the trade to draft him that even when he was struggling, it wasn't a point where we started to backpedal on what we thought he was going to be. We knew it was just a matter of him getting baptized."

.   .   .

IN A WAY, that makes Gilbride the Godfather, since he's the one who held Eli up when the water poured in over his head. Years later, sitting at a table in the Giants' team hotel at Super Bowl XLII, Gilbride was asked if he thought the conversation he had with Eli on that train was the turning point in the young quarterback's career.

"That's putting maybe a little too much credit into that conversation," he said.

Maybe so, but even Gilbride admitted their talk was something "that needed to take place." It was part of the growing process that every young quarterback has to go through. There comes a point when they all—or at least most of them—need a little push. And it's not always a push in a specific direction. Sometimes it's just a gentle little kick in the pants.

"He needed to get a sense of what he could and couldn't do within the framework of our preparation," Gilbride said. "'Do I have any say in this, or don't I?' The bottom line is your players have to be able to do what you're asking them to do, and I think he finally realized that if there were certain things he didn't necessarily feel good about, he could say it.

"He may have known it, but maybe he needed to be prodded just a little bit. I think maybe it helped a little bit."

Eli agreed. "That was maybe the first step of getting that relationship with my coaches and kind of getting that comfort level where you can tell people what you think is best," the quarterback said. "And not just for me, but for the team. You have to build that relationship with all your offensive coaches and be on the same page. That can be a start."

Eleven: "You hope he can be like his brother"

PEYTON MANNING IS a presence. He's always in control, and that's clear the moment he walks into a room. He's confident, smiling, willing to show off a little of his famous personality to anyone who asks—or even to those who don't. Eli? He's the stereotypical little brother, standing in the background as if he's trying to hide, eyes down to the ground, kicking his feet at nothing in particular and seemingly unwilling to speak out of turn.

It's the spring of 2006, and the two brothers are sitting in the basement of a house in North Caldwell, New Jersey, just across the street from the house they used for Johnny Sack in *The Sopranos*. They've taken over this house for a day to shoot a Reebok commercial with their father. During a break in the shooting they head downstairs to the spacious basement and plop themselves down on the couch.

As similar as they look, they don't need name tags for guests to tell who the two-time NFL MVP is and who is the kid still struggling to find his way. During a rare joint interview, Peyton answers nearly every question—even if it's explicitly directed toward Eli. His answers are long, detailed, and filled with flashes of his personality. He's friendly, engaging, and relaxed.

Eli, meanwhile, sits to his brother's right, rarely attempting to make eye contact with anyone except Peyton. He appears to gaze away into some far-off place. When he does decide to take his turn speaking, his answers are shorter, more boring, filled with platitudes and clichés. He reveals little more than he does in his typical media sessions during the season, when he manages to find a way to say, "I just need to make good decisions," no matter what question is asked.

The comparison between the two won't end on the couch, of course. Three months later, the brothers in arms will play one of the most hyped season openers in NFL history. It will be dubbed "The Manning Bowl." Eli vs. Peyton. Giants vs. Colts. It'll be in prime time—NBC's first *Sunday Night Football* telecast, in fact. And while there may be 106 players on the rosters that night and twenty-two on the field at any given time, the only two anyone will care about will come from the First Family of the NFL.

To Peyton, the whole idea is "fun" and "unique." He even seems to be embracing the hype that he knows will only strengthen like a hurricane as the summer goes along. He seems happiest for Eli, who'll be getting a lot of national attention, even though Eli doesn't seem very happy for himself. To the youngest Manning, the idea of more hype, more questions, and more pressure is repulsive. When the schedule came out in April and he saw what game was scheduled for the opener, he dreaded the idea of having five months to discuss it. It would've been easier for him if the game were buried in week six, where they hype might only last one week.

Instead … well, the look on his face makes it clear this whole thing feels like he's having a root canal again.

"The build-up, we could do without that," Eli said. "That's not what we're about. We're going to be asked tons of questions about it and we'll probably give the same answer over and over and over again."

In fact, that's exactly what he does in that interview, and in dozens more he'll do over the next few months. The answers will become remarkably familiar. He even has a practiced joke all prepared about how he wishes Peyton was playing defense for the Colts. "That," he says, "would really help us out." It gets a laugh every time, except from those who had heard it before.

Still, Eli finds nothing funny about the incessant comparisons to his much more accomplished brother. And who could blame him? He was supposed to be the second coming of Peyton. OK, he didn't look like a Manning as he struggled through his rookie year in 2004. But in 2005, his first full season as a starter, he not only won eleven games but threw for more yards than Peyton (3,762 to 3,747) and nearly as many touchdowns (24 to big brother's 28)—not bad, considering Peyton was an eight-year vet at the time. He even compared favorably to Peyton's first full season as a starter—his rookie year in 1998—when he threw for 3,739 yards and 26 touchdowns (with 28 interceptions).

There were some brilliant performances in year two, as well. How about the 352 yards he threw for in his first trip to San Diego, the city he famously spurned, in front of a hostile crowd that booed him from the start, held up signs questioning his family tree, and even hung him in effigy? It was, in many ways, his coming-out party, even though the Giants lost 45–23. One week later, he threw for four touchdowns and 296 yards in a win at home over St. Louis. A few weeks later, he had a three-touchdown performance in a win against the Eagles despite being sacked five times. He threw for 344 yards the next week in what would have been an NFC-changing win in Seattle if it hadn't been for three missed Jay Feely field goals. He'd have three 300-yard games in all, and another three over 250. The numbers and performance sure seemed to indicate that Eli, two years into his career, was off to a pretty good start.

But it wasn't good enough for the media and fans who couldn't forget his awful, season-ending, six-game slide in which he threw ten interceptions and only four touchdowns (the Giants still won four of those games). It ended with an ugly 23–0 loss in the first round to the Carolina Panthers. Eli was 10 of 18 for 113 yards and intercepted three times in what was only the second shutout play-off loss at home in the franchise's history, and first since 1943.

Peyton? All he was doing at the time was leading a team that threatened to go undefeated and came within one missed Mike Vanderjagt field goal of reaching the AFC title game. Sure, Eli and Peyton had comparable numbers through twenty-three starts, but Peyton already held the single-season record for touchdown passes (49) and had topped 4,000 yards in six straight seasons.

Is it unfair to compare him to possibly one of the greatest quarterbacks ever just because they share genes? Sure. But that wasn't going to stop anybody from making the link.

"You see his brother playing and you see all the success he's had and you just kind of wonder," teammate Jeremy Shockey said during Eli's rookie season. "You hope he can be like his brother."

Talk about pressure. Hey Eli, your brother is well on his way to the Pro Football Hall of Fame. So what have you got?

"I've always said that if I'm being compared to Peyton in any way then I take that as a compliment," Eli said. "He's at the top of the game and the top of the league in what he does. He plays quarterback and does it better than anybody else. Obviously that's just part of the deal. I'm going to be compared to him. There are similarities and differences. I guess I've just accepted it."

Oh, if it would only be that easy.

• • •

THERE PROBABLY WON'T be a day in Eli Manning's career when he's compared to Angelo Bertelli. But in at least one way the two will forever be linked. They are each among the twenty-six quarterbacks who have been selected first overall in the seventy-three NFL drafts that were held through 2008. In fact, when the Boston Yanks called Bertelli's name in 1944, he became the first quarterback ever to be taken first.

The pick didn't turn out to be a good one. Bertelli, the "Springfield Rifle," was the reigning Heisman Trophy winner, but he only played six games for Notre Dame in 1943 before he was activated by the Marines. He never played a down for the Yanks. Pro football was hardly a lucrative career at the time, so nobody could blame him. And, not surprisingly, the Yanks didn't recover from striking out at the top of that draft and they had the number one pick again two years later. Also not surprisingly, they had little choice but to select another quarterback—Frank "Boley" Dancewicz, Bertelli's successor at Notre Dame.

(The Yanks, by the way, eventually became the Dallas Texans, whose holdings were sold to Carroll Rosenbloom in 1953. Rosenbloom restarted the franchise in Baltimore, called them the Colts and eventually hired a young public relations director named Ernie Accorsi, who would eventually become their general manager and draft another quarterback first overall in 1983. And, like Bertelli, that quarterback—John Elway—would never play a down for the team that drafted him.)

The names on the list of quarterbacks drafted first overall from Bertelli to Manning and beyond are hardly an advertisement for using the top pick at that position. The first Hall of Famer on the list is Terry Bradshaw, who was taken out of Louisiana Tech by the Steelers in 1970. He was the tenth quarterback to ever go number one overall. There are only two other Hall of Famers on the list—Elway in 1983 and Troy Aikman in 1989 (though Peyton Manning, 1998, is well on his way).

For every quarterback on the list who had even a good NFL career, there's a Steve Bartkowski (Atlanta, 1975), whose NFL career was mediocre, or Tim Couch (Cleveland, 1999), whose NFL career barely existed. Yet despite all the evidence that being the number one overall pick isn't a guarantee of any kind of success, the honor still conjures up images of Aikman and Elway. For Eli, that's where the bar was set.

If that wasn't enough, there had been forty-five quarterbacks taken in the first round in Eli's lifetime alone, and his performance would always remind people of the best or the worst. Is he the second coming of Elway or is he another Akili Smith? Those were the players to which he'd always be compared. And there were sixteen other quarterbacks taken after him in the 2004 draft, not to mention several more that went undrafted but managed to find an NFL home—like Jared Lorenzen, the strong-armed, big-bodied fan favorite from Kentucky, who signed on to be Eli's backup in New York.

Eli, the number one pick, would have to out-perform them all. Nothing less would do.

And the comparisons weren't just from columnists or sports–talk radio callers. Even when talking to members of the Giants—players, coaches, and management—the measuring sticks seemed to work their way into every conversation. Shockey hopes he'll be like Peyton. Tiki Barber, talking about Eli's first start, said he hoped he'd turn out like Roethlisberger. And look at the names Accorsi tossed into the mix when reviewing Eli's rookie year.

"If you throw out Roethlisberger and Marino, he's basically had a better first two years than any quarterback—Elway, Eli's brother, Aikman," Accorsi said. "He has to play to a different standard because of his name and because of the trade."

That is certainly true. It didn't help that he was playing in an era where the sports news cycle is twenty-four hours and everyone with a telephone gets to voice their criticism at 50,000 watts. It didn't help that he was playing in New York, with more bully pulpits per capita than anywhere in the world. Elway had a nightmare of a rookie season in 1983, but it was in the relative isolation of Denver and a decade or so before there was a twenty-four-hour sports-talk station on every radio dial. Johnny Unitas—a ninth-round draft choice—was cut from the first NFL team he tried to make, but the year was 1955 and there weren't a million people rushing to the internet to find a blog where they could declare him a bust and pronounce the end of his NFL career.

Still, Eli might have been able to endure the typical rookie struggles in peace if it weren't for one very big problem: Big Ben Roethlisberger, the quarterback every Giants fan knew their team could have had—and without giving up any draft picks—was on his way to a 13–0 start as a rookie and would eventually lead his team to the AFC championship game.

Roethlisberger was a different animal, too. He had the "it" factor people love to see in their quarterbacks. He had the confidence, the swagger, and the presence all down pat. Eli was the master of the cliché, trying desperately to say nothing that could generate a headline. Roethlisberger, meanwhile, unabashedly wore his confidence on his sleeve. At Super Bowl XXXVIII in Houston, a few months before he was drafted, Roethlisberger was led around the floor of the Astrodome by his agent, Leigh Steinberg, at the NFL's annual commissioner's party. He looked out of place at the catered, shirt-and-tie event for the rich and famous, and in a quiet moment admitted that he'd rather be someplace—anyplace—else.

There was considerable debate back then about whether Roethlisberger, who played in the Mid-American Conference, could transfer his considerable skills to the NFL and how ready to do that he really was. Yet when he was asked if he'd mind coming to New York, where he might get to spend a year sitting behind Kerry Collins, he said "I'm not sitting behind anybody. I'm going somewhere to play right away."

So much for political correctness. So much for clichés. So much for easing his way into the league.

Could anyone imagine hearing Eli Manning say something like that?

That brashness was part of what endeared Roethlisberger to blue-collar Pittsburgh, at least at first. He was the leather-jacketed, motorcycle-riding tough guy in the draft, a stark contrast to Eli's class president image. And Western Pennsylvania—home of Marino, Unitas, Montana, and Namath—loved it. The winning helped, to be sure. So did Eli's struggles 375 miles away in New York. But Pittsburgh ate it up—literally. Three wins into his career, the Brentwood Express, a restaurant located just outside of Pittsburgh, debuted the Roethlis-burger—complete with bacon, barbecue sauce, ranch dressing, cheddar and provolone, all for $3.95.

Meanwhile, over at Giants Stadium …

"I think Tom and Ernie have to be sitting there saying to themselves, 'Why can't Eli be like Ben?'" Joe Theismann said. "You can't avoid it."

Well, that's not exactly what they were thinking. Under escalating pressure from the impatient fan base and the restless media, the Giants' executives had rallied around their increasingly embattled quarterback. It wasn't a public relations campaign either. When Accorsi insisted that neither he nor Coughlin had lost any confidence in Eli, he meant it. And no one in the organization ever looked back at their 2004 draft board and wondered where they went wrong.

"Most NFL teams had Manning rated over Roethlisberger," co-owner John Mara said. "Most would have taken Manning over

Roethlisberger. Revisit this in a few years and make the judgment then."

Unfortunately for Eli, nobody outside the organization was willing to wait, and the comparison smacked him in the face early, in his fifth NFL start when Roethlisberger rolled into town with a gaudy 11–0 record and Eli was still scraping pieces of himself off the Baltimore turf. They faced off just six days after Eli was benched and battered by the Ravens. On that same day, December 12, Roethlisberger hadn't exactly been Montana-esque. He had completed only 9 of 19 passes for 144 yards and two interceptions against the Jets. But his team won 17–6 and he was still undefeated, which was more than enough for everyone to hold over Eli's head.

Not that it was fair. While the Giants were overloading Eli with information, the Steelers were bending over backwards to protect Roethlisberger, to not put him in a position where he might lose a game for his team. Plus, the simple fact was that the Steelers' offense was a thousand times easier to run. "People want to compare him to Ben Roethlisberger," Tim Hasselbeck said. "Well, I played in the offense that Ben runs in Pittsburgh [under former Steelers offensive coordinator Ken Whisenhunt, who is now head coach of the Arizona Cardinals] and he is asked to do not even a fraction mentally of what Eli is asked to do."

Of course, nobody ever mentioned that in the comparisons. They just mentioned the stats, the wins, and the way they looked on the field. Meanwhile, it seemed the pressure of all that was getting to Eli. He had been remarkably accessible to the media during the early stages of his career, but this time he was kept away from the press until Thursday of that week—and it was a Saturday game. The Giants' media relations staff insisted it had more to do with scheduling during a short week and wasn't an attempt to shield their young quarterback. But nobody bought the explanation.

None of the questions facing Eli were going to be pleasant or easy, and he clearly already had enough problems of his own. It was the first sign—albeit a small one—that maybe Eli was feeling a little heat.

"He's not going to show you, but you know he's not impervious to the pressure," Gilbride said. "No one is. But it didn't seem to affect him, certainly not in a negative way, the way he performed."

Eli stood toe-to-toe with Roethlisberger that night. The Steelers won the game, but Eli won something else with his impressive performance: some confidence and some much-needed respect. He played hard and looked more determined than he had at any point during his rookie year.

"That's why I say sometimes you can underestimate his competitiveness," Gilbride said. "Because he went out anxious to show 'Hey, I deserved to be drafted where I was.' He's never going to verbalize that. He's never going to say that. His body language is never going to say that. But I thought with his play he attempted to say that."

That game sparked a season-ending surge for Eli that carried over into season two, his first full season as a starter. With the distraction of Warner gone (Hasselbeck was his new backup) and some new toys in place (right tackle Kareem McKenzie and receiver Plaxico Burress were signed in the off-season), Eli started off the 2005 season on fire. In his first four games his numbers were excellent compared to what he had done his rookie year: a completion rate of 53.6 percent (66 of 123), 985 yards, nine touchdowns, and just two interceptions. And that included that remarkable performance in unusually hostile San Diego. Even with his season-ending slump, the Giants went on to finish 11–5 and win the NFC East. But whatever positive vibes were coming out of that were ruined by his playoff disaster in the game where Tiki Barber famously said the

Giants were "out-coached," the first sign the wheels were coming off Coughlin's chaotic bus. The image of Eli, which earlier in the season was that of a confident star in the making, was now one of him shaking his head and looking down at the ground as if he were saying, "What is going on here?" He was, in many ways, the bumbling, befuddled captain of a fast-sinking ship.

Roethlisberger? Well, the news just kept getting worse for Eli. Roethlisberger wasn't as good in his second year as he was in the first, but he still led the Steelers on a tear through the playoffs—winning three games on the road—and didn't stop until they had beaten the Seattle Seahawks 21–10 in Super Bowl XL. Never mind that Roethlisberger was only 9 of 21 for 123 yards and two interceptions in that game, or that he was helped out by some questionable calls and bunch of drops by Seahawks receivers. All that really mattered was that the quarterback the Giants could have had, the one taken ten spots below Eli, had just won a Super Bowl in his second season. That he did it wearing the number 7 in honor of his childhood hero, Elway, was just another little dagger in the heart of Accorsi, whose signature trade was quickly looking worse and worse.

And thus a new bar was set: For Eli's career to be considered a success, he now had no choice but to win a Super Bowl. To validate the trade and all the draft picks Accorsi surrendered to get him, he probably had to win two, because the legend of Big Ben was growing fast. In the days before the 2005 AFC championship—Roethlisberger's second straight appearance in the game—one of the greatest quarterbacks in Giants history was already comparing Roethlisberger to a player already on the way to being one of the all-time greats.

"I hate to compare," Phil Simms said, a few days before calling that game for CBS. "But he does have one thing in common with Tom Brady. They have a tremendous sense of being calm on the field. It shows. He doesn't get rattled, and that's pretty unique for a second-year player like him."

. . .

THE GOOD NEWS for Eli? Well, he dodged at least one bullet because Philip Rivers wasn't doing anything in San Diego. Early success for the guy the Giants traded for Eli could have been disastrous. But the unexpected emergence of Drew Brees gave the Chargers the opportunity to sit Rivers on their bench until they were sure he was ready. In his first two seasons, while Eli was struggling, Rivers attempted only thirty passes (completing seventeen, with one touchdown and one interception).

Even the biggest Eli bashers in the world weren't going to get too worked up over that.

Rivers became an issue in year three, 2006, when Eli was still struggling to get his footing in the NFL. Eli would have stretches of absolute brilliance. He had games that left fans drooling for more, like his week two overtime win in Philadelphia when he led the Giants back from a seventeen-point, fourth-quarter deficit. Eli completed 31 of his 43 passes that day (72.1 percent) for 371 yards, three touchdowns, and only one interception, despite being sacked a ridiculous eight times. He even stood in the pocket in the face of a blitz, absorbed a hit, and still completed the game-winning thirty-one-yard touchdown pass to Burress in overtime.

But too much of his third season was the picture of mediocrity. He even ended with another second-half swoon. With a playoff berth on the line in week sixteen he went out in a home game against the woeful New Orleans Saints and completed 9 of 25 passes for 74 yards—a performance so awful that it prompted the ever-loyal Coughlin to effectively fire his offensive coordinator, the unpopular John Hufnagel, later that night. But even with Gilbride calling the plays, the change didn't exactly pay quick dividends for Eli. The next week, while Barber was carrying the Giants to a play-off berth with a franchise-record 234 yards rushing in Washington, Eli was completing just 12 of 26 passes for 101 yards.

That those were his thirty-eighth and thirty-ninth starts were alarming, especially considering what Rivers was doing in San Diego. The "painful but priceless" experience that Coughlin always talked about for Eli surely didn't appear to be working out very well. Yet Rivers walked onto the field after two years on the sidelines and had a higher completion percentage than Eli (61.7 to 57.7), and threw for more yards (3,388 to 3,244) and a much better touchdown-to-interception ratio (22-to-9 for Rivers, 24-to-18 for Eli).

Oh, and the Chargers under Rivers's direction were 14–2.

Rivers made the Pro Bowl that year (though he didn't play because of a foot injury). So did linebacker Shawne Merriman and kicker Nate Keading, who had been selected by the Chargers with two of the picks acquired in the Eli deal. And if you don't think the comparisons were starting to get to everyone involved, consider what was going through Accorsi's mind a little over a year later, on January 20, 2008, a few hours before he was going to watch Eli play in Green Bay in the NFC championship game. First, he sat down to watch Rivers and the Chargers play the Patriots in the AFC championship. And for a brief moment, when Accorsi thought the Chargers had a chance to win and make the Super Bowl, he couldn't help but think, "Oh no, they're both going to go."

First Roethlisberger, now Rivers? And Eli had to win in frigid Green Bay, which, as Accorsi said, was "not exactly a gimmie putt."

Until Eli's Super Bowl run, the comparisons he faced would come up at every statistical milestone. After sixteen starts, how did Eli compare to Elway, Peyton, Simms, Roethlisberger, and all the others? How about after two years? Three years? Twenty-five games? Fifty? He couldn't duck them. Ever. And at each milepost, Eli appeared to drop further behind them all.

The worst comparison? Easily it was after his fiftieth start, an arbitrary and meaningless point in time that's only significance was the roundness of its number. It just so happens, unfortunately for Eli, that his fiftieth career start, late in the 2007 season, was one of his worst—a four-interception disaster at home against the Minnesota Vikings in which three of those picks were returned for touchdowns in a brutal 41–17 loss.

He was booed off the field. Even Accorsi left the building at halftime. And the aftermath was made worse when comparisons were made with other quarterbacks in their first fifty starts.

It wasn't pretty. Through those starts, Eli had completed just 55.1 percent of his passes (907 of 1,647) for 10,425 yards, 70 touchdowns, 59 interceptions, and a quarterback rating of 73.6. The numbers weren't bad, until you factored in all the other things you have to factor in with Eli. He was nowhere near meeting expectations. Yes, he was a little better than Simms was through fifty starts, and Simms managed to meet expectations rather nicely (eventually). But Simms played in a different era, so his passing numbers were naturally lower. And alarmingly, Eli's first fifty starts weren't quite as good as those of Kerry Collins, the quarterback he essentially drove out of town. And Peyton, Roethlisberger, Tom Brady, Brett Favre, Marc Bulger, Carson Palmer, and Donovan McNabb were among his contemporaries whose first fifty starts were better. Even Eli's win-loss record—27–23—was bettered by most of them.

Meanwhile, it was hard not to notice the name at the top of those "first fifty start" charts. Roethlisberger, with a completion percentage of 63.0 (819 of 1,299), 10,734 passing yards, 75 touchdowns, and 51 interceptions, had a passer rating of 91.9. Bulger and Palmer were close, but none of the others—including Peyton (86.3)—were over 90. Passer rating may be a flawed statistic, but still …

"That's the whole thing," Theismann said. "If you're a number one pick, I don't care who you are, you're never going to live up to the expectations that have been set for you. Ever. I don't care who you are, as a number one pick, it ain't going to happen. But at this stage of Eli's career, I would expect him to play better football. And I'm sure he would, too."

Here's the irony, though. Unfair expectations and comparisons aside, Eli was still pretty good. Theismann said he'd "easily" put Eli in his top ten of current quarterbacks. Boomer Esiason agreed, saying at least twenty-two of the thirty-two NFL teams late in the 2007 season would prefer to have Eli over their current starter.

"Do you want to wake up and have David Carr [the number one overall pick in 2002] as your quarterback?" Esiason said. "Or J.P. Losman [taken twenty-second in the first round in 2004]? There are not a lot of guys out there that you're going to say look better than Eli."

Well, there was always at least one.

. . .

AFTER ALL THE comparisons, it still always came back to one thing for Eli: He's a Manning, and he's supposed to be like his brother. Even those who dismissed the comparison as unfair still could be caught searching for similarities. There had to be something, anything, to prove that Eli didn't get stuck in the shallow end of the Manning gene pool.

By the time the Manning Bowl rolled around on September 10, 2006, Eli had already heard all the jokes and read all the signs that suggested he was adopted. If it bothered him, if he came into the game with a chip on his shoulder or something to prove, it was impossible to tell.

"If there is, you'll never know," Gilbride said. "He plays his cards very close to the vest, even with me."

Some of that was because Eli never bought into the gene theory. He never thought he was guaranteed stardom because of his last name. "I don't think he had any illusions that 'Oh, because I'm Peyton's brother or Archie's son, it's just a given,'" Gilbride said. "I think he knew that it was going to take some time and some hard work to get this thing done."

Still, there was no doubt that somewhere—maybe deep inside— he viewed the Manning Bowl as his chance to show … something. Maybe it was just to his older brother. Maybe it was just to himself. Maybe it was even just the competitiveness of their backyard games kicking in, or the frustration of being beaten by his older brother in sports year after year after year. But those closest to him suspected it was a little more than that. It was a chance to prove he belonged.

"There is something in him that he just wants it," Gilbride said. "'I'm good. I'm going to show you guys. You don't think I am? I'm going to show you.' He'll never say it. He'll never act that way. But it's there."

And so it was that night when he opened his third NFL season with a decent performance—20 of 34 for 247 yards, two touchdowns, and one interception. Peyton was slightly better (25 for 41, 276 yards, one touchdown, one interception) and won the game 26–21. The Colts needed an Adam Vinatieri field goal with 1:12 remaining to put Eli in a position where he'd need a touchdown to win it in the end. And the game still wasn't over until Eli's center, Shaun O'Hara, was called for a strange and controversial "illegal snap" penalty with seventeen seconds left and the Giants standing at their own forty-six-yard line with only one play left.

After the game, the Giants were furious, complaining loudly that the game had been stolen by the officials (who made several controversial calls). Eli took the high road, lamenting earlier missed opportunities. Peyton, meanwhile, gushed about the performance of his little brother.

"He's every bit as good as he looked on TV," Peyton said. "He's going to be a great player. I'm proud to be related to the guy. I'm proud to be his brother."

Eli would never see it this way, but he won a big victory that night, too. For the first time, the brothers were right there, together on a football field for everyone to see, and amazingly they looked pretty comparable. Yes, Eli was still the little brother lagging behind, getting knocked down in the end by his older, more accomplished sibling. But Peyton still had six years on Eli. And for the first time, Eli looked like he was closing fast.

Some, in fact—but not all—thought he was on the way to becoming a star.

"I'd be careful with the word star," said former Bengals receiver-turned-broadcaster Cris Collinsworth. "His brother is a star. There are probably four or five stars. He's got a long way to go to get to there. But I think he can be an upper middle-class quarterback, and if the light bulb starts to come on there's no question he could be one of the top-end guys. But the Tom Bradys, the Peyton Mannings, you could see it some in their first year and some in their second year. Usually it's a little clearer cut right off the bat.

"But who knows? Steve Young took a while to develop, too."

Twelve: "You can't measure things like heart"

THE FIRST QUARTERBACK wasn't taken in the 2000 draft until the eighteenth pick, when the Jets took Chad Pennington out of Marshall. It would be another two rounds and forty-seven more picks before another quarterback was taken. Do you remember Giovanni Carmazzi? He was a record-setting quarterback from that noted football powerhouse, Hofstra University in Long Island, New York.

Carmazzi was taken with the third pick of the third round—sixty-fifth overall. Chris Redman went next, ten picks later, to the Baltimore Ravens. With one of the last picks in round five, the Steelers took Tennessee quarterback Tee Martin 163rd overall. Five picks after that, at the start of round six, the Saints took Marc Bulger 168th. And finally, fifteen picks later, 183rd overall, the Cleveland Browns dipped into the talent pool at Southwest Texas State and grabbed Spergon Wynn.

Meanwhile, experts everywhere were baffled by one question: Is there nobody out there who wants Joe Hamilton, the quarterback from Georgia Tech?

Hamilton finished second in the Heisman Trophy voting that year, right behind running back Ron Dayne—who was drafted eleventh overall by the New York Giants—and ahead of a slew of future NFL players, including quarterbacks Drew Brees and Michael Vick. Hamilton was only 5-foot-10—not exactly ideal size for a quarterback—but he was the most dynamic player in the Atlantic Coast Conference, having set a record with more than 10,000 career total yards. And wasn't the new NFL looking for quarterbacks who were dangerous on the run? Plus, he could throw pretty well, too. He won the Davey O'Brien Award as the best collegiate quarterback in the land.

It boggled the mind of many that he lasted so long, not getting selected until the Tampa Bay Buccaneers took him in the seventh round, 234th overall. He was the twelfth quarterback taken. He even went thirty-five picks after some lightly regarded quarterback from the University of Michigan—you know, that kid who wasn't supposed to be as good as his backup, Drew Henson.

Some kid named Tom Brady.

It has become the ultimate example of how inexact a science picking a quarterback really is—the flip side of Ryan Leaf, who was the number two pick of the 1998 draft, right behind Peyton Manning. But Leaf was a head case whose NFL career became a disaster that set the San Diego Chargers back six years. Meanwhile, there was Brady, the ultimate diamond in the rough, going to the New England Patriots 199th overall. All thirty-one teams passed on him over and over again, round after round, hour after hour, ignoring his poise, character, composure, accuracy. The Patriots weren't sold on him either, by the way. They were considering passing on him and taking Louisiana Tech's Tim Rattay.

It seems ridiculous now, of course. Four Pro Bowls, three Super Bowl championships, and one NFL MVP award later he's only one of the greatest quarterbacks of this (or any) generation. He's already punched his ticket for the Pro Football Hall of Fame. Yet six quarterbacks went before him in the draft? Tee Martin? Spergon Wynn?

Combined, the two of them made all of three NFL starts (all by Wynn) and completed 76 of 168 passes (45.2 percent) for 654 yards, one touchdown, and eight interceptions. For them, that's a career (two careers, really). For Brady, that's a horrible month.

And Carmazzi? To San Francisco? Brady was born in San Mateo, a suburb of San Francisco, for crying out loud. Carmazzi went into Brady's backyard and ended up getting beaten out by Rattay, the 49ers' seventh-round selection. Carmazzi wasn't even good enough to stick in the Canadian Football League. That's why, the geniuses say, you don't need to take a quarterback in the first round of the NFL draft. Just look at all the mistakes that are made up high. And look at all the late-round gems teams unearth. Jake Delhomme was undrafted and so was Kurt Warner, and they both took their teams to the Super Bowl. Brett Favre, a future Hall of Famer, was a second-round pick. Matt Hasselbeck, who took the Seahawks to the Super Bowl, was a sixth-rounder. Joe Montana was a third-rounder. Roger Staubach was a tenth-rounder. Johnny Unitas went in round nine.

"The fact that some of the guys in later rounds have made it just shows that the system is not foolproof," said Seahawks coach and general manager Mike Holmgren. "There are human beings making human errors."

"It really is an inexact science," added Cowboys coach Wade Phillips. "You can't measure things like heart."

• • •

THERE WERE SOME concerns about Ryan Leaf when he was coming out of Washington State, but nothing that would really make anyone overly nervous. The consensus around the league was that he and Peyton Manning were the two best quarterbacks in the 1998 draft, maybe the two best players. Leaf was 6-foot-5, 240, had a strong arm, and he did what great quarterbacks are supposed to do—he carried his undermanned Washington State team all the way to the Rose Bowl.

"You know what?" Accorsi said. "If you gave us all truth serums there isn't anybody who wouldn't say, 'He looked like he was going to be a great player.' There were people in this league who said that was a toss up."

Obviously that's what the San Diego Chargers thought. Their general manager, Bobby Beathard, made a blockbuster deal to move up from third spot in the draft to second, just to guarantee he'd get one of the two quarterbacks. He sent Arizona his first and second round picks in '98, a first-round pick in '99, a backup linebacker named Patrick Sapp, and a three-time Pro Bowl, return man in Eric Metcalf. At the time, Beathard didn't know what the Indianapolis Colts were going to do with the first overall pick, and it seemed pretty clear that Beathard didn't really care.

It didn't seem to matter to anyone that there were whispers about Leaf's character and maybe even his mental stability. Teams overlooked the horrible impression he made at the NFL's annual scouting combine, with his casual attitude and even more casual appearance. While Peyton Manning was going from room to room, acting each time like he was a businessman on the most important job interview of his life, Leaf was sauntering in and out as if it was a nuisance to be there at all.

It's all hindsight, of course, but maybe nobody should have been surprised that Leaf suffered one of the most famous meltdowns in NFL history. He started off on the wrong foot by skipping the NFL's annual rookie symposium, drawing an unwanted fine. In his three seasons in San Diego he was caught on camera shouting at and physically threatening a reporter, and later being restrained by coaches as he tried to go after a fan. While on injured reserve in 1999, he drew a fine and a suspension for a shouting match with Beathard, and was forced to issue a painful-looking public apology. He was even caught on camera playing flag football when he was supposed to be rehabbing his shoulder and wrist.

He was a mess. That pick went down as one of the worst in the history of the NFL draft. Years later, the question still lingers: How is it that the Chargers—and the rest of the league, for that matter—didn't see it coming? How could they not know?

"You know, it's so hard to tell the inside of a person," said Gilbride, who was the Chargers head coach for the first six games of Leaf's rookie season. "As much as we evaluate their cognitive abilities and their arm strength and their height and their weight and this and that, you can't look inside the guy. We give him psychological profiles, but no matter what you just can't tell with certain guys."

Of course, it's all magnified with a quarterback. He's counted on to be cool under pressure, mature, and a team leader. All Leaf did was alienate everyone in the organization. The Chargers were a struggling franchise and the expectations on Leaf were enormous. No one expects a left tackle or a linebacker or a receiver to single-handedly turn around the fortunes of a franchise. But a quarterback is supposed to be a savior. A lot of people thought Leaf was. A lot of people were wrong.

"Most of the time if you're a top draft pick, you're going to a team that's not very good, that's why they got you," Gilbride said. "Do you have the resiliency, the inner toughness, the inner strength to get through what guaranteed is going to be a very difficult transition process? Quite frankly, I'm not sure that everyone does. The ones that can somehow withstand and weather that trying period. Do they have the equanimity, the poise, the composure, the inner stability to just kind of hang through the tough times? Eventually it gets better. The supporting cast gets better. And then as a group they grow and become what everybody hoped they would when they drafted them that high."

Sometimes they can't even handle success. Todd Marinovich was groomed his whole life to be an NFL quarterback by a father who closely monitored his workouts and diet from the time he was a baby. He was so groomed for athletic and NFL success that Todd became known as the "Robo QB." He set passing records in high school and was a budding star at USC—so good, in fact, that the Raiders were willing to ignore his poor relationship with his coaches and the rumors of his marijuana use and make him the twenty-fourth pick of the 1991 draft. But after eight career starts he lost his job to Jay Schroeder in his second season, never played again, and killed any chances of resurfacing in the NFL with numerous run-ins with the law.

Sometimes the mental issues aren't as black and white. Some young quarterbacks may avoid the legal troubles and the public meltdowns, but they still find it impossible to handle the scrutiny just the same.

Of course, they're not all head cases, either. Some—like Andre Ware (seventh overall to Detroit in 1990), David Klingler (sixth to Cincinnati in 1992), Heath Shuler (third overall to Washington in 1994), Jim Druckenmiller (twenty-sixth to San Francisco in 1997), Tim Couch (first to Cleveland in 1999), and Akili Smith (third to Cincinnati in 1999)—simply didn't appear to have the talent, despite impressive college résumés. Somehow, very smart people in the NFL simply just misjudged how good those quarterbacks were.

"I think where players and teams run into problems is, when you take a quarterback who's had great success throughout his whole career, high school, college, won a lot of games, it's almost come easy," said Cleveland Browns general manager Phil Savage. "But generally the teams picking at the top aren't coming off good years and they're in a rebuilding mode. So the quarterbacks go to those teams and the team is not prepared to be able to handle a rookie quarterback in terms of having a line or the skill players around him. So I think the expectations are way up there and in reality they should be lowered. But that's a hard thing to do when you look at all the attention that the draft is getting and then all the money that's paid to those top picks, in particular the quarterbacks that are seen as the savior of the organization."

And there's nowhere to hide, even if they're not playing as a rookie. There are media demands, intense classroom sessions, and more playbook studying than the average player. They are being prepared to take over the team and the franchise. That means the coaches are paying more attention to them than the guard they drafted in the seventh round. And the more the coaches try to take the pressure off, the more it's obviously there.

That's why, in some ways, it was easier for Brady. He was buried deep on the Patriots' depth chart when he arrived in New England. He was no lock to make the final roster. No one was handing him the keys to the franchise.

"When I came to the Patriots I was the fourth-string quarterback," Brady said. "I was eating nachos before the games, watching us in 2000, just hoping that one day I would get the opportunity. I think with a lot of athletes, you're always the best athlete through high school and college. Then you come to the professional level and you realize, you look around and go, 'Man, all these other guys are good, too.' You begin to think, 'Can I make it?' or 'Am I good enough?' or 'How do I find the work ethic to compete with these guys?'

"I don't think that was ever really the case for me, and I'm lucky that wasn't the case. I always felt I needed to work extremely hard to get whatever opportunity there may have been. I always used to look at the other players in college and think, 'Man, they got it easy. This guy gets every rep in practice, all the chances and opportunities, and I only get two reps.' Then I'd begin to look at it very thankfully. 'I get two reps now and I'm going to do the best with the two I've got.'"

• • •

THERE ARE THIRTY quarterbacks in the Pro Football Hall of Fame. Fourteen of those were selected in the first round. And in the first forty-two Super Bowls, there were twenty-seven different winning quarterbacks. Fifteen of those were first-round selections. That means only twelve Super Bowl-winning quarterbacks have come from rounds two and beyond. In other words, a lot of hard work by a lot of scouts turned up a lot of low-round quarterbacks that were less-than-championship-caliber.

But it only takes one gem—one Unitas or Brady or Warner—to convince teams they don't need to go for the high-ranked, high-priced superstar.

"There are so many good players that have come from the bottom," said former St. Louis Rams head coach Mike Martz. "And I think teams now understand that, particularly with Brady, and Kurt Warner, and some of those other guys that have done so well, guys really understand how hard it is to evaluate that position. Just because you take him in the first round doesn't mean he's going to make it at that level. You have a real chance of missing there, too. There are very few Peyton Mannings, Ben Roethlisbergers."

Warner was the first one to really start the debate, at least the modern version of it. He was an obscure quarterback from Northern Iowa who had played in the Arena League and NFL Europe and failed in several tryouts for the NFL. He was only supposed to be the Rams' backup quarterback in 1999, but was thrust into the lineup in the preseason when the starter, Trent Green (himself an eighth-round pick), injured his knee.

The rest was historic—one of the greatest Cinderella stories of all-time. Warner helped turn the Rams into the Greatest Show on Turf, throwing for 4,353 yards and 41 touchdowns while completing 65.1 percent of his passes. He even led the Rams all the way to the Super Bowl, where he threw for two touchdowns and a record 414 yards in a win over the Tennessee Titans. He became the sixth player (and fifth quarterback) to be named the league MVP and Super Bowl MVP in the same season.

While that was happening, general managers and scouts were falling all over each other, digging through their old reports on the newest overnight sensation. Many of them had seen Warner in college or in the Arena League. And if they didn't, they certainly saw him Europe. They all needed to know how they misjudged him so badly. And for some, it made them reevaluate how they judged whether a quarterback could make it in the league.

"Do you need a quarterback that everybody rates in the top five? No you don't," said Atlanta Falcons general manager Rich McKay, who won a Super Bowl in Tampa Bay a few years later with Brad Johnson, a ninth-round pick, at quarterback. "Do you need a quarterback that fits what you do on offense? Yes. He's got to fit what you do and be very proficient at the way he fits it. But I've never believed you need a 'franchise quarterback' to win a Super Bowl."

"There certainly have been a lot of guys that have been in Super Bowls or taken their teams deep into the playoffs that by most people's account wouldn't be in a category of 'This guy is a difference-maker,' 'This guy is a Hall of Famer,' or 'This guy is a franchise quarterback,'" said former Browns head coach Butch Davis. "But they know how to win."

Run that theory by Accorsi, and he just shakes his head.

"I know that some teams win [without a great quarterback], but I always ask the same question," he said. "If you have an average quarterback and you think you can win a Super Bowl if he just stays within himself and you don't ask him to win it for you, if I'm handing you Elway, would you take him?"

. . .

QUICK. NAME THE biggest quarterback busts in the history of the sixth and seventh rounds. None come to mind because no pick that late has ever been considered a bust. They are long shots to begin with in most people's minds, so it hardly matters if a team makes a mistake that low, even at a position as important as quarterback. And the truth is, the odds of hitting on a quarterback in the later rounds are even longer than they are at the top of the draft. But teams have cover fire down low. There wasn't much of an uproar in San Francisco when Carmazzi was beaten out by Rattay. Carmazzi was only a third-round pick and was never hailed as a savior. The hopes and dreams of the 49ers were never pinned solely on him.

The same wasn't true in San Diego, and look what happened to the Chargers as a result of the Leaf disaster. They were 4–12 the year before he arrived, which is why they were picking so high in the 1998 draft. They were 5–11, 8–8, and then 1–15 in the next three seasons. They traded the number one overall pick in the 2001 draft—a brilliant move, as it turned out, since they gave up the rights to Michael Vick and ended up with future MVP running back LaDainian Tomlinson. But their seemingly never-ending search for a quarterback led them to three more disappointing seasons at 5–11, 8–8, and then 4–12 in 2003, when they were positioned right back at the top of the draft. They had selected quarterback Drew Brees in the second round in 2001, but he hadn't developed as fast as expected. So six years after Leaf, the Chargers were forced to pick a quarterback near the top of the draft again.

"Not only is it much harder to pick quarterbacks, if you're wrong it's more damaging," Accorsi said. "You expect even Elway to start slow, so then you forgive them for that. So you're going to say, 'Well, he'll be better.' If he's not going to make it, you've just blown five years."

That was the dilemma Accorsi had put the Giants in with Eli. By going for the guy at the top in 2004, he was locking them into that choice through at least 2009, maybe longer. Yes, if they were wrong they'd have to eventually start all over again. But they had to wait him out. They had to show patience and give Eli every possible chance to succeed.

"You have got to commit to that guy," Holmgren said. "And sometimes you go down with the ship."

Thirteen: "The best free-agent signing we ever made"

THE PLAY THAT was called didn't always matter. Sometimes all Joe Montana had to do was look at Jerry Rice and they both immediately knew what was going to happen next. "Eye to eye contact," Rice said. "And you know exactly what your quarterback wants you to do." That's as good an explanation as any for how that dynamic duo accomplished so much.

Nearly two decades later, Rice still struggles to explain that connection, that indescribable chemistry that a quarterback can (and should) develop with his number-one receiver. And he knows more about it than anyone in history. For seven years he teamed with Montana to form one of the most exciting, productive quarterback–receiver tandems ever. Then, when Montana wasn't around, Rice spent twelve years doing the same things with Steve Young.

He attributes his connections with both of those Hall of Fame quarterbacks to hard work, endless practice sessions, and thousands and thousands of non-game-day throws, even during the long off-seasons. But even hard work can't explain everything.

"You look back in awe and amazement at times when you see stuff you've done during football games," Rice said. "You're like, 'Man, how did we do that?' It's almost like it becomes magical. It's just amazing to see some of the things that happen on the football field. It's like magic, man."

It's why all these years later, it's impossible to think of Montana or Young without thinking of Rice. Two Hall of Fame quarterbacks and one soon-to-be Hall of Fame receiver, they are forever linked by hundreds of catches, thousands of yards, and 140 touchdowns passes (85 from Young, 55 from Montana). It's the same way with Troy Aikman and Michael Irvin, Terry Bradshaw and Lynn Swann, Dan Marino and Mark Clayton, Peyton Manning and Marvin Harrison. The story of one isn't complete without the other. A quarterback without a top receiver he can count on time and time again, more often than not isn't much of a quarterback at all.

"You have to have a guy who you don't have to make perfect throws to," Accorsi said. "You have to have a guy who'll get you cheap touchdowns, who turns a lob pass into a sixty-yard touchdown. Almost every quarterback has had that receiver, that you know when the game is on the line, you trust him."

It's why one of the most important days in the development of Eli Manning was March 17, 2005, the day when Accorsi made what he considers "the best free-agent signing we ever made." He had already bought linebacker Antonio Pierce for his defense and added Kareem McKenzie at right tackle that off-season. But on that date, after a long and strange courtship that nearly ended before it began, he signed Plaxico Burress to a six-year, $25 million contract. Burress was a 6-foot-5, 230-pound receiver with enormous arms and an alarming reputation for being a complainer. But he was also only twenty-seven and three years removed from an impressive 78-catch, 1,325-yard, seven-touchdown season with the Pittsburgh Steelers. The Giants had just released Ike Hilliard, whose body they felt had been too broken down by injuries for him to continue to be effective. All they really had left was Amani Toomer, a thirty-year-old with a lot of miles on his body and what they considered to be diminishing speed.

Burress, they believed, was exactly what Eli needed. After all, remember Accorsi's original scouting report? When Eli was off-target he was usually high. And Burress, just by reaching up with his long arms, became an elastic seven-foot-plus target. Plus he had great hands and an impressive vertical leap. One thing Eli had failed to do during his seven starts as a rookie was develop a go-to receiver. Burress clearly was going to be that guy.

It almost didn't happen, though. Burress missed his first scheduled free-agent visit to the Giants because he had the flu. When he finally arrived three days later, he was an instant hit inside the Giants' offices. Knowing his reputation, Accorsi had called the Steelers—an organization he trusted more than any other—and spoke with their coach, Bill Cowher, and their general manager, Kevin Colbert. They couldn't say enough nice things about Burress, even though he no longer fit into their financial plans. And Accorsi and Coughlin could see why when they met with the receiver and took him to dinner at Smith & Wollensky's steak house in Manhattan. They put on the full-court press, too. They sent him to a New Jersey Nets game that night, and brought in Tiki Barber to help recruit him the next day. They were all set to sign him. In fact, they were sure they were going to sign him.

Then he just left.

His agent, Michael Harrison, apparently wanted to keep the Giants on the hook while shopping Burress to the Minnesota Vikings. But all that did was tick Accorsi off. So he did something he had never done before. He issued a statement publicly declaring he had withdrawn the Giants' offer to Burress. He wanted to remove Burress's leverage and cut the agent off at his knees.

"As soon as I pulled the plug on the offer, I get word that Philadelphia is willing to throw a lot of money at him for just one year," Accorsi said. "I went to Tom and said, 'Tom, if we have to play against him and Terrell Owens, we're in deep trouble.'"

A few days later, Jerry Reese was on a scouting trip when he ran into Harrison, who began to plead his case. During the conversation, Reese looked up and saw another agent, Drew Rosenhaus, sitting in a car behind him, apparently spying on their conversation. Two days after that, word got out that Burress has dumped Harrison, and soon Rosenhaus was on the phone with Accorsi selling his newest client, even though NFL rules forced teams to wait before opening negotiations after a player had switched agents.

"He calls me and says, 'We're not allowed to negotiate for forty-eight hours,'" Accorsi said. "I said, 'OK.' And for the record, we don't. Then, when he's finally allowed to negotiate, we make the deal in fifteen minutes."

The Giants were thrilled, and so was Burress, who had grown frustrated with his role and his life in Pittsburgh. He didn't like the Steelers' offense, which had become even more conservative and run-based than ever as they tried to ease in Roethlisberger. And he felt that his outspoken nature had been misunderstood by a town that he thought hated him because of the way he dressed and maybe even because of his race. People had questioned his toughness because of the hamstring injury that cost him five games of the 2004 season. All in all, Accorsi called him "the most misunderstood player we've ever had," and that was a big reason why he was so unwanted around the NFL, and why the Giants were still able to grab him more than two weeks after free agency began.

When he finally arrived, one of the first things Burress said was "hopefully Manning-to-Burress will become a big thing around here." That was music to the organization's ears. The coaches quickly began designing plays for their new toy, which they knew was a walking mismatch for defensive backs all over the league.

"You put him on a 5-9 corner," said tight ends coach Mike Pope, "and it looks like a father-son banquet."

Meanwhile, Eli began dreaming of a connection like the one his brother had forged with Marvin Harrison. But he knew it wouldn't be instantaneous. He had spoken with Peyton many times about how he and Harrison had become one of the most prolific quarterback-receiving tandems in the history of the NFL, and the answer was always the same: hard work.

"You're talking about a guy who, for some reason, you have a great feel with," Eli said. "It's a guy where for some reason, if you've never run that play before, something new has happened, and you can just tell from his body. He just has a great feel for the game and you can feel it with him. You have that special connection. Sometimes it's hard to explain.

"But it's something that doesn't happen in a month or two. It doesn't happen automatically. After being with someone for a long period of time you start to get it."

. . .

UPON SIGNING HIS contract, Burress disappeared.

There was a lot to do, of course. He had to take care of his personal affairs in Pittsburgh, and he preferred to spend his off-seasons in Miami anyway. Never mind that Eli was in New Jersey, anxiously awaiting the chance to work with his newest receiver, and that he kept saying as much to anyone who would listen. "You can have all the players in the world, but it's no good if you don't work hard with them," Eli said. "And it starts in the off-season."

Even his father, Archie agreed, that "just because you signed someone doesn't mean you all of a sudden have a great offense. It's all about work and chemistry. They've got a lot of work to do."

That would be a running theme through Eli's early years. Burress and Shockey preferred to spend their off-seasons working out on their own, rarely showing up for more than the one mandatory mini-camp, maybe for another day or two of throwing. Toomer wasn't always in attendance either, due to an ambitious world travel schedule he pursued each off-season. More often than not, Eli was left throwing to rookies and other players he wasn't likely to rely on during a game.

"The reason why a quarterback–receiver combination becomes great is because of the chemistry and that time you put in," Rice said. "Then once you get on that football field, you know exactly what your quarterback is thinking all the time. It's almost as if you guys are as one on the football field. And the incredible plays you made, people look at it and they say, 'Wow.' They're really in awe. But you've made those plays over and over so many times in practice. It comes from practice—repetition, over and over again.

"I know Eli has Plaxico Burress, but they really don't work together too much during the off-season. It makes it a little bit more difficult. To be a combination like that you have to work together all the time."

Throughout their years together, it was as if Eli and Burress were determined to test that theory. In their first summer camp together, Burress hurt his hip early, then Manning sprained his elbow late. But despite that, look what they did in their first season as teammates: seventy-six catches for Burress, 1,214 yards, and seven touchdowns. Players and coaches glowed about how much their newest receiver contributed even when he wasn't catching passes. He was an underrated downfield blocker and drew constant double coverage from worried defenses, opening things up all over the field for Toomer, Shockey, and even Barber.

But another theme was starting to develop. That reputation Burress had of being a complainer? It didn't seem unwarranted in his first few years with the Giants. He was flaunting some of

Coughlin's legendary rules. He was even punished by being benched for the first quarter of the Giants' game in San Diego because he had been more than five minutes late to two team meetings. He had no qualms about telling the media he didn't get along with his coach. If he had a complaint about the offense, he would voice it.

Burress defended himself by insisting, "I speak from my heart. A lot of people don't like that. They see it as complaining: 'Oh, he's a problem.' But when you're actually telling the truth and being factual, that's not complaining, it's just being honest."

Unfortunately, his honesty, if that's what he wants to call it, was showing on the field, too. If Eli overthrew him—or worse, didn't throw to him when he was open—the whole stadium was going to know it. The sight of Burress flapping his arms, stomping his feet and shaking his head became familiar. The idea that he and Eli could build any sort of chemistry seemed ridiculous, and Burress's public praise of Eli sounded hollow. On the field they always seemed to be at odds.

But the production continued. He caught sixty-three passes for 988 yards and ten touchdowns in 2006. That included a remarkable game in Philly in week two when he caught six passes for 114 yards, including a thirty-one-yard touchdown pass to win the game in overtime. That pass was emblematic of their chemistry: On a day when Eli was being battered by the Eagles' blitz, he was able to stand in the pocket with two defenders about to crush him and just float the ball up towards the end zone. It was a risky pass in overtime, but he believed that Burress was going to be there and had confidence that he'd catch it. He did, of course, and the Giants escaped with a 30–24 win.

That was another season, though, that ended in disappointment and chaos. The Giants lost in the first round of the playoffs again, the offense struggled down the stretch, their coach was maybe on the verge of being fired, and the whole organization was concerned that Eli looked lost. Meanwhile, the more they struggled, the more Burress flapped his arms and stomped his feet. It was hard to tell what New York was more worked up about—Burress's histrionics or the fact that Eli refused to put him in his place.

Maybe even worse, whenever he was asked about it, Burress was defiant. "When I get the ball early, I get hot," he said. "I'm into the game and I get better throughout the game. But some games, I get a pass in the first quarter and I won't get another ball thrown to me until the third or fourth quarter. Those are things that I think shouldn't happen.

"People get upset when I throw my hands up when I'm open. But if I'm not getting open I'm getting criticized, too. So that right there is a lose-lose situation. They see the hands and they say, 'Oh he's complaining.' It wasn't my fault I was open."

Maybe that made sense to Burress, but it certainly didn't to Eli.

"When Plax was showing him up, it was driving him crazy," Hasselbeck said. "Fortunately, Plax was able to realize that it wasn't good. It was bad for Eli. [The coaches] talked to Plax about it and he stopped, for the most part."

Eli and Burress talked about it, too, after the 2006 season, which is right about when something seemed to change in Burress. Maybe it was the fact that his first son was born—named Elijah, though apparently not after his quarterback. Maybe it was the fact that he saw the age of thirty coming at him fast. Maybe it was that Hufnagel, the offensive coordinator he didn't like, got fired and was replaced by Gilbride, who was the Steelers' offensive coordinator when Burress was a rookie in 2000.

Or maybe it was that when Burress watched highlights of himself in 2006, he didn't like what he saw. He finally could see what everyone else had, that he was acting like a big baby. So he told Eli he was determined to change.

"He's grown up," Eli said. "He's a tremendous athlete, but since we've been here, he's kind of become a different person. He's gotten married. He's had his first kid. He's grown up a lot. He understands his role. He knows he's our playmaker. We try to get the ball to him when the opportunity presents itself."

As for the arm-waving and foot-stomping, Eli said that Burress understood: "He wouldn't want me to do that to him."

. . .

THERE WASN'T MUCH arm-waving and foot-stomping during the 2007 season, mostly because Burress sprained his right ankle in training camp on August 2—a cruel twist since he was still rehabbing from off-season surgery on his left ankle. The Giants downplayed the sprain, but Burress would later admit he tore ligaments. As a result, he didn't practice all summer and ended up only practicing a handful of times all season.

That could have ruined any opportunity they had to work on their chemistry, but the new, improved Burress wouldn't allow that to happen. He had always been a meticulous note-taker in team meetings—a little-known and surprising fact about him—but when he was unable to practice, he became a more attentive student than ever. He was an active participant in discussions about the offense, especially with Eli. And when he could, he made sure to catch passes from Eli out on the field about two hours before each game.

The result was this: seventy catches, 1,025 yards and twelve touchdowns in what should have been a Pro Bowl season. Then he had another eighteen catches for 221 yards and a touchdown in the Giants' Super Bowl run. The touchdown, of course, was the one that sealed the championship. But his greatest performance came two weeks earlier in Green Bay when he endured the bitter cold that had to make every step feel like a hammer was coming down on his ankle as he caught eleven passes for 151 yards.

In three years, Eli and Burress have played in fifty-three games together (including the playoffs) and combined for 232 catches, 3,537 yards, and thirty-two touchdowns. That's not quite in the Peyton-to-Harrison class—a combo that Rice said is the only one he sees in the NFL that can compare with the chemistry and production he had with Montana or Young. But it's still pretty good. And Burress's impact has gone beyond the numbers, to the way he cuts across the middle, reaches up high and corrals a pass that was destined to land deep in the defensive backfield. Or how he outjumps a smaller corner (and they're all smaller to Burress) for a pass that floats just a little too much out of Eli's hands.

All the great quarterbacks have had a receiver like him. Maybe not with the same height or reach, but the point was still the same. They all had a guy who they felt they could just toss the ball to time and time again, and they didn't have to worry about the rest. Look at Marino, who threw 420 career touchdown passes in his brilliant career. An astonishing seventy-nine of those—or 18.8 percent— went to Clayton, who was so much a part of Marino's legacy that the quarterback celebrated his induction into the Hall of Fame by throwing Clayton one last pass from the stage. Is there an Aikman without an Irvin? A Dan Fouts without a Charlie Joiner?

Even Unitas had Raymond Berry, who caught sixty-three of his quarterback's 290 touchdowns—an absolutely incredible number in the '50s and '60s before the NFL's passing revolution began.

"It's amazing to me," Theismann said. "You look at Steve Smith in Carolina. When he's healthy they're a different offense. Randy Moss up in New England—that's an entirely different offense than it was [before he got there]. You take one guy in that receiving corps and you change that and all of a sudden you don't get the big plays."

Having that receiver means everything to a quarterback, just like having the right quarterback can mean everything to a receiver. Burress certainly appreciates that. He had four different starting quarterbacks during his five years in Pittsburgh. He had no chance to develop a connection with any of them.

With Eli, that connection is clearly there.

"It just came to a point where Eli and I just said we want to come off the ball and feel it," Burress said. "It wasn't so much of us even running plays. We were freelancing and having fun. I think that's when you start to see a quarterback and wide receiver duo grow. We just go to the sideline and say, 'Hey, we're just going to feel it. If he goes one way, you react and I'm going to react to you.'"

Fourteen: "It's going to be torture"

THE SHARKS WERE circling, as they always do when they sense blood in the water. The Giants were falling apart in 2004, but the media wasn't really interested in the big picture. So the whole group made its way right past most of the players—and some pretty inviting targets—and made a big circle around the biggest piece of chum. Eli Manning had just smashed face-first into rock bottom, with that nightmare of a performance in Baltimore during his rookie year. It had been four days since he faced the press, and believe it or not there were still many unanswered questions. So they stood there, five and six deep around his locker, tape recorders on and cameras rolling, just waiting for him to come out.

Michael Strahan, one of the real and established stars on the team, wandered by the pack and no one even glanced in his direction. That's something that didn't happen in the locker room every day.

"Who's everyone waiting for?" Strahan asked.

"Eli Manning," said one reporter.

Strahan chuckled and shook his head in wonder.

"I wonder if Eli knew what he was getting into," he said.

How could he possibly know? How could anyone know what it would be like to be a magnet and a piñata at the same time? Because he was the future, the young star quarterback, the number one pick, a Manning, he couldn't be ignored. Fans and media gravitated towards him. His every move generated a remarkable—and unwanted and often ridiculous—amount of interest. And though there was very little substance to debate at first, he was still being regularly torn to shreds. His mechanics, his demeanor, his words, his throws … every second of his existence seemed to provide another sign that he was either a superstar in the making or that for the Giants the apocalypse had arrived. To the outside world there was no in-between.

Yes, he came from a famous football family and had been rich and famous all his life, so this wasn't completely unfamiliar territory. But his father played football for a losing team in the polite Deep South, in New Orleans, a city that at the time was about one-twentieth the size of the New York–metro area. His brother played in Indianapolis, a city maybe twice as big as New Orleans, but still a tame one-newspaper town. And Eli went to college in Oxford, Mississippi, a sleepy hamlet by comparison where the football players were revered as heroes. Now he was in New York—big, angry New York—with its nine major newspapers covering his team every day (often with more than one person), its twelve television networks (not including nearby ESPN), and its two all-sports talk radio stations that provided constant analysis and psycho-babble twenty-four hours a day.

And every outlet expected the world from him. New York really hadn't had a true superstar quarterback—a celebrity at the position—since the flashy Joe Namath left the scene in 1977. The city hadn't even had a quarterback it loved since Simms was unceremoniously cut in 1994. Every quarterback since was measured against those two, and Eli had to be everything all at once, instantly. All New York wanted was a quotable celebrity with a winning personality who was tough, determined, strong-armed, and won way more than he lost. And New York wanted it fast. It wanted it now.

And if it didn't get it? Well, there were plenty of outlets to discuss and analyze why not.

"I remember somebody asked me, 'What advice would you give Eli?'" Simms recalled. "I said, 'It's going to be torture.' You know, 3–6, 6–3, it's all the same. You're going to get it and there's going to be tremendous ups and downs as far as how you're perceived and how the media and fans treat you. That's going to go up and down. That's just the way it is. Until you become a tremendously established player who has won playoffs and Super Bowls and continues to play for a good football team it's just a week-to-week deal."

Simms should know. When he was selected seventh overall in 1979 out of tiny Morehead State, he wasn't exactly the most popular pick. As the early years went on and injuries and inconsistency made his future murky, some fans sided with the likes of Scott Brunner and Jeff Rutledge as Simms battled for his job. And while he did, it escaped no one's notice that Joe Montana had been selected two rounds and seventy-five picks later in the same draft, and that he was out in San Francisco collecting Super Bowl rings.

Even after Simms won his Super Bowl it wasn't easy, though his performance in Super Bowl XXI was as close to perfect (22 of 25, 268 yards) as any quarterback is likely to ever get. But that only got him a few hassle-free years until a broken foot robbed him of a chance to lead the Giants to victory in Super Bowl XXV. Jeff Hostetler led them to that title, after Simms had taken the Giants to eleven regular-season wins. And when Hostetler did, it was as if half the town had suddenly discovered Simms's replacement. The Simms–Hostetler controversy got ugly, divided the city, and inevitably set back the franchise. It also underscored New York's inability to settle on a quarterback it could be identified with. Denver had Elway. Miami had Marino. San Francisco had Montana. Buffalo had Kelly. Dallas would soon have Aikman and Green Bay would soon have Favre.

But New York? It had Simms for a while, and New York loved him. He won his Super Bowl, went to Disneyland, and even earned his stripes with some caught-on-camera battles with Bill Parcells. But New York, the ultimate what-have-you-done-for-me-lately town, was alarmingly quick to discard him. It was still searching for a worthy heir to the Namath throne.

That's what Eli was up against. He couldn't just be a quarterback. He had to be a great quarterback, a championship quarterback, and a charming celebrity. He had to be Namath and Simms. And he had to do it every week. Otherwise New York would gladly and often focus its attention on his flaws.

"There are some people in New York who would throw Raquel Welch out of bed because she couldn't cook," said quarterbacks coach Chris Palmer. "You know what I mean?"

• • •

THE FIRST TIME Pat Hanlon met the Manning family was in 1993, when prior to a Giants game against the Saints he went with then Giants head coach Dan Reeves to watch Peyton Manning receive a high school player of the year award. As the Giants' public relations chief stood there watching that eighteen-year-old kid hold his press conference, he was amazed by his professionalism and poise. "He handled himself better than ninety-five percent of the professional athletes I had dealt with up to that point," Hanlon said. "He was very polished, very polite, very articulate, very composed."

He expected Eli to be the same way when he arrived, and of course he was. But there were still New York–specific things the kid and his family had never dealt with before. Not the least of which was the controversial draft-day trade that he forced, which made his introduction to the city anything but smooth.

So soon after Eli arrived at Giants Stadium, Hanlon sat him down for their one and only conversation about how to handle the press in New York. He told him he wasn't going to offer him any advice because "You've got enough people already chirping in your ear." But he told him, "I'll be thinking of you every minute of every day. I'll be thinking about what you're saying. I'll be thinking about things that maybe you could say better. It's not like I'm not thinking about what you're going through. But I'm not going to force my thoughts on you. If you need some advice or want to talk about something, all you've got to do is grab me."

"He has yet to ask me about anything," Hanlon said in 2008. "And I'm not surprised by that."

Eli's approach to handling the press was to be accessible and polite, but to reveal little about what he's thinking, his personal life, or his personality. He didn't want anyone to see him sweat—particularly the media. He wasn't going to react to praise or overreact to criticism. He was just going to take whatever came his way, the good and the bad. And for a while it was mostly bad.

Of course, what he thought was a laid-back, Southern-gentlemanly, steely public approach was often misinterpreted for aloofness or disinterest. The less he reacted to what was going on around him, the more it seemed as if the fans and media tried to draw his reaction out.

"I wonder if that was part of it," Gilbride said. "Maybe people think, 'We're not getting to him. We've got to go after him harder.' I don't know. I've just never seen anything like what this poor guy's been exposed to."

"The problem is, this is New York," said Esiason, the Long Island native and former Bengals and Jets quarterback turned radio host, not long after the fiftieth game of Eli's career. "This is not Kansas City. This is not the Midwest—Cincinnati, Cleveland—that are going to appreciate how Eli is, his personality. There's just so many critics, so many people talking about it, so many people writing about it, that the kid unfortunately, unfairly gets judged.

"Now, if he were Derek Anderson, or if he were Tom Brady when he first started, or Tony Romo—just an afterthought or a late-round draft pick or not even drafted at all—nobody would say anything. But when you orchestrate a trade on draft day and tell a team that you don't want to go play for it, you put yourself squarely in the midst of it. I wonder if Archie was thinking, 'My son, with his personality, can handle New York.' I don't know what he was thinking about. Maybe he should be in Jacksonville. Maybe he should be in Atlanta or New Orleans."

. . .

SIMMS TOOK A beating from the fans and press at times. So did almost every Jets or Giants quarterback in the post-Namath era. It was impossible, they learned, to ever live up to expectations. And failure—even slight failure—was rarely tolerated in the media capital of the world. But as Eli's career went on, and as he began to look more and more like a disappointment, it became a popular theory that he was getting it worst of all. His numbers weren't terrible. He won a division title. He even led his team to the playoffs in two of his first three years. But because he was the first-overall pick, had that famous last name, and had a bland personality, he was being hit with everything the city had. And in the decade-plus since Simms's career was at its low-point, the media had exploded. The all-sports talk of WFAN radio had become a staple of people's lives, and now they had an ESPN radio alternative, too. Also, thanks to the internet with its fan message boards and blogs, everyone with a keyboard—or worse, a cell-phone camera—could pretend to be a reporter. And everyone now had a ready-made, lightning-quick, electronic pulpit to swat Eli down or tell him where he went wrong.

At the Super Bowl, of course, when the national media surrounded Eli in a much more pleasant setting, they wanted to know what it was like being eaten alive by the New York media hounds. They asked everyone around him if it was really true that Eli had gotten worse treatment than any New York quarterback ever had.

"I don't know," said receiver Amani Toomer. "We did have a quarterback here named Dave Brown."

Poor Dave Brown, a local kid made good from Westfield, New Jersey, who came to New York in the first round of the 1992 supplemental draft out of Duke. Such a nice guy, too. Very personable and likeable. But in hindsight he had no shot. He was like a comedian who was forced to follow Elvis to the stage.

He was given the job, for all intents and purposes, on June 15, 1994. The dawn of free agency was cracking in the NFL and salary caps were creating a new reality. For George Young, the general manager who helped restore the Giants to glory, that new reality meant releasing Simms. He was getting too expensive, too old, and there were concerns about his shoulder. Plus, the Giants now had a number one pick sitting on the bench.

On that terrible day, in the Giants' cramped press room, Young made his stunning announcement. He was followed to the podium by Wellington Mara, who very uncharacteristically let everyone know he wasn't in favor of the move by reading from a prepared statement and calling it "a day of overwhelming sadness." In fact, in front of the eyes of New York, just talking about the release of Simms brought Mara to tears. Of course, by then Simms had reclaimed his place as a fan favorite. Now he was cut and the move made the famously stoic Mara cry.

A few months earlier, Lawrence Taylor—one of the greatest players in Giants and NFL history—had retired, so the Giants were stuck without their two best players, and two unbelievably popular links to their championship years. Worse, there was a mess brewing in the front office. The relationship between Mara and Young was never the same after Simms's release, and there was a growing feud between Young and Dan Reeves, too. On top of that, the Giants weren't exactly overflowing with talent.

And now, ladies and gentlemen, here's Dave Brown!

Of course, it didn't help that he was awful. In his three full years at the helm, the best the Giants could do was 9–7—and it took a six-game winning streak at the end of the 1994 season to do that. In his best season he barely topped 2,800 yards, and never threw more than twelve touchdown passes. He balanced that in 1996 by throwing twenty interceptions. It was no wonder that when Accorsi succeeded Young as general manager in 1998, the very first thing he did was give Brown his release.

"When he wasn't playing well, there were times I think people felt sorry for him," Hanlon recalled. "Dave Brown did get the short end of the stick on a lot of things. But the scrutiny that Eli's been under since he's been here, and the over-analysis of his personality and his demeanor, I don't think what Dave Brown went through compares to that."

•   •   •

ALL ELI HAD to do to get the fans and the media and all his critics off his back, for a few minutes at least, was win the Super Bowl.

Win the MVP. Beat an undefeated team with a last-minute drive. Really, there wasn't much else that was going to make New York completely happy. Don't bother reading off the stats or saying how even the greatest NFL quarterbacks struggled early in their careers. New York doesn't want excuses. New York wants results. And eleven-win seasons or playoff berths really don't matter if you're not going to put together a string of playoff wins, too.

Oh, and never, ever, ever have a bad game. Maybe in baseball a player can get away with that, because in that sport there's always a game (and a chance for redemption) the next night. But a stinker in football gives every reporter and fan a seven-day window to become some odd combination of psychiatrist and quarterback coach.

Take the awful experience Eli had in his fiftieth career start, during the 2007 season, when he threw those four interceptions against the Vikings. He would have drawn less attention if he had sat naked on a stool in Times Square and painted a target on his back. He would have drawn less ire if he had stolen toys from a nursery school. It was so bad, there's a video on the Internet of a fan burning his Manning jersey in the parking lot after the game.

"But I've got to tell you, he wanted to be traded to New York," Esiason said. "He didn't want to play in San Diego. He pulled a John Elway. And, you know, along with that comes the scrutiny of having a lousy game. His brother threw six interceptions the other day and his brother is the preeminent quarterback in football right now. So it happens to everybody. It's not like it's just confined to Eli. But that's the hard thing you try to tell Giants fans, especially on the radio at seven in the morning. They're calling in going, 'We're paying this guy how much? He wanted to come here as a first-round pick and we're going to have to owe him $22 million over the next three years? You've got to be kidding me!'"

At that moment, there were a lot of people that thought Eli was all wrong for New York. His personality and his lack of reaction just didn't go over well with the media and fans. He looked like he was a turtle retreating into his shell. But that wasn't exactly true. What Eli was doing was standing there, taking whatever New York had to offer, and refusing to let it affect him. What fans mistook for a lack of emotion was just him concentrating on how he could find his way out of this mess. What was mistaken for a lack of emotion was just his stubborn refusal to overreact. New York was hitting him with everything and he was refusing to be knocked over.

Wrong for New York? At that moment, it should have been clear that his personality was just right.

"I see no reason to think he has not handled it anything but perfectly," Simms said. "He watches what he says. He conducts himself the right way. Tom Coughlin says he works hard and he's humble, and those are always good traits to have as a quarterback. That is how most teams want their quarterback to be. And I really think down deep most fans want their quarterback to be that way, too.

"Actually, let me rephrase a little bit. You've got to do what fits you the best. If you're Joe Namath, being humble might not be the greatest thing in the world for you, because you're a different type of player and you were willing to say and stand out there alone by yourself for the attention or whatever. But that's not Eli Manning's way. And history says that's not the Giants' way either. You represent the team the way they'd want to be represented, and that's what he does. I'm sure the Maras and the Giants are proud of the way he acts."

His coaches and teammates were proud of him, too. In fact, more than that, they were amazed.

"If you read all of this stuff about him and you listened to all the talk radio, you might have to put him in a white jacket," Palmer said. "You know, I'm sure there are players in the locker room who've said, 'Boy I'm glad I'm not Eli, because I don't know if I could take that abuse.'"

. . .

THERE WAS ONE time when the pressure did seem to get to him, not that anyone outside his inner circle knew it. Not that most people inside that circle knew it either. But there was one time during the tumultuous 2006 season when the Giants' players held a team meeting to try to glue their fractured locker room back together. The meeting was ugly and there was a lot of finger-pointing and accusations, and the sins of some of Eli's teammates—like not reading their playbooks, not studying film enough—were exposed. Publicly, the leaders of the team were trying to squash reports of a team in turmoil. Privately, things were actually a little worse than even Eli knew.

The meeting took place after a horrible Giants' loss in Tennessee, in which they blew a twenty-one-point lead in the final ten minutes and lost 24–21. That was the game where then-rookie defensive end Mathias Kiwanuka had Titans quarterback Vince Young wrapped up for a game-clinching fourth-down sack, then inexplicably let him go before the whistle. It was the game where Hufnagel called for a ridiculous downfield pass on a second-and-four play with the Giants at their own thirty-five-yard line and leading 21–0, resulting in an interception that changed the whole game. It was the game where Burress didn't even bother to try to tackle Pacman Jones after he picked off that pass. And to top it off, Eli threw another interception in the final minute, setting up the Titans' game-winning field goal.

Eli felt bad enough about his own performance. He dutifully took the blame for his teammates' failures, too. Now he found out that some of his teammates weren't exactly turning in a full week's work?

"There was so much drama going on around there, it was tough," Hasselbeck said. "And things were said and certain things were exposed about guys and what they were or weren't doing in terms of their preparation. Eli said to me after the meeting, 'I'm fighting my butt off and trying to do everything I can, people in the city are calling me a bust and all these things, and we've got people doing this? I'm ultimately the one that ends up falling on the sword?'

"Guys were in the meeting saying, 'I didn't really look at my playbook,' and he was like, 'I'm counting on this guy and this is what he was doing? No one's talking about this guy. They're talking about me. But what am I going to do? I have to take the blame. I'm the guy.'"

And he couldn't avoid it either. Where was he supposed to hide?

"At the time, every newspaper was like, 'This kid's a bust,'" Hasselbeck recalled. "People say they don't read it, and I don't think he necessarily reads it. But in the cafeteria there's five New York papers and a couple of New Jersey papers. You see it. It's sitting there right next to the oatmeal.

"And for him, he's local *and* national. You can't say, 'I'm not going to read the local paper, but I'll pick up a *Sports Illustrated* and I'll be OK.' He's everywhere. There's no way he can avoid it."

. . .

THERE WAS ONE more time when the media glare appeared to get to Eli. It happened during his rookie season when he went out to a club in New York City and was introduced to actress Lindsay

Lohan. It didn't take long for the gossip columns in the New York tabloids to create a romantic link. He reportedly got her phone number. They were sure to be an item soon.

Months later, Eli admitted "that wasn't a good scene," but he still refused to throw a fit or issue any public denials—even though the report bothered his future wife, then-girlfriend and college sweetheart Abby McGrew.

"I think for the most part you just have to forget about it," he said. "Obviously it's easier for me to forget about it than the girlfriend. She wants to make a deal about it, so that's just something I'm going to have to get used to. That's why you have to be careful about who you're talking to and where you are."

A similar incident forty years earlier might have brought boasts from the hard-partying Namath. For Eli, though, all it did was drive him further into his shell. It made an already careful man even more wary of the world around him. He had enough friends already. He didn't need to let any more outsiders in.

That private nature and ability to retreat is why even his father had a tinge of doubt about how his youngest boy would handle the Gotham spotlight and whether the glare would be too much for his droopy eyes. When they were making the decision to force their way away from San Diego, Archie recalled pulling out a big legal pad and drawing a line down the middle. He listed the pros of the deal on one side, the cons on the other. Dealing with the media was definitely on the "con" side for his son.

"I am not sure what kind of disposition a person needs to have to handle this best," Archie said on the day Eli was drafted. "But he is a pretty level guy and he knows what got him here to this point. That was hard work. He won't stop that. So you just have to roll up your sleeves and let it happen."

Meanwhile, New York went to work on him, chewing him up and spitting him out, raising him up and dropping him off a cliff. And it did it over and over and over again. He just took it and kept getting up, coming back for more, never changing his personality, never getting mad.

"He doesn't let anything bother him," Strahan said. "It's very hard for me to understand how he does that."

They don't call him "Easy" for nothing, after all.

"E's such an easy-going guy, none of that affects him," said running back Brandon Jacobs. "Sometimes he can care less what's going on around him. None of it has really bothered him. So if people want to stop now they really can because they're wasting their time."

Fifteen: "You're not the little brother here"

NONE OF THE Giants were watching when their former teammate, Tiki Barber, made his NBC *Sunday Night Football* debut during halftime of a meaningless Giants–Ravens preseason game on August 19, 2007. Barber had burned a few bridges on his way out the door, and more than a few players were glad he would now be doing his talking far from their ears. They figured he would probably criticize the Giants at some point, but they assumed his shots would be directed at his favorite target—the coaches. Players-turned-TV-stars rarely enter the media with guns blazing, anyway, and they almost never attack old teammates, especially not right away.

So imagine Eli Manning's surprise when, hours after that game, people started calling him asking him if he heard what Barber had said. He was even more shocked when he read the comments the next day. The shot had come from a panel discussion about Manning and his leadership—a discussion Barber knew was coming from the production meetings before the show. He had been given time to prepare his remarks and choose his words carefully. Knowing that just made the attack worse.

"Last year about week twelve I turned over the offensive motivational speech to Eli," Barber said that night. "And he was gung-ho to do it. But he was uncomfortable doing it. I think a lot of it had to do with vets being around—myself, Jeremy Shockey, Plaxico Burress. He didn't feel like his voice was going to be strong enough and it showed."

Then Barber issued his most damning statement, including the word that would cause months' worth of trouble. "Sometimes," Barber added, "it was almost comical the way that he would say things."

Comical? Barber's friends would later admit it was a terrible choice of words (though he never retracted them). Eli's leadership was a subject for debate in New York to begin with, and was the source of at least some concern in the Giants organization. Now, a former team leader, one of the Giants' all-time greats, was insinuating his attempts at leadership were a joke?

"That," said Hasselbeck, his training camp roommate, "pissed Eli off."

It pissed him off so much, in fact, that the kid quarterback who rarely reacted to anything began considering his reaction. He told his roommate that he didn't want to say anything until he actually saw the tape of Barber saying it, so he could absorb the entire context. Even in his anger he was analytical in his approach. Once he heard it, he went back and forth on what to say in response, and even on whether it would be appropriate to say anything at all.

"Listen," Hasselbeck told him, "no one's going to get mad at you for firing back, because it's so out of character."

Hasselbeck was right, of course. So a day after that conversation, Eli took his usual slow stroll to the dining hall in the middle of the University at Albany campus where a throng of reporters and cameras were waiting for him to arrive. They surrounded him under the hot sun, fully expecting him to dismiss Barber's barbs as no big deal. Nobody thought he would fire back. And when he did, many jaws hit the floor.

"I guess I'm just happy for Tiki that he's making a smooth transition into the media world," Eli began. "You know, I'll be interested to see if he has anything to say [about a team] besides the Giants, and what his comments will be on that.

"I'm not going to lose any sleep about what Tiki has to say," he continued. "I guess I could have questioned his leadership skills last year with calling out the coach and having articles about him retiring in the middle of the season, and [how] he's lost the heart [to play]. As a quarterback you're reading that your running back has lost the heart to play the game and it's about the tenth week. I can see that a little bit at times."

Clearly this wasn't a Reggie Jackson–George Steinbrenner-caliber war of words, but consider who was doing the speaking. Quiet, shy, reserved Eli Manning making an awkwardly worded statement questioning the leadership of Tiki Barber? Saying he could see that Barber had lost the heart to play with six games to go last season? Insinuating that all his retirement talk, which had been an ongoing story throughout the 2006 season, was a distraction? This wasn't Shockey or Burress or even Coughlin, who had more than a few public and private wars with Barber. This was Eli? Really?

When word rang forth of this unexpected event, there were people in the front office who were nearly dancing with joy. Finally, they thought, their shy, reserved quarterback was showing signs of life. And it didn't hurt that they overwhelmingly approved of his target. His teammates, who were already preparing to defend their quarterback, couldn't stop talking about what Eli said.

"Didn't they say there was fire in his eyes and roaring from his mouth like a dragon or something?" asked linebacker Antonio Pierce. "I think that's what everyone wanted to see."

Eli might not have been breathing fire, but at least he was breathing—and that was something a lot of people were happy to see. It was a sign of life. A sign that he was ready to hit back, and that he wasn't going to take it passively anymore. It was a big deal and even Eli knew it, though he was a bit amused at how big a story it became. It didn't take long at all for his words to reach Indianapolis, where his father and brother were hosting a charity event. By late afternoon, Archie was on the phone with Eli asking "What happened? Why are all the New York media calling me now?"

"It just came out," Eli said the next day. "I don't know. It was just one of those deals where it seemed like the right thing to do. I guess I've always been even-keeled, never really responded back, [and] tried to always make things smooth and easy. That's probably the first time I've kind of fired back a little bit. It's one of those things I felt the need to do."

. . .

It takes incredible athletic talent and a brain that works in ways most of us can't imagine for someone to become an NFL quarterback. But for the great ones—really even just the good ones—it's about more than that. It's about leadership. It's about finding ways to pull the team together, to drag them down the field together towards the same goal. It's about looking them in the eye and getting them to follow. It's about them looking in your eyes and knowing they can win.

And there's no right or wrong way to be a leader, either. There have been leaders who got people to follow them because of their work ethic and their calm under fire. Those are the reasons Joe Montana was able to lead a great player like Jerry Rice. Some leaders do it with emotion. After all, who wouldn't follow Brett Favre as he runs down the field after a big pass with his fist pumping up in the air? Some lead by example. Some lead with a loud voice.

Eli throwing a warm-up pass before the NFC wild card playoff game against the Atlanta Falcons. *(Courtesy of AP Images)*

During a quiet first half, Eli was able to connect with Hakeem Nicks on one of his two receiving touchdowns in the second quarter. *(Courtesy of AP Images)*

Demonstrating his agility, Eli was able to fight off a tackle from strong safety James Sanders (36) and was only sacked once the entire game. *(Courtesy of AP Images)*

Flaunting his skills outside of the pocket, Eli attempts a difficult pass in the NFC Divisional round against the 15–1 Green Bay Packers. *(Courtesy of AP Images)*

Showing his composure, Eli lit up the Falcons defense in the second half, and finished the day with 277 passing yards and three touchdowns, two to Nicks and one to Manningham. *(Courtesy of AP Images)*

Unfazed by the NFL favorites and perennial MVP Aaron Rogers, Eli finished his day by throwing more yards than Rogers (300 to 264) and more touchdowns (three to two). *(Courtesy of AP Images)*

While his brother Peyton is known for calling audibles and changing the play at the line of scrimmage, Eli has not only adapted his brother's skill set, but also come close to mastering it. *(Courtesy of AP Images)*

Showing faith in his young wide receivers, Eli once again hit Nicks in the end zone twice and Manningham once. *(Courtesy of AP Images)*

Under pressure for most of the game, Eli was sacked six times against the San Francisco 49ers in the NFC Conference Championship. *(Courtesy of AP Images)*

Initially considered too quiet to be the leader of a team, Eli has shown that his leadership skills have developed, and that his team is behind him 100 percent. *(Courtesy of AP Images)*

Keeping the defense on the field was the key to the Giants game plan, holding the ball for almost forty minutes. *(Courtesy of AP Images)*

Eli ended this epic game by going 32 for 58 with 316 yards and two touchdowns (Manningham and Pascoe). *(Courtesy of AP Images)*

Completing 75 percent of his passes, Eli showed that he's a force to be reckoned with in Super Bowl XLVI against the New England Patriots.
(Courtesy of AP Images)

Eli elebrating after fitting a perfect pass to Victor Cruz for his first touchdown of the
game and giving the Giants an early 9–0 lead. *(Courtesy of AP Images)*

Eli celebrates with defensive end Justin Tuck after he led the Giants eighty-eight yards on nine plays to set up what would be the game-winning score. *(Courtesy of AP Images)*

Named the Super Bowl MVP for the second time in his career, Eli Manning joined Hall of Famers Bart Starr, Terry Bradshaw, Joe Montana (3), and Super Bowl XLII and XLVI opponent Tom Brady. *(Courtesy of AP Images)*

"If you buy any business books, there are 101 ways to lead," said Chris Palmer. "Everybody leads in a different way."

But how was Eli supposed to be a leader of the veteran-heavy Giants team he took over in 2004? Clearly he had to wait his turn, until Warner had been benched and later let go. But even then, he was stuck on a team with some imposing veterans with loud voices and big presences. If the Giants were anybody's team, it belonged to Shockey or Barber or Strahan. And really it belonged to Coughlin, an imposing vocal presence himself who yelled often and carried an enormous rulebook and wasn't afraid to wield it as a weapon. Eli was quiet by nature. He preferred to lead by example, by work ethic, and to wait his turn to become the man.

"He was smart about the politics of the locker room," said Jim Miller. "He knew Tiki, Strahan, and all those guys were running it. He had to earn his keep."

And so he did. But he was too quiet, really. Too reserved. Too shy and unwilling to speak up. That was the whole point of the long conversation that Gilbride had with him on that train ride back from his horrible performance in Baltimore his rookie year. He didn't tell Eli to start yelling at his teammates, just to start speaking up for himself. If there was something in the offense he didn't like, he needed to say it. And he did—briefly. Then, before long, he seemed to go back into his shell.

Hasselbeck was brought on board after Eli's rookie season, when Miller tore his hip in the spring, and the coaches quickly began relying on him to help lure out Eli's personality and leadership skills. They even pulled Hasselbeck aside several times and said, "I want to know if he likes this play. I need him to speak up." But Hasselbeck could only do so much.

Like in their first year together, 2005, the Giants were preparing to play in San Francisco nearly halfway through the season. The night before the game, at the team hotel, they got the script for their first fifteen plays from John Hufnagel, and the first one was a play Hasselbeck knew Eli didn't like.

"I'm sitting there waiting for him to say something, but he doesn't say anything," Hasselbeck said. "So I say to Kevin [Gilbride, the quarterbacks coach], 'Ask Eli if he likes that play.'"

That may seem like a small point, but it can be an enormous deal. Forced to speak up, Eli told his coaches what he didn't like about the play, which side of the field he preferred to run it toward, and how he thought it could work. The next day, the Giants opened with the play anyway, but tweaked it with Eli's suggestions. The result? A completed pass to Shockey for twenty-eight yards.

But moments like that were rare. Eli preferred to do what he was told, to find a way to make it work even if he was uncomfortable. He took the same approach with teammates, rarely scolding them for running an incorrect route, missing an assignment, or doing something he just thought was wrong.

A lot of that was because during the first few years of his career he wasn't always exactly sure what to do himself. He admitted there were times where he sat in a meeting thinking, "I don't want to say this out loud. What if I'm wrong? What if he did the right thing and I'm the one mistaken?" He couldn't dictate anything to teammates with any authority if he wasn't sure of himself.

"Leadership just comes with how confident you are in what you're doing, how you're playing, whether you're confident that what you're doing is the right thing and you can fix things," Eli said. "That confidence comes with experience. It comes with success. And it just takes time. You've just got to see so many different defenses, run your offense, get more practice, learn more ways you can fix things. And you've got to get comfortable to where you know what you're doing, what blitz they're bringing and where you're going with the ball even before anything happens."

None of that was easy in the Giants' complicated offense and all the pressure it put on the quarterback, who is forced to make the calls and adjustments for all eleven players on the field. And veterans can smell weakness. Some of them had their doubts about their quarterback to begin with, and not only could they see him struggling, but Eli *knew* they could see it. How is he supposed to lead a group of accomplished players who deep down aren't sure he's the guy they should be following? Even Gilbride called it "an ongoing process" into his third season and conceded "the Tiki Barbers, the Michael Strahans, the guys that have been here, it's still their team."

"I'll tell you what I did say to him at one time," Gilbride said. "I said, 'You may be the little brother of the Manning family, but you're our big brother here. Every one of those guys need to know that you're the guy, you're the leader. You're not the little brother here. You're the guy everyone is looking to, and when things are not going well they need to see a toughness about you, a determination about you that there's no questioning you're going to get this done.' He's the only guy facing those other ten guys and they need to look in his eyes and say, 'Hey, he hasn't been shaken by what's happened. He's going to fight through this. Let's just do our job.'"

But how? His personality just seemed to be so … blah. It wasn't an act for the press, either. Sure, he could loosen up in private, knock down a few beers, belt out a few karaoke tunes. He was a huge fan of *Seinfeld* and was big into repeating funny movie lines to his friends. He had become a bit of a wine connoisseur as he got older—much to the amazement of his two older brothers. He always had a little more personality than he was willing to share. And he was strong-willed. He could even occasionally give the appearance that he was in charge in the huddle. But everyone wanted more, and not just the media and the fans. The coaches wanted him to wear his heart on his sleeve a little more, too.

"I got called into the coaches' office once and they told me, 'Hey listen, we need him to show more emotion, to talk more and say more,'" Hasselbeck said. "They felt like 'This team needs something.'"

. . .

THE FIRST SIGN of leadership that Eli Manning showed came in an unlikely setting, sitting at his locker with a handful of reporters standing around him in what had become less of an interview and more like a casual conversation. It was early April of 2005, about three weeks into the off-season program and there wasn't much news to discuss. But Eli surprised everyone by creating some when he was asked about Shockey's decision to workout on his own in Miami, rather than work in New Jersey with a young quarterback heading into the second year of his career.

Eli called Shockey out and talked about how imperative it was for the two to work out together. He revealed he had been calling his tight end every day, leaving him messages, hoping against hope he might get through. He even showed a reasonable side, saying all he wanted was for Shockey to show up in a few weeks when he transferred his workouts from the weight room to the field. He even pointed to the sixty-one catches Shockey had during the 2004 season and said, "He could've had maybe fifteen more if we were on the same page."

It was an impressive show of bravado for the then-twenty-four-year-old. But it didn't go over well down in Coral Gables, Florida, where Shockey was at the University of Miami working out with his old college teammates and a personal trainer. The tight end wasn't happy—not so much with the constant badgering of his quarterback, but with the fact that he was just called out in public. He was sensitive to media criticism, especially after a rocky rookie season in which he drew plenty of it, mostly for his mouth. He certainly didn't like having the spotlight shone on him for this, especially given the implication that he wasn't willing to do what was best for his team.

So even though Shockey downplayed the incident, he let Eli know how unhappy he was. Then he put on a show. His agent leaked word to the media that he was returning to the off-season program, even though his trip to New Jersey was only so he could take care of some private business. He made sure to show up at Giants Stadium on a day when the media had access, and he held a short press conference where he defended his workout habits and famously said, "I'm just trying to do what's best for me."

It was the perfect example of why Eli was having trouble emerging as a leader. Even when he tried, he had veterans who weren't ready or willing to follow. And the hit he took from Shockey only seemed to knock him further back into his shell. One year later, when Shockey again skipped the off-season program, Eli didn't even bother standing up for what he believed in.

"Last year it became an issue," he said. "But it was my first season as a starter. I don't feel it's as important to me [now] as it was [then]."

• • •

Is THERE VIDEO somewhere of Unitas screaming like a lunatic on the sideline, waving his hands around, getting in the face of a coach or throwing his helmet in the direction of a teammate? Did Montana do that as he marched the 49ers down the field at the end of Super Bowl XXIII? Sure, Simms had his sideline blow-ups with Parcells, and New York loved it when it was caught on camera. And as Namath knows, no town in America loves a bold guarantee more. Tough talk, demonstrative actions, that's the image of what a leader is all about.

The problem, of course, is that's not always necessarily what a leader really is.

"The best guys I've had have all been quiet," Gilbride said. "Warren Moon was not a screamer. He was low key. But there was an aura about him. He was almost regal in a way. Mark Brunell was not a yeller or a screamer. But they had a knack that when they said something, teammates said, 'OK. Let's go.'"

That's the kind of knack Eli was trying to develop. The problem was his teammates didn't get it at first. His low-key, even-keeled personality—or lack thereof—was a source of wonder and amusement, even in the locker room. Gilbride recalled the gift Warner gave to Eli for Christmas in 2004. It was a "mood shirt" that changed colors to show whether Eli was happy, angry, or sad. "It would've worked if you could see it," Gilbride recalled. "But he kept it covered up."

He did that with his emotions, too, and it was most definitely on purpose. "I'm not a screamer and a yeller," Eli said. "I get fired up. I get mad. I get intense. I try not to let things discourage me. I try not to let the defense or the coaches or players see me down. I think that kind of gives a negative aspect. It gets the [opposing] defense fired up. It gets your players worried that something has gone wrong. So you just try to stay even-keeled. When things are going well I'm excited. I can be energetic. I'm just going about it the way I always have."

Teammates grew to appreciate that. When Eli was blindsided by the Barber attack, current players rushed to his defense, even though that caused them to attack an old friend. And Barber did still have a few friends in the Giants' locker room despite his messy exit. But when he jumped on Eli, nobody was on his side.

Why? Because Eli always had their back, and they knew it. The thing his teammates loved most about him was the way he took the blame and the heat for everything. If a receiver ran the wrong route and his pass was picked off, he called it a bad throw. If he was sacked because an offensive lineman blew an assignment, he said he needed to do a better job of avoiding the rush. He did that publicly and privately and then would spend extra hours trying to fix whatever problems there were. He rarely, if ever, complained about anyone or anything.

Like late in the 2007 season, during the Vikings game that got him dubbed "Eli the Terrible" on the back page of the *Daily News*. Two of the interceptions happened because Shockey and Burress ran the wrong route.

"He got blamed for a lot of things that weren't his fault," Hasselbeck said. "Now, every quarterback throws interceptions that end up being someone else's fault. But not everyone just sucks it up and says, 'I've got to play better. I just can't throw four interceptions.' He could've said, 'The first one was my bad, but the next two, if the guys are doing their job we don't have this problem and we're not sitting here with a loss.' It's very tempting to want to say that stuff. There have been plenty of guys that said, 'Wait a second. Don't blame me.'"

And there are a lot of guys who would rant and rave and act like a crazed dog on the sidelines, playing as much to the fans as anything else. "That's not something you can fake," said tackle David Diehl. "If he feels he needs to say something and needs to talk, he does. And everybody rallies around him."

Or as Accorsi put it, "Do you want somebody that jumps up in the air like Kent Graham and plays like Kent Graham?"

. . .

ON CHRISTMAS EVE, 2005, the Giants were down in Washington with a chance to wrap up the NFC East title—an amazing accomplishment considering it was Coughlin's second year with the Giants and Eli's second year in the NFL. Eli wasn't bad that day— 23 of 41, 244 yards, one touchdown, and one interception. And it was only 14–10 late in the first half when Eli threw his worst pass of the day—a low duck, seemingly intended for Shockey but thrown well behind him and picked off by Redskins linebacker Lemar Marshall, who returned it to the Giants' twenty-yard line and set up another touchdown.

Who knows, though, how it would've turned out if Shockey's head had been screwed on straight? He was completely unaware of where the ball was and, while it was still in play, was busy arguing with the officials that Marshall had shoved him in the mouth. It was a typical Shockey moment, where his emotions got the best of him and he just lost control. Too often it was to the detriment of his team.

Not long after that play, Shockey hurt his ankle while committing a pass interference penalty forcing his backup, Visanthe Shiancoe, into action. Shiancoe, who was known for having some of the best hands on the team, came in and caught three passes for forty yards. But he made his presence felt by not making his presence felt.

"There were plays where he was running free down the middle of the field," Hasselbeck said. "Shank would come back and say, 'I think you had me, but don't worry, we'll get it.' If that's Jeremy, he's thinking, 'I just had a sixty-yard touchdown that Eli didn't throw to me. I'm pissed.' Then he comes back saying, 'I'm wide open!'"

When that game ended in a 35–20 loss, teammates were discussing the pre-Shock and post-Shock difference. Said one Giant: "There was a calm on the sidelines that was never there before."

Shockey is without a doubt the biggest enigma in the Giants' organization. An incredibly talented tight end with the potential to be one of the best in the league, he's frequently injured and rarely comes close to maximizing his talent. When he was drafted in the first round in 2002, Accorsi said they drafted him as a playmaker, not a tight end, because then-coach Jim Fassel wanted a Shannon Sharpe–like player to be the centerpiece of his offense. But Coughlin's offense used the tight end much more often as a blocker, and Shockey made it clear that while he was outstanding at that skill, it was a role he didn't like.

He also never knew when to shut up. Though he cut way down on media interviews after his turbulent rookie season, he almost always managed to create a headline whenever he spoke. Sometimes he did it even when he wasn't being interviewed, like after a blowout loss in Seattle early in 2006 when reporters were surrounding the locker of left tackle Luke Petitgout. Without being prompted, Shockey— steaming over a 42–30 loss that wasn't even that close (the Giants trailed 42–3 when the fourth quarter began)—decided to jump in and declare the Giants had been "outcoached." Petitgout, other teammates, and even a public relations official tried to stop him but he kept going, even continuing his rant on the way to the team bus.

Shockey—a long-haired, tattooed, freak of nature—wasn't without his supporters in the Giants' locker room. There were some players who swore that the team fed off his on-field energy. And even in disappointing seasons he put up numbers that placed him among the top ten tight ends in the league. He wasn't completely happy with life as a Giant and his role in their offense and he certainly could be a pain the neck, but he still was a valuable part of the team.

ELI MANNING

His value was tested—and questioned—when Shockey broke his leg in week fifteen of the 2007 season, one week before the Giants clinched a playoff berth. The week after that they nearly beat undefeated New England in the regular-season finale, and the next week they started their Super Bowl run. Hasselbeck, Shockey's old friend and teammate, went on the radio with the idea that Eli was blossoming because he didn't have Shockey constantly chirping in his ear, always demanding the ball. Eli called it "a stupid theory," but it seemed clear that he was performing better with Shockey out. And privately, more than a few people in the organization agreed with Hasselbeck. Shockey wasn't mean to Eli on the sidelines, but whenever something went wrong he felt the solution was to get the ball into his hands. When he wasn't getting the ball, he sulked, even when the Giants were winning. He'd stomp his feet and wave his hands and complain about it on the sidelines. And even when he was making an effort to fire up his teammates, it would be done in a negative way. Instead of clapping his hands and encouraging his teammates, he'd be yelling, screaming, slamming his helmet, and telling everyone how bad they were.

Shockey's antics weren't nearly as bad in 2007 as they had been in previous years, but it was noticeable to many that with Shockey on crutches and far away from the team, there was none of that at all. Eli was free from his obligation to make Shockey happy by throwing him the ball early and often. He was free to approach any problems that arose in his quiet, calm, analytical way.

"Some of the volatility was gone," Gilbride said. "So it made it a little easier."

• • •

IT WAS DEFINITELY the word "comical" that really stung Eli. If Barber had used almost any other description on that summer night, Eli might not have felt the need to fire back. After all, his old friend wasn't saying anything he hadn't heard a thousand times before. He needed to show more leadership, needed to take charge, needed more of a personality. But comical? It left everyone with the image of this droopy-eyed, shy Southern kid doing a General Patton imitation in front of a room full of hysterical teammates. Or worse, it gave the impression that after he made a serious attempt to lead, his teammates would be cracking up behind his back. Either way, it wasn't a good image for the face of the franchise.

Given what came next—a remarkable Super Bowl championship season—there's a good chance Eli's response to Barber will be remembered as the turning point of his leadership ascent. For years, so many people were spoiling for a fight, waiting for Eli to raise his voice, take someone on and show some signs of life. Finally he did, and everyone inside and outside of the organization was pleased.

But it's not as if taking on Barber suddenly changed Eli's personality or his philosophy on how to lead. He still tried to lead by example, to show his teammates he was working to get things right so they would believe in him and follow him. He didn't feel the need to yell and scream.

"Eli's always going to be quieter about it," Gilbride said. "He's always going to be one on one. He's always going to try to make it in a way that nobody sees it except the guy that he's talking to. That's his MO. He is never going to stand up and be Jim Kelly. That's not him. He doesn't want to be that way. But, little by little, within the parameters of his personality, you see him begin to assert himself in a very Eli Manning way.

"And there's no question, that's part of his strength. He doesn't show a lot of emotion and when things are going bad that's kind of the way you'd like to have it, a guy that just says, 'Hey, I can deal with this. Just hang with me, guys. We'll get through this.'"

That, of course, is exactly what happened in Super Bowl XLII when the Giants took the field trailing an undefeated team 14–10 with 2:39 remaining. It was the perfect moment for a calm, cool, and collected quarterback to prosper. And, of course, he did. That really was the true moment that Eli became the unquestioned leader of his offense, of the Giants and of the franchise. It was truly the moment where he finally seized command.

"Right now there is not one guy on that offense that can say shit," Miller said. "And that includes Jeremy Shockey. He will come back in that locker room and by default he's got to defer to Eli Manning. That guy runs that offensive team now. Not Amani Toomer. Not Plax. None of those guys. Eli commands it all and those guys will listen to anything he says and it will go that way from here on out."

Sixteen: "The most significant relationship in all of sports"

THE PROFESSOR ARRIVED on campus early in the summer having already done most of his research. He was a soft-spoken, bespectacled man who seemed to want to blend into the sidelines, even though he had been given the most important job in the franchise. He was brought in to fix Eli Manning, which to many seemed like an impossible task.

But not to Chris Palmer, the fifty-seven-year-old coach with seventeen NFL seasons and plenty of young quarterbacks on his résumé. In fact, the Giants' new quarterbacks coach disagreed that Eli needed any fixing at all. And he knew because he had spent thirteen long, grueling hours studying film of every pass Eli threw in 2006, with Eli sitting at his side. They had spent two weeks on the field together, too, and Palmer was seeing things he didn't often see in quarterbacks Eli's age. "He made some throws that maybe two or three guys can make in this league," Palmer said. "I'm not saying every throw, but you sit there and say to yourself, 'Hey, that's a big-time throw.'"

So in his first public review of his newest pupil, Palmer declared Eli not only to be "an excellent quarterback who'll be very, very good in this league," but also "one who'll lead his team to the Promised Land." Those were words that quickly made their way right up Interstate 87 to the tiny town of Saratoga Springs, New York, summer home of Palmer's former boss.

"I went up to visit Bill Parcells in Saratoga on a Sunday afternoon we had off, and he kind of chastised me for being so upbeat about Eli and what he could do," Palmer recalled. "He did it in his own way. He'd say, 'I've been reading a lot about what you've been saying about the quarterback …'

"I couldn't help but think of that after we won the Super Bowl."

. . .

PALMER WASN'T THE first coach to get a crack at Eli. The honor of that, in the NFL at least, went to Gilbride. He had been mostly an offensive coordinator in his career, but had pretty good success with Drew Bledsoe in Buffalo, Warren Moon in Houston, and Mark Brunell in Jacksonville where Coughlin was the head coach. The black mark on his résumé came from San Diego, where he was the head coach and his quarterback was the disastrous Ryan Leaf. But Gilbride only coached Leaf's first six NFL games before he was fired. To this day he insists he could have helped Leaf save his career, if only he had been given more time.

When Coughlin was hired in 2004, he promised his bosses he'd assemble the best coaching staff in the NFL. Nobody seemed to have a problem with the addition of Gilbride. But Coughlin's choice of offensive coordinator was immediately controversial. He wanted John Hufnagel, one of his former quarterbacks coaches in Jacksonville who was at the time holding the same job for the New England Patriots. He was a former Canadian Football League quarterback and coach who had spent the past five years as a quarterbacks coach for four different NFL teams.

That should have been a warning sign. But the numbers said he was successful. Other than his first two years in Cleveland, where he worked for Palmer and could not get the overrated Tim Couch to perform to his full potential, Hufnagel's quarterbacks all had successful seasons. Then again, he was dealing with Peyton Manning in Indianapolis (2001), Mark Brunell in Jacksonville (2002), and Tom Brady in New England (2003)—two future Hall of Famers and one three-time Pro Bowler. Who could screw up a lineup like that?

At some of his former stops he just wasn't well-respected, according to some of his former pupils. Brady, in particular, didn't like his coaching style. "They couldn't wait to get rid of him in New England," said one NFL source. Said another, "They just didn't feel he had a clue about how to attack defenses. He was inflexible. He said, 'Well, we're just going to stick with our game plan and run it.'" That rigid approach would end up haunting him through his three turbulent years in New York.

The Giants' front office was aware of the concerns and they certainly weren't sold on Hufnagel either, but they allowed Coughlin to hire him for a couple of reasons. One was that they didn't want to undermine their new coach by meddling with his new staff. But more importantly, Accorsi and the owners believed Coughlin would be the one really running the offense. That's what he did in Jacksonville, and they had been impressed by the scheme, its flexibility, and how difficult it was to prepare for. Hufnagel was just going to be an assistant. Coughlin was going to run the show.

In reality, that was never the case.

• • •

ACCORSI BELIEVES THE relationship between a coach and a quarterback is "the most significant relationship in all of sports," and given the importance he places on the quarterback position, it's hard to argue. Not every quarterback is a fit in every scheme, and a good coach finds ways to get the most out of his players' talents. These are unanswerable questions, perhaps, but would Joe Montana have been a Hall of Famer if he hadn't landed with Bill Walsh? Where would Jim Kelly have been without Marv Levy and his offensive coordinator, Ted Marchibroda?

For Jim Miller, the definition of the perfect coach for a quarterback was Ron Erhardt, the offensive coordinator of the Giants' first two Super Bowl teams who coached Miller in Pittsburgh in the mid-'90s. Erhardt was a teacher, even more than he was a coach, and that's something he felt every quarterback really needs.

"He was just good at breaking it down and teaching you how to read defenses," Miller said. "They could show you the playbook and it says, 'Read 1 to 2 to 3 in a progression.' But he would actually break it down for you to where it's really easy and really try to strip you down and teach you his way. I've been some places where it's been 'Hey, here's the playbook. Learn it. Go out and execute it.' They don't really cover it. They just give you the plays and you go out and run it. It's not easy to do."

A truly good coach can even get results out of a quarterback he doesn't believe in. After the Browns drafted Bernie Kosar in 1985, Accorsi and Marty Schottenheimer decided he needed help, so one year later they hired Lindy Infante, "the best offensive coordinator I've ever been around in my life," Accorsi said. But Infante had seen Kosar with his wacky, side-armed throwing style and wasn't sure if Accorsi had really found the right guy. And as the Browns were preparing for the draft the next year, Infante took his concerns about Kosar to Browns owner Art Modell.

"When [Modell] heard something from the new guy on the block, that had more weight," Accorsi said. "So David [Modell] comes up and says, 'My dad wants to see you.' Art is ashen-faced. I said, 'What's wrong, Art?' He says, 'I just asked Lindy if he felt we could win with Kosar and he said, "No way."' I said, 'We didn't hire Lindy to evaluate him. We hired him to coach him.'

"Now we have our first training camp meeting and all the position coaches are talking about players and Lindy says, 'If you think this guy is taking you to the Promised Land, you're kidding yourself.'"

Over the next two seasons, Kosar completed 60 percent of his passes for more than 6,000 yards, with thirty-nine touchdowns and nineteen interceptions. "Kosar essentially gets Lindy the Packers head coaching job because we led the league in scoring," Accorsi said. "So Lindy, with all his class, came in and said, 'Look, I wanted to tell you I was wrong about Kosar,'" Accorsi recalled. "I said, 'Lindy, one of the reasons you were wrong was you. Your coaching made you wrong.'

"Now, the reason I say that is there have been some quarterbacks in my lifetime that I would say, 'I don't care who coaches them.' Elway was one of those. He was such a super talent. He could've played single wing tailback. He could run. He was big. It didn't make any difference. Montana? It's a damn good thing he went to Walsh because he did not have a great arm. He had a frail body. I asked Bill Walsh about it one time. I said, 'I saw him play high school football, I saw him in college. He was good and all, but …' Walsh said, 'I saw his feet. A quarterback plays with his feet. And I don't mean running, I mean rhythm.' The point being, he went to the right place. Even with all his ability, he went to the right coach."

. . .

IT WAS CLEAR to almost everyone that Hufnagel's pass-happy, downfield-throwing offense wasn't working for Eli. It put way too much pressure on the shoulders of a young quarterback still trying to find his way. There was no effort to protect Eli, to let a powerful, Tiki Barber–led running game be the centerpiece of the offense. Hufnagel was so pass-happy, in fact, that some members of the front office took to referring to him derisively as "the Canadian quarterback." Players—most notably Barber, but certainly others—expressed great frustration at Hufnagel's penchant for abandoning the run. When things went wrong, if the running game didn't click right from the beginning, he started dusting off his down-field passes.

"And guess what?" Accorsi said. "The defense knew it."

It was a three-year trend that first became evident at the end of the 2005 season when Barber famously said the Giants were "out-coached" in an embarrassing 23–0 home playoff loss to the Carolina Panthers. He wasn't pointing the finger at Coughlin, necessarily—he had Hufnagel in his sights. And his offense and play calls were really wearing on the players in 2006, when Coughlin was clearly on the hot seat and players grumbled daily. Shockey went on a similar "out-coached" rampage after the week three loss at Seattle, when—among other things—he seemed to criticize Hufnagel for being woefully unprepared.

"They were in defenses that we didn't know they were going to be in," Shockey said. "They did different things that we hadn't seen. You can make adjustments all you want, but when they switch things up we can't do anything. The coaches' jobs are supposed to be to put us in the best situations to succeed."

Later in the season, after a particularly ugly game against Jacksonville in which the Giants lost 26–10 and Barber rushed only ten times, the star running back again lined Hufnagel up in his sights and said the play-calling left him feeling "insignificant." The next week Hufnagel called that ill-advised downfield pass in Tennessee with the Giants up 21–0, resulting in an interception that sparked the Titans' miraculous comeback. And four weeks later, in the penultimate game of the season—a 30–7 loss to New Orleans—the patience was completely gone. Players were trying to tell Hufnagel what was happening on the field, why their offense wasn't working. But he didn't listen and, according to players, continued to call plays that had no chance of working against the Saints' scheme. At one point the frustration was clear to everyone in Giants Stadium when Barber reacted to the play call by standing up in the huddle and waving his arms towards the sidelines as if he was saying, "Why are you calling that again?"

"I was never a big fan of Hufnagel—everybody knows that, including Tom," Accorsi said. "To me, that offense was designed for Eli to do it all. Everything was hard. I had always learned— Sonny Jurgensen told me this—'Make it easy on the quarterback.' Eli was asked to do so much. The way the offense was constructed made it easier for him to fail."

It wasn't just the downfield passing, either. Simple things were becoming too confusing for everyone involved. In 2005, after Warner was released, the Giants signed Miller to be Eli's backup and mentor, to help him through his problems and to work through issues with the offense that nobody could seem to solve.

One particular problem, Miller recalled, was an issue Eli was having with calling the offensive line's protection scheme. He'd approach the line of scrimmage, make a call, and then freeze when the defense would appear to change their scheme. That was partic- ularly evident his rookie season during the Baltimore disaster. He'd make a call, the Ravens would switch to a blitz or a scheme that Eli knew was going to mean disaster, but he couldn't figure out a way to get back to the original protection call in time.

"Eli was struggling with that," Miller said. "So I told them, 'Well, all you've got to do is make a 'reload' call.' So if I go up there and say, 'Reload, reload, reload,' now everybody knows that even though I audibled, we're going back to what I originally called."

That seems simple, right? "Yeah," Miller said. "But they just struggled with it. They couldn't figure it out. Those coaches are so engrossed in everything, sometimes you make it harder than what it is. Sometimes it really is: Just keep it simple."

Not surprisingly, the worse things got for the offense and the more confused Eli became, the worse he looked. And he was having trouble speaking up and asking questions or offering his opinion because, as Gilbride said, "You can't ask questions about calculus until you've gone through the introduction to math." As a result, his mechanics suffered. And though Eli wouldn't admit it, it sure looked like his confidence waned. He had respect for Gilbride, then his quarterbacks coach, but he began to seek answers elsewhere. In the off-seasons he'd head to Tennessee where he met with his former Ole Miss coach, David Cutcliffe, to go over film. They'd talk on the phone to discuss what went wrong, too.

The front office wasn't oblivious to any of that, nor were they dismissive of the effect it was having on their franchise quarterback. They hinted to Coughlin after the 2004 season that maybe he should think about changing coordinators. They pushed him a little more to do it after 2005. Then, as 2006 was winding down and Coughlin's job was clearly in jeopardy, they had decided that if they brought the coach back he was going to have to fire Hufnagel.

But Coughlin beat them to the punch and, with one game left in the season, he took the play-calling duties away from his old friend, effectively firing him (Hufnagel would soon resign). Gilbride, his offensive coordinator in Jacksonville from 1995–96, was promoted to the job and immediately earned rave reviews.

"He's one of the few guys that you can walk up to and talk to during the course of the game, tell him what the defense is doing and tell him what's open," said Burress. "I wasn't able to do that with the previous coordinators I've had. I can actually talk to him like I'm talking to you during the game. I don't have to be throwing my helmet or throwing a fit because I can walk over and talk to him."

Obviously, he felt he couldn't do that with Hufnagel. "We kind of tried," Burress said. "But it wasn't a really open relationship."

"You want to have a close relationship with your coordinator," Eli said. "You want to talk over things and make sure you're on the same page while you're doing certain things. You don't question what he's doing, but just understand the thought process of why certain things are put in place."

That he could do that with Gilbride came as no surprise to Warren Moon, one of Gilbride's previous students. "Kevin has a good rapport with his quarterbacks," Moon said. "But he also has a good feel for what defenses do and how to attack them. His offenses have always been so multi-faceted, especially with the leeway that he gives receivers to adjust routes. And I think it's going to help Eli knowing 'I don't have to do it all myself the way the game is going to be called. I just need to be efficient and not lose the football game.'"

. . .

THE RELATIONSHIP BETWEEN Palmer and Gilbride goes back a long way, to when they were teammates at Southern Connecticut State University. Palmer once replaced Gilbride as the offensive coordinator in Jacksonville when the latter took the job as the head coach in San Diego. Now he was going to replace Gilbride as the quarterbacks coach, too.

It was a dicey situation. The fact that he was being hailed as the man who could fix Eli Manning didn't reflect well on Gilbride, who had three years to get the quarterback on the right path. At the end of the 2006 season, no one in the organization thought Eli was where he should be. Nobody blamed Gilbride exclusively, but the implication was clear that he hadn't done enough.

Gilbride, though, would have to have a hand in any Eli resurrection. The biggest reason for optimism was that he knew Eli better than anyone, that he would have a better feel for which plays the quarterback liked and which he didn't. He had a much better chance of tailoring an offensive game plan that actually fit Eli's strengths.

"The teams that have success on the field, there is a very clear understanding by the quarterback of what it is you're trying to achieve as an offense," Gilbride said. "He has to understand that we're doing these plays or using this formation, this personnel grouping, or this motion for this reason. If you don't have that, I think you're dead. Conversely, the coach has to have a sense of what he can do and what he can't do, and try to tailor to the best of his ability, because it's such a key position. You tailor your approach to the things that he can do, that he's comfortable with."

Again, a simple theory that the Giants had not put into practice. Accorsi had watched with a bit of awe how Bill Cowher let Ken Whisenhunt, his offensive coordinator in Pittsburgh, design and run their offense to protect Roethlisberger, to minimize the damage he could do in the offense. Others noticed that, too.

"It's kind of fascinating listening to Cowher when he talks about Ben Roethlisberger early in his career," said Boomer Esiason. "He knew what Ben could do and he knew when he'd go to the well too often and asked Ben to do something in the midst of a game he probably shouldn't have asked him to do it because it would lead to a mistake. The coaches need to know that, too. They need to understand when a kid is not playing well and doesn't look like he has it. You either take the ball out of his hands and protect him, or you get him off the field."

For a change it appeared that the Giants might actually do that, but there was still the matter of "fixing" Eli. How shot were his mechanics? How far gone was his confidence? Did he need to be rebuilt? It would be Palmer's job to find out.

And so he did, diving right into the job after he was hired, looking at every pass Eli had thrown, spending those thirteen painful hours in the film room with the twenty-six year old, reliving every errant pass over and over again. Of course there was no need for fixing, Palmer concluded. Tweaking, yes. Perhaps even some reminding of fundamentals. But fixing? Quarterbacks at the NFL level rarely need to be fixed. And if they do, they're probably already too far gone.

Nick Saban, who was nearly the Giants coach on two separate occasions, recalled his days as an assistant in Houston, when he had to help come up with ways to defend against Kosar when they played the Browns. Kosar's throwing mechanics looked awful on film, he said, "but if you didn't watch the motion, and you watched where the ball went and how accurately it went, that was much more important than the motion itself. I was told as a golfer, 'You'll never get any better with the golf swing you have.' I had a little outside-in fade, Lee Trevino–style. The guy taught me how to swing inside-out, and I've never scored nearly as well as I did with my old fade that I learned on the side of the hill in West Virginia by watching somebody else do it."

In other words, if Eli's mechanics looked bad, so what? If he threw off his back foot, who cared? All that was important was whether the ball reached its intended target. Of course, that wasn't happening with any consistency, but the Giants were hoping the problem was more mental than anything else. And they were banking everything—most notably Coughlin's future—on the belief that Palmer could sort everything out.

• • •

"What are you as a coach?" Gilbride asked. "You're a glorified teacher. That's all you are. To be able to be part of and be able to contribute to the development of a guy as a teacher, that's what everybody goes into this profession for to begin with. You enjoy working with young people and seeing them get better and feeling like you have some knowledge and can assist them as they grow. It's always fun to have a student/player that's very open to what you have to say, which is as good as it gets, and to feel like you helped make a difference. On the other side, when you have some guy that you couldn't [help], and you saw some ability but you just couldn't get it out of him, there's nothing more frustrating."

Gilbride was in Buffalo when Bledsoe arrived there and proved he could still be a viable NFL starter after losing his job to Brady in New England. He helped turn Brunell into a Pro Bowler. Moon adores him from their days together in Houston. He even helped Kordell Stewart rebound from a benching when he was left crying on the sidelines and helped turn him into a Pro Bowler again.

Then there was Leaf, a black mark on more than a few NFL résumés. "Really, I felt had I stayed with San Diego that I could've made a difference with Ryan Leaf," Gilbride said. "Now I know I'm in the minority, and maybe that's overly optimistic on my part, but I thought that."

Coaches always think they can make something out of nothing, and they rarely see the flaws in their players that outsiders see. That's probably why Parcells was gently prodding Palmer during that lazy Sunday in Saratoga. To almost everyone on the outside, Eli was a mess whose potential had been vastly overstated. Palmer was no longer an outsider, though. He was seeing Eli from the inside—and he didn't see his potential as being overstated at all.

But he knew there was work to do. He also had to gain Eli's trust—not exactly an easy task. Eli was a private, closely-guarded person with more than enough potential advisors. He had a college coach he trusted, a brother on his way to the Hall of Fame, and a father who knew a little something about being a quarterback, too. Eli, in his own subtle way, had to find out what Palmer was about, too.

"I was being tested by Eli," Palmer said. "'What kind of coach is this guy? Can he help me or can't he help me?' I always felt that if you had good players and if the players thought you were helping them, they listened to you. If the players did not think you were helping them, they turned you off very, very quickly."

Eli didn't turn Palmer off at all. He even welcomed his quirky summer drills, including the one the fans at the University at Albany loved where the quarterbacks would spin, run around a few obstacles, and then fire at a net twenty or so yards away. Every time the ball hit the net, the fans would cheer. What they didn't know was Palmer was calling out a number or a color and the quarterbacks were supposed to fire at a very specific target. Most of the time they missed.

The drill wasn't only a crowd favorite it was a player favorite, too. They enjoyed working the fans, making them think they scored even when they missed. They played to the cheers, much to

Palmer's fake dismay. They were having fun, but they were learning something, too.

"A long time ago when I got into teaching, I learned you try to make people work and don't let them know they're working," Palmer said. "So they go over and they work on their movement in the pocket, they work on their accuracy, and they're having fun doing it."

Seventeen: "This is where you want to be"

HE WAS IN the middle of a sea of humanity, with fans screaming at the tops of their lungs, workers hurrying to set up a stage, photographers snapping pictures of everyone, and confetti flying all around. Some of the losers were still making their way off the field, heads low, helmets in hand. The winners were passing out championship hats and T-shirts and offering hugs and smiles all around.

It was a great moment for the Manning family. Or at least most of them.

For Eli, it was oddly bittersweet.

Together, the Mannings had spent more than a generation waiting for one of them to ascend to the ultimate game, and Peyton finally did on January 21, 2007. He knocked off his nemesis, Tom Brady and the New England Patriots, in the AFC championship, 38–34, and he did it in dramatic fashion. The Colts were down 21–3 at one point. They didn't have the lead for good until a Joseph Addai three-yard touchdown run with one minute remaining. It wasn't over until Brady, of all people, was picked off with sixteen seconds to play.

Peyton had a brilliant game. He was 27 for 47 for 349 yards with a touchdown and an interception. Now, he was on his way to the top of the podium to receive the Lamar Hunt Trophy. Soon he'd be on his way to Miami for Super Bowl XLI.

And there was Eli, down on the turf at the RCA Dome in Indianapolis, watching the whole scene, taking it all in. As a brother, he was proud beyond words of what Peyton had just accomplished. But as a quarterback?

Jealousy was all he could feel.

"As you watch it happen, you realize that this is where you want to be," Eli said. "You kind of want to go through the same emotions that he's going through and have that same excitement. To be there and see it happen, it makes you want it even more."

Two weeks later, on February 4 at Dolphin Stadium in Miami, Eli had the same things going through his mind as he pushed his way through the crowd in the hallways and then inside the Colts' locker room. He brushed off reporters as he searched for his brother, who was elsewhere in the chaos doing interviews and accepting congratulations.

There may have been pride in Eli's heart, but there was nothing but determination on his face. The wheels were already turning in his head as he thought about next year.

. . .

ASK SOMEONE TO name the greatest quarterbacks of the Super Bowl era, and it won't be difficult to find a similar list in the NFL record books. It will be found under Super Bowl–winning quarterbacks. It will probably be duplicated under Super Bowl MVPs.

There are exceptions of course, but not many. Any list of the greatest of the last forty-two years undoubtedly starts with Montana (four championships) and probably includes Terry Bradshaw (four), Elway (two), Roger Staubach (two), Bart Starr (two), and Brett Favre (one).

Pretty quickly, the list would move on to Dan Marino, Jim Kelly, Fran Tarkenton—three Hall of Famers who have no rings, but they do have eight Super Bowl appearances between them. But they are the exceptions. Marino, with 61,361 career yards and 420 touchdown passes, will go down as one of the most prolific passers in NFL history. Kelly took his team to four straight Super Bowls. Tarkenton was there three times in four years.

Those three are, undoubtedly, among the all-time greats. But how much would just one Super Bowl win have changed the way they're perceived? Marino might have been considered the greatest of all-time given all the passing records he set. Kelly, a first-ballot Hall of Famer as it was, might have been in the upper tier of that conversation, too.

Is it unfair that history gives them a demerit for winning no championships in a team sport? Sure. Just ask Peyton Manning, who was clearly on his way to the Hall of Fame and was already starting to rewrite the NFL's passing record book before he led the Colts to his Super Bowl championship in 2006. But up until the moment he finally dismissed Brady—and really, until he hoisted the Lombardi Trophy—you might have gotten an argument if you dared to suggest he had a chance to be one of the greatest quarterbacks ever. Until then, he was too busy being saddled with the dreaded "can't win the big game" tag. He was even asked about that just moments after he finally won a big one, in that 2006 AFC championship game.

"That's been the number one question I've been asked so far," Peyton said. "But I don't get into monkeys and vindication. I don't play that card."

That's easy to say after winning a big game, of course. It's even easier to say while wearing a Super Bowl ring.

Giants fans never needed to be reminded of how important a ring is. Many of them still make a convincing argument that Simms belongs in the Hall, despite career statistics (55.4 completion percentage, 33,462 yards, 199 touchdowns, 157 interceptions) that the voters have never deemed to be even close to Hall-worthy. In fact, had injuries not robbed him of his part in the Giants' Super Bowl XXV championship, his fans believe he might have been a Hall of Fame lock.

But that's still a slight case of selective memory. Up until the Giants' magical 1986 season, Giants fans had spent much of Simms' first eight years in New York booing him and trying to run him out of town. But one championship made him a legend, especially after he had arguably the greatest Super Bowl performance of any quarterback in history. He was almost perfect in the Giants' 39–20 win over the Denver Broncos in Super Bowl XXI—22 of 25 for 268 yards and three touchdown passes. He had a Super Bowl-record ten straight completions, and he still holds the record for completion percentage (88) and passer rating (150.9), too. And all of a sudden he was one of the most beloved Giants of all time.

One ring had similar effects on the careers of Jim McMahon, Mark Rypien, Jeff Hostetler (the man who filled in for Simms in 1990), Doug Williams, and Kurt Warner. Maybe none of them are headed to the Hall of Fame either, but they will also never be forgotten. Take away their rings and their significance in history, for the most part, is gone.

To a lesser extent the same is true for Brad Johnson and Trent Dilfer, two of the worst quarterbacks to ever win a Super Bowl championship. That's fine, though, because they still have something that an overwhelming majority of NFL quarterbacks will never have: a ring.

. . .

How important is that Super Bowl ring? Consider this: There have been twenty-seven winning quarterbacks in the first forty-two

Super Bowls, and eleven of them are in the Hall of Fame. That's a startling 40.7 percent. And the percentage goes even higher—to 57.9 percent—when you consider that eight Super Bowl–winning quarterbacks were still active in the 2007 season. That means eleven of the nineteen Super Bowl–winning quarterbacks who have already retired are in the Hall. And it's a pretty safe bet that Tom Brady, Peyton Manning, and Brett Favre will someday be there, too. And Brady, with three championships already, could probably be inducted today, considering that every quarterback that won more than one championship, with the lone exception of Jim Plunkett, is in the Hall.

In all, quarterbacks make up 12.4 percent of the Hall—thirty of the 241 members. That includes eighteen quarterbacks who played in the Super Bowl era, and fourteen who played in a Super Bowl game. The only four Hall of Fame quarterbacks who played in 1967 and beyond but never reached the Super Bowl are George Blanda, who was forty years old by the time the first Super Bowl was played; Sonny Jurgensen, who battled injuries late in his career, including when Billy Kilmer led the Redskins to a loss in Super Bowl VII; Warren Moon, who played the first six years of his pro career in the Canadian Football League; and Dan Fouts, whose only excuse was that he played for the snake-bitten Chargers.

Look beyond those numbers, though, and see what a Super Bowl can really do. Take Joe Namath, probably the most famous quarterback in the history of New York football. He's the patron saint of upsets, famously guaranteeing victory by the upstart Jets of the AFL over the NFL's powerful Baltimore Colts in Super Bowl III. With that one game, he's sometimes single-handedly—and mistakenly—credited for sparking the NFL's modern era and the NFL–AFL merger that changed the landscape and shaped the game of today.

His guarantee, and the way he backed it up, is one of the most famous moments in NFL history and the signature of the Super Bowl era.

Now take that moment away. Would Namath still be in the Hall of Fame?

It's a debatable point. He spent thirteen years in pro football (1965–77), including the first five years of his career when the Jets were still in the American Football League. It was a pass-happy league, at least compared to the stodgier NFL. And in 1967, Namath became the first pro quarterback to ever top 4,000 yards in a single season (4,007). But still, he only had six seasons where his completion percentage was 50 percent or higher, and it was never higher than 52.9 (in 1974). There were exactly two seasons in his career (his rookie year in 1965 and again in 1969) where he threw more touchdowns than he did interceptions. For his career, Namath completed 50.1 percent of his passes for 27,663 yards, 173 touchdowns, and 220 interceptions.

How borderline are his credentials, even with the ring? His statistical equivalent from the same era is, roughly, Kenny "The Snake" Stabler, who succeeded Namath as the quarterback at Alabama. He had a slightly longer pro career than Namath (fifteen years, 1970–84), but finished with similar numbers—27,938 yards, 194 touchdowns, 222 interceptions.

Namath went to four AFL All-Star games and a Pro Bowl. Stabler went to four Pro Bowls. Stabler was named one of the three quarterbacks on the NFL's all-1970s team, as selected by the voters for the Hall of Fame. Namath, stuck between decades, made neither the team of the '60s or '70s. Stabler, at one point, was the quickest quarterback to win 100 games, doing it in 150—three quicker than Johnny Unitas. They both even won a Super Bowl, with Stabler getting his in the less-remembered Super Bowl XI.

Yet Stabler, with similar—some would argue better—credentials has never been deemed worthy of the Hall. Maybe that's an indictment of Hall voters, or at least a sign of how inexact the science of selection can be. But what if Namath had never won Super Bowl III? Which of the two quarterbacks would be in the Hall then?

Want another example? How about former St. Louis Cardinals quarterback Jim Hart? He was a four-time Pro Bowler with very Namath-like stats. He stuck around longer (nineteen years, from 1966–84), though he didn't play much at the end. He had a better completion percentage (51.1) and more yards (34,665) than Namath, and a similar touchdown-to-interception ratio (209–247). He did win two division titles with the Cardinals in the mid-1970s, quite an achievement with that miserable franchise. But he never won a playoff game and never even sniffed a Super Bowl.

Does anyone but the most die-hard of St. Louis Cardinals fans (if there are such people) even remember him?

For another example, look at the curious case of Boomer Esiason, a veteran of fourteen NFL seasons and one of the finest left-handed quarterbacks in NFL history. He finished with 37,920 yards, 2,969 completions, and 247 touchdown passes—all records for left-handed quarterbacks. He made four Pro Bowls, was the NFL MVP in 1988, and even led the hapless Cincinnati Bengals to Super Bowl XXIII. In fact, he led them to a fourth-quarter lead in that game. The Bengals were up 16–13 after a field goal with 3:20 remaining and the ensuing kickoff pinned the 49ers way back at their own eight-yard line. From there, Montana led the Niners on an eleven-play, ninety-two-yard drive that finished with a ten-yard touchdown pass to John Taylor with thirty-four seconds remaining. It was the only time in the first forty-one Super Bowls that the game was won by a touchdown pass in the final minute.

"But because Montana takes that last drive, it could keep [Esiason] out," Accorsi said. "And he had nothing to do with it."

Of course, Accorsi's Browns did dominate Esiason's Bengals during the latter half of the '80s in the AFC's Central Division. But still, Esiason finished his career an impressive thirteenth on the NFL's all-time passing yardage list, ahead of Kelly (four Super Bowls, all losses, and a Hall of Famer), and fourteenth on the all-time passing touchdown list (ahead of Kelly and fellow Hall of Famers Len Dawson and Steve Young). The only men above him on either list that aren't in or headed to the Hall are Vinny Testaverde, Drew Bledsoe, and Dave Krieg.

Put a ring on Esiason's finger and does history view him differently? Does he get considered for the Hall?

Of course, a ring doesn't work magic for everyone. It's hard to believe that if David Woodley (Miami, XVII), Joe Kapp (Minnesota, IV), Vince Ferragamo (L.A. Rams, XIV), Stan Humphries (San Diego, XXIX), or Rex Grossman (Chicago, XLI) had won his Super Bowl that he would be remembered as anything other than one of the worst quarterbacks ever to appear in the big game. And even winning the ring certainly didn't work for Trent Dilfer, who is also a charter member of that "worst quarterbacks to win a Super Bowl" group.

In fact, Dilfer is remembered for being mostly along for the ride when the Baltimore Ravens pounded the Giants in Super Bowl XXXV. The oft-struggling quarterback completed just 12 of 25 passes for 153 yards and a touchdown that day, and nearly threw the game away with an interception that would have been returned for a touchdown by Giants linebacker Jessie Armstead if it hadn't been wiped out by a horrible holding call on defensive tackle Keith Hamilton.

Even Dilfer understands why he rarely gets much credit for a championship run that was decidedly led by his defense.

He also doesn't care.

"Who cares if you have one completion?" Dilfer said several years later. "At the end of the day, if you're hoisting the Lombardi trophy, you did what you wanted to do."

. . .

ELI HAD TO see that in Indianapolis that day, how the weight of the world was finally lifted from Peyton's shoulders. The quarterback who couldn't win the big one had finally won a big one, and was two weeks away from winning an even bigger game. Peyton was already a huge star, the commercial darling of the NFL and one of its best and brightest personalities. But the 29–17 win he led over the Bears in Super Bowl XLI made his career seem more complete.

He would be no Marino—as if it was somehow an insult to be one of the most prolific passers in the history of the NFL—now that he had his ring.

"I know everything Peyton's been through," Eli said while his brother celebrated someplace else. "I've been to the playoffs, been disappointed. It's tough. I know how hard he's worked, how much he's wanted this and what he's put forth to get it."

Then came a rare moment of public introspection—a rare glimpse into what was really going on inside Eli's heart and mind.

"When it comes time for next year, I'll know what that feeling is and know that I don't want to be shaking hands and have people congratulate me about Peyton and what he's doing," Eli said. "I want to be on the other side and not have to be going to events.

I want to be in the hotel studying film and getting ready to play for a championship.

"Seeing the grin on his face, his smile after the game, and the relief and enjoyment he had put something in my heart that said 'this is where you want to be.' It definitely sparked something with me. It definitely made me want it even more."

Eighteen: "The post-game press conference isn't the problem"

THE FIRST THREE seasons of Eli's career were analyzed, dissected, torn apart, and shredded by everyone—not just by the media and the fans. He was also being pulled apart, broken down, and re-analyzed by the men who signed his massive checks.

His third season—the one where he was expected to come of age—came crashing to a disappointing end on January 7 with a 23–20 loss in Philadelphia, where he played fairly well (16 for 27, 161 yards, two touchdowns, one interception) but the Giants' defense didn't. Year three of the Eli era, though, had become a circus in the Giants' locker room as they limped to an 8–8 record. Coughlin was being hammered by the press and in the press by mostly anonymous players. His bosses didn't help matters by refusing to discuss his tenuous job status, which team sources insisted was hanging by a fraying thread.

In the middle of all that chaos, Eli limped down the stretch saving his worst performances for the most crucial times in the regular season. There was serious concern—even inside the organization—about whether he'd ever develop into anything more than an average NFL quarterback. Privately, some executives began conceding that the initial expectations were way too high. They could win with Eli, they insisted, but they weren't sure he was the type of quarterback who could carry the team on his shoulders. It was a startling admission, considering that had always been exactly what they thought he'd be able to do.

It's not that they didn't believe in his talent. In his first three seasons he had shown more than a few flashes of brilliance. Who could ever forget the game that everyone thought finally signaled his arrival, at Giants Stadium on October 23, 2005, just thirteen starts into his NFL career? The Giants were trailing the powerful Denver Broncos 23–10 with thirteen minutes remaining when Eli started a miraculous comeback. First he led the Giants down the field for a short touchdown run by Tiki Barber. Then, still trailing 23–17, he got the ball back on the Giants' seventeen with 3:29 to play. He took them down the field looking far too calm for a second-year player, and then zipped a game-winning, two-yard touchdown pass to Amani Toomer with just five seconds to play.

Even during the chaotic 2006 season there were several performances they just couldn't get out of their minds. Like the second game of the season on September 17 in Philadelphia when he rallied the Giants out of a seventeen-point fourth-quarter hole. He completed 31 of 43 passes for 371 yards, three touchdowns, and one interception. He did all that despite being battered by eight sacks. And even at the end, in what Accorsi would later call "the earliest must-win game of my career," Eli had the toughness and the resiliency to stand in the pocket with two Eagles blitzing and throw a perfect thirty-one-yard touchdown pass to Burress in overtime to seal the 30–24 win.

"That was really one of the remarkable performances by any quarterback that we've seen this year," said Cris Collinsworth, the former NFL receiver and television analyst. "He showed a toughness in that game that, quite frankly, I thought faded away at the end of the season. I really thought that game might have been the game that turned the corner for him and made him into a star quarterback."

It didn't happen, of course. That game was part of a season-opening four-game stretch in which he completed 67.1 percent of his passes, was over 250 yards in three of the four games, and threw nine touchdown passes and only five interceptions. The rest of Eli's 2006 season, though, was hardly star material. He was under 200 yards passing in nine of the final twelve games, under a 50 percent completion percentage in five of them. He threw nearly as many interceptions (thirteen) as touchdowns (fifteen) the rest of the way, too. Neither that Eagles game nor his red-hot start was a sign he had turned a corner toward stardom. And the Giants ended up losing in the first round of the playoffs again.

Still, Eli was being paid like a star, which all of a sudden was becoming one of his many public-perception issues. A couple of months after the season ended, he got a $5 million "buy-back bonus"—part of his complicated rookie contract that also locked him into the Giants through 2009, and bumped his 2007–09 salaries to $6 million, $8 million, and $8.5 million. The Giants had no issue with paying him the money, but when the numbers made the rounds in the press it ignited another debate about whether he was worth it all.

Meanwhile, Eli's situation was about to get tougher now that Tiki Barber—who accounted for 2,127 of the Giants' 5,214 yards, single-handedly carried them into the playoffs with a 234-yard rushing performance in the season finale, and caught 58 of Eli's 301 completions—was about to retire. Barber wasn't just the best player on the Giants, he was also one of Eli's favorite receivers, and an important safety valve for him to dump the ball to when nobody else was open. Some argued that getting Barber out of the locker room—where he was one of Coughlin's most vocal critics—would be a plus. But to Eli, losing him on the field couldn't be anything but a huge loss.

Knowing all that, co-owner John Mara spent three days huddling in the Giants Stadium offices in the days after the end of the 2006 season with team treasurer Jonathan Tisch, who was representing his brother Steve, and the embattled Coughlin. They talked about Coughlin's prickly personality, the grip he was apparently losing on his locker room, a need for the sixty-year-old coach to alter his behavior and be nicer to his players and the press.

And they talked and talked and talked about the $45–54 million elephant in the room—the startling, frustrating lack of development of their franchise quarterback. They needed to hear—they needed to know—whether Coughlin thought Eli could ever be what they thought he would be. And they needed to know Coughlin had a realistic plan to make it happen. Tom had tried everything to get the most out of his struggling protégé. He had brought him along slowly, given him pep talks and assigned him mentors. He even once tried a direct and more painful approach, after an ugly, season-changing loss to the Chicago Bears at home in the middle of the '06 season. Eli had been awful, completing just 14 of 32 passes for 121 yards and two interceptions. The next day, Coughlin called him into his office for a stern lecture in which he told him the loss was his fault—an approach that didn't sit well with some members of the front office. But Eli's shaky performance, as much as anything, was what had Coughlin on the firing line and the coach was desperate. The quarterback's ability to improve, more than anything, would determine whether Coughlin would be back on that line again in one year.

"Obviously that was a major part of our discussions," Mara said. "Eli needs to play more consistently. He would be the first one to admit that. There is nobody in this building that doubts his ability and that feels like he is not the guy to lead us to where we want to get to. But he has to play more consistently."

The same concern was addressed a week later when the Giants introduced Jerry Reese as their new general manager, replacing the retiring Accorsi. "Eli's progress right now is not where we want him to be," Reese said. "We want him to be a Pro Bowl guy that can lead us to the Super Bowl."

There wasn't despair in any of those words. Just concern. Reese insisted that the quarterbacks still in the playoffs weren't much better than Eli. Mara insisted, "We know the talent is there because we've seen him do it." He even defiantly said, "I don't want there to be any doubt about the fact that everybody in this organization is committed to this quarterback and believes that this quarterback is going to be a great one for many years to come."

But hadn't they also just placed the weight of the world on Eli's twenty-six-year-old shoulders? Hadn't they just labeled Eli a disappointment and said his failures were a big reason why his coach was almost fired? And didn't Reese just set the bar for Eli absurdly high saying they expected him to make the Pro Bowl and win a Super Bowl, too? Presumably soon?

Even Accorsi, during his retirement speech to the Giants after they lost that playoff game in Philadelphia, raised the bar when he addressed a group of players who would hardly remind anyone of a band of brothers, and told them: "There's a championship in this room."

Oh yeah? Where? And who would be the leaders? Even Accorsi later admitted that when he made that statement, he wasn't exactly thinking in the short term.

. . .

THE SUMMER DIDN'T exactly go smoothly for the Giants, which didn't help Eli's cause. There were mini-fires everywhere in camp, starting with the summer-long holdout of Strahan, the biggest personality on the now Tiki-less team. He said he was considering retirement. Management believed he was looking for money it never planned to give him. His holdout even featured a few contentious phone conversations with Reese, who angered Strahan with his tough talk to the press.

Then there was Barber's "comical" shot at Eli, which ignited a month-long debate. And as if that wasn't enough, Eli's number one target, Burress, who was already recovering from off-season surgery on his left ankle, sprained his other ankle during an evening practice at training camp at the University at Albany on August 2. The Giants downplayed the injury, but he wouldn't practice again until a few days before the regular-season opener. In fact, he'd practice only a handful of times over the next five months.

Despite all that, Eli did appear to be making progress under the stewardship of Palmer, the "quarterback guru," as Reese called him, that Coughlin hired to replace Gilbride, who was officially promoted to replace Hufnagel as the team's offensive coordinator. For what it's worth, in four preseason games the previously inaccurate Eli completed 68.6 percent of his passes. And his progress seemed even clearer in the regular season opener on a Sunday night in Dallas. The game was a shootout—and a brutal one, at that. The Giants had already lost running back Brandon Jacobs and defensive end Osi Umenyiora to knee injuries thanks, in part, to the unforgiving Texas Stadium turf.

The big scare, though, came with 7:20 remaining in a game in which Eli would complete 28 of 41 passes for 312 yards and four touchdowns, including a sixty-yard touchdown pass to Burress on the initial series—an absolutely brilliant opening to a critical season. His third touchdown pass was a nine-yarder to running back Derrick Ward, which closed the score to 38–28, pending the two-point conversion.

But on that failed conversion attempt, the season—and Coughlin's career—flashed before everyone's eyes. Eli was slammed to the turf by rookie defensive end Anthony Spencer, suffering what was feared to be a season-ending torn labrum but would later prove to be just a painful second-degree shoulder separation (the Giants called it a bruise). Eli got up, went to the sidelines and could be seen stretching his shoulder. The pain seemed to be obvious in his face.

Yet he went back in the game and threw a ten-yard touchdown pass to Burress to bring the Giants to within three points at 38–35. And he didn't come out until there was 2:34 left and the Giants were down ten and he decided to "make the smart decision" because his shoulder was getting tight.

According to people in the organization, Eli was acting anxious (and in considerable pain) the next day when he went for an MRI, and again one day later when the Giants sent the results to Dr. James Andrews, the famed orthopedic surgeon in Alabama. His father, Archie, was nervous because the Giants' doctor, Dr. Russell Warren, told him that Eli could end up missing three to four weeks. That prognosis made its way to Chris Mortensen, who reported it on ESPN, and hung over Eli all week long like a dark cloud.

But the diagnosis from East Rutherford to Birmingham was actually the same: no structural damage, and if Eli could tolerate the pain he could play. One week later, Eli was still in considerable pain, but he did play, struggling through a 16-for-29, 211-yard performance in a 35–13 loss to the Green Bay Packers. He kept insisting his shoulder was fine, even as he meandered through the next four weeks and the expression on his face and the lack of power on his throws said otherwise. The Giants did rebound from that 0–2 start—which was nearly 0–3 when they trailed the Redskins 17–3 at halftime in week three—and were actually 3–2 five weeks into the season. But Eli wasn't doing much. He had one good day for the rest of the first half of the season—a 27-for-39, 303-yard performance in Atlanta. Most of his days were average, like his 13-for-25, 186-yard day in a win against the Jets.

Though he refused to admit it at the time, it seemed clear his shoulder needed a rest.

"Yeah, it was sore for the next couple of weeks," Eli admitted a few months later. "During practice, any time we had a deep throw, I couldn't make the throw. I'd kind of say, 'Hey, I would have thrown it to the post,' but I'd take the five-yard check down. Probably after three or four weeks it felt fine. And I don't think it affected me as the season went on."

· · ·

HERE'S THE TRULY maddening thing about Eli Manning. He can go from outstanding to terrible in the blink of an eye. He started off the second half of the 2007 season by completing 23 of 34 passes in a loss to Dallas, and followed that up by completing 28 of 39 in a win in Detroit. That's a two-week completion percentage of 69.9.

Seven days later, he was Eli the Terrible. At home, against the 4–6 Minnesota Vikings and their thirty-first-ranked passing defense, he somehow managed to complete only 42.9 percent of his passes (21 for 49) and he threw those four interceptions. It was the second four-interception game of his career, and his first since November 13, 2005 (his second season in the NFL) when he tossed four at home against those same Vikings. It was a cruel way for history to repeat itself, which made it even more painful for everyone involved.

Accorsi was in the stands that day. For a little while, anyway. "I left with two and a half minutes to go in the second quarter," he said. "And it got worse in the car. Not only did I leave, but before the Lincoln Tunnel I turned it off." And it wasn't as if Accorsi had someplace better to be. "I just couldn't bear to see anymore," he said.

And the hits from that game kept coming. Darren Sharper, the Vikings safety who had three of the picks back in 2005 and another in this game, hinted that Eli was tipping where he was going with his passes. He said he looked "gun shy" after the first interception. Dwight Smith, the other safety, said it looked like Eli "just didn't want to get hit," and said their strategy was to sit back and wait because they knew eventually Eli would panic and throw the ball to the wrong team.

It was a humiliating turn of events, considering it was Eli's fiftieth NFL start and he was outplayed badly by the Vikings' unheralded first-year starting quarterback, Tarvaris Jackson. The Giants lost 41–17 that day, and it harkened back to the Baltimore disaster his rookie year.

But here's the truly absurd part: The next day the big issue in New York wasn't Eli's penchant for throwing to the wrong team, his startlingly wobbly throws, his humiliating inaccuracy, or the promising season that was suddenly slipping away. Instead, the calls that flooded the radio stations, the posts on message boards, and the blogs all had to do with something else:

His post-game press conference.

After that game, Eli looked like Eli always does—completely and maddeningly unaffected. On the field, after each miscue, he shook his head, pointed his chin towards the ground, and walked quietly off the field. No helmet throwing, no stomping, no visible signs of the hurt the fans were obviously feeling. He appeared oblivious to the boos. Then, in the interview room moments after it was over, he was calm, analytical, and seemed to show no emotion at all.

Asked what happened on the field, he said "They just had a good plan." Asked to assess his performance, he said "When you throw four interceptions, it's never a good day." Asked specifically if that horrible showing left him embarrassed, angry, shocked, surprised, or anything at all, he replied, "You know, just disappointed."

To many, it was as if he just said, "You know what? I don't really care."

Obviously that wasn't the case, but New York had long been frustrated with his aw-shucks demeanor—"Aw Shucks," in fact, was the nickname given to him by Craig Carton, the co-host of WFAN's morning show with Boomer Esiason. There were fans of the Giants whose week would be ruined by the loss. They'd sink into a funk that would weigh on them until the next Sunday. They felt embarrassed, angry, shocked, surprised and would feel that way all week long. Then to hear that Eli was "just disappointed"? How were they supposed to root for a quarterback who didn't hurt from a loss as much as they did?

The next day, that was all anyone talked about. Manning's demeanor was dissected on the radio, not his mechanics. His words were analyzed, not his decisions. He even held a press conference to explain what happened in his press conference, which might have been a first—even for New York.

"Yeah, the post-game press conference isn't the problem," Eli said. "I don't get to watch film on my post-game press conference. I guess I'll start doing that now."

Pretty soon, everyone was piling on. As Eli was down in the locker room explaining his behavior, Reese was up in his office telling *Newsday* that Eli looked "skittish" against the Vikings—an accurate assessment that nevertheless was damning coming from the general manager. It was a word Reese didn't retract either, and with good reason—a lot of people thought he was exactly right. In fact, one month earlier in a *Sports Illustrated* poll that asked NFL players "Who is the easiest NFL quarterback to intimidate?" Eli came in second, right behind the much-maligned Rex Grossman. Eli got twenty percent of the vote from the 278 players who responded. Worse, he got 30.8 percent of the vote from other NFL quarterbacks—an embarrassing and damning assessment from his own peers.

"I just think there are times in games where he looks like he completely loses focus," said Esiason. "When I watched him against Minnesota, he had that deer-in-the-headlights look. We had a caller that told us, 'He was rattled against Minnesota,' and I thought that was the perfect assessment of his performance against the Vikings. Completely confused and rattled."

"You never see him just stay in there and, literally, as he's throwing it, somebody just wallops him—he always will back out and fade away from the throw," added former NFL offensive lineman Brian Baldinger, an analyst for both Fox and the NFL Network. "That's on tape and that's one reason the Vikings were blitzing."

Being obviously skittish in the pocket was bad enough and would have put Eli on the defensive, if he hadn't already been backpedaling from his post-game press conference. So bland, so monotone, so emotionless, so … nothing.

Could such a painful loss really hurt as little as it appeared?

"If you go into a tantrum, it doesn't make anything better," Eli explained, to the satisfaction of no one. "It doesn't correct the last play or the last few that happened. I figure if I start going crazy and getting wild, it's just going to make everybody else go into a tantrum. And I'm trying to keep everybody calm."

Calm is fine. But he took it to a Hannibal Lecter–like extreme. His fans weren't looking for a tantrum. They were looking for a pulse.

His teammates had his back—"All that stuff about the look on his face, why does he look like that? That's just people trying to find something to pick on him for," Brandon Jacobs said—but few others did. The Giants were 7–4, but they had the look of a team headed for yet another second-half stumble. Worse, nearly four years and fifty games into Eli's career, he appeared to be back at rock bottom. Again.

"There's a little thing I used to put in my locker," Theismann said. "'You never have to be the reason a team wins. You just can't be the reason it loses.' And right now, with some of the throws he's making, the decisions he's making, he's contributing to a large degree of what's going on."

The world, at that point, was completely against Eli. Even Accorsi started to feel badly about the mess his quarterback project had become.

"I said to John Mara, 'I'm sorry this is happening this way,'" Accorsi recalled. "He said, 'Ernie, I was as much in favor of this as you were.'"

. . .

THERE WERE FIVE games left in the regular season at that point, and there couldn't have been a single person on the planet who believed the Giants were a Super Bowl team. The mere suggestion would've been laughable—a cruel joke—especially since even the playoffs suddenly looked to be in doubt. And now Coughlin's job status was once again an issue. No one in management would commit to him returning in 2008. There were even rumblings that the Giants were going to consider bringing in another quarterback next season, not to backup Eli, but to compete for his job.

The whole master plan for building the organization seemed to be teetering on the brink of collapse.

When the Giants trailed the Bears in Chicago 16–7 in the fourth quarter one week later, the collapse appeared to have begun. Eli had even already blown a chance to tighten the game when he got the Giants to the Bears' one-yard line, only to underthrow Burress in the end zone where he was picked off. Another terrible interception. Another bad pass. Just another day at the office for a quarterback in a rut.

But when Eli got the ball back with 11:45 left in that game, he led the Giants on a quick drive that ended with a six-yard touchdown pass to Amani Toomer. And when he got the ball back again with 4:55 left, he drove the Giants seventy-seven yards and threw a gutsy fifteen-yard pass to Burress at the Bears' two. It was a skinny post into the wind that Peyton would later label "an impressive throw," and not just because it set up Reuben Droughns' game-winning touchdown run. It was impressive because of the conditions, the way Eli had been playing and the whole precarious situation the Giants were in.

"This is just kind of as a fellow NFL quarterback," Peyton said. "I certainly watch other games and have an appreciation when Tom Brady makes a great throw or when Tony Romo makes a great throw, Favre, whoever it may be. So watching Eli in that game, it really stood out how he kind of stayed tough and put the previous plays behind him. I think that's one of the most important characteristics of a quarterback—to put the previous play behind you, good or bad. I think Eli does that as well as anybody."

It obviously felt good to put the whole previous ugly week behind him. A palpable weight had been lifted off the Giants' shoulders.

The post-game locker room was the loudest and most delirious it had been all season, and most of the joy was directed Eli's way.

"That just tells you the mentality of that guy," said linebacker Antonio Pierce. "All the critics and hell is coming down on him. He could have easily flopped over, put his head down and put the game away. But he didn't."

"He kept the same demeanor," added guard Chris Snee. "He wasn't rattled or skittish. He was confident."

While watching that game, Peyton was sending text messages to his father. "I remember sending one to my dad saying 'Eli has big ... I guess the proper way to say it is it rhymes with 'guts,'" Peyton said. "That's all I can tell you. That's something that I think is real true in describing Eli."

Here's something else that's true about Eli: Good or bad, he's still who he is. In the post-game press conference in Chicago, seven days after his post-game press conference from hell, he was as bland and as boring and as seemingly unaffected as ever. Asked how it felt to redeem himself and save his season, Eli—wearing the same droopy-eyed expression as always—said, "Well, it's nice."

Of course, there was still some work to be done. Eli didn't exactly rebound from the Minnesota mauling with a game for the ages. He was 16 of 27 for 195 yards with one touchdown and two interceptions. One week later, he was equally mediocre in a 16–13 win in Philly, going 17 for 31 for 219 yards and a touchdown.

And he didn't exactly end the season on a high-note either. In another horrible home loss, this time 22–10 to the Redskins, he was once again booed off the field after a remarkably bad 18-for-53 performance. His thirty-five incompletions on that incredibly windy day were the most in the NFL in forty years. And though there wasn't the same firestorm about his demeanor, he appeared to be his usual unaffected self. Gilbride actually took most of the heat for that performance, with questions about why he had let a struggling, inaccurate quarterback throw that much on a day with steady twenty-mile-per-hour winds and gusts so strong they had knocked down and ripped apart the Giants' indoor practice bubble earlier in the day.

With a questionable game plan and a shaky quarterback, the season was obviously in jeopardy, especially since the Giants also lost Shockey (57 catches, 619 yards) that day to a broken left fibula. And, with the undefeated Patriots looming in the season finale, they were now facing a must-win week sixteen game in Buffalo. The playoffs and possibly Coughlin's job were on the line.

The Giants won in Buffalo, 38–21, after falling behind 14–0 in the opening quarter before a wild weather swing saw fifty-mile-per-hour winds, rain, snow, and a temperature drop of more than twenty degrees during the course of the game. Eli had remarkably little to do with that win, going just 7 of 15 for 111 yards with two interceptions and five fumbles. It was really an awful performance, but he was bailed out by a defense that scored twice, 145 yards and two touchdowns by Brandon Jacobs, and 151 yards, including an eighty-eight-yard touchdown run, by rookie running back Ahmad Bradshaw.

A playoff berth had been clinched, but Eli seemed to be regressing—at least according to the numbers. But a few people looked through the wind against the Redskins and the snow in Buffalo and saw a quarterback who was starting to look a little more like a quarterback should.

"It never turned around with four touchdowns, 380 yards. It never turns around that way," Accorsi said. "The Bears game probably started it, don't you think? It was sudden death on all the road games, but he had that one drive, he made a drive at the end, a play at the end. That's usually how it happens. Because if you have a big, huge game—five touchdowns—and then have a bad game, you really haven't gone to another level. It's slow building. I just could see him getting more confident."

And there was still one more game to go, one more game for Eli to build on—that is, if Coughlin would even let him play. The shoulder injury he suffered sixteen weeks earlier still loomed over everything like a lighthouse warning everyone of the impending danger. The Giants' week seventeen game against the 15–0 Patriots didn't matter to them. Their playoff spot, seeding, and first-round game in Tampa were all secure. Why risk the health and availability of Eli—or any of the regulars, for that matter—in a game that was completely meaningless?

Of course, it would turn out to be one of the most meaningful meaningless games ever played.

Nineteen: "For whatever reason, it's clicking"

IT'S IRONIC THAT the flash point for the Giants' championship run came in a season-ending loss, at the end of a stretch that was as miserable as any Eli ever had in the NFL. Two weeks earlier was the windswept incompletion fest against the Redskins. One week earlier was his five-fumble near-disaster in the snow in Buffalo. In a five-game stretch, dating back to the four-interception nightmare against Minnesota, he was completing just 45.4 percent of his passes (79 for 174) and had thrown just four touchdowns to his eight interceptions. It was yet another ugly second half of the season. Another miserable slide.

There wasn't a single sign anywhere that it was all just about to come together for the erratic twenty-six-year-old who tied Jon Kitna and Carson Palmer for the league lead in interceptions and who had become the most over-analyzed, dissected, and criticized athlete in town.

So what was the moment when the light went on? Or was there even such a moment?

"I compare it to those Hollywood overnight sensations that you never heard of," Gilbride said. "Then they tell their life story and you find out they've been laboring in anonymity the last fifteen years. That's what I feel like. Here's a guy that's been doing everything to get ready, and now all of a sudden it's all crystallized for him and come into focus."

There seems to be no doubt the eye of the coming storm formed on December 29—or maybe even four days before when, facing a game against the powerful, undefeated, New England Patriots that meant absolutely nothing to the Giants in terms of their playoff position, Coughlin stood in front of his players at their Wednesday morning meeting and announced, "We're playing to win the game."

There would be no resting players unless the game got out of hand. There would be no playing with caution just to preserve players' health. They didn't need the game. They weren't expected to win anyway. They could just go out and play, free of pressure, expectations, or any of the other usual stuff weighing them down.

To Eli, what could be better? No one had ever played with more pressure on a daily basis than him. Now, he was facing a game where if he played poorly, he'd be pulled to preserve his health and it wouldn't matter to anyone. In fact, another poor performance in his season of struggles oddly might not even get much notice. The Giants were expected to lose. The New York media had already turned its attention, somewhat, to the Giants' playoff opener. The fans had even started looking ahead, making unhappy headlines during the week because they were selling off their tickets in droves to Patriots fans who wanted to be at Giants Stadium to see them complete the first 16–0 regular-season in the history of the NFL.

In other words, Eli had a free pass.

And here's what he did with it: 22 for 32 (68.8 percent), 251 yards, four touchdowns, and only one interception. He helped the Giants build a twelve-point lead in the second half, and they still held a 28–23 lead about three minutes into the fourth quarter. Eli did make one critical mistake: On a second and six from the Giants' twenty-seven with ten minutes remaining, he overlooked a wide open Brandon Jacobs underneath, and instead overthrew

Burress on the sidelines. The ball landed in the hands of Patriots cornerback Ellis Hobbs, and a little more than five minutes later the Patriots had an insurmountable ten-point lead. Eli had one more touchdown drive in him, but it was too little, too late and the Pats won 38–35.

But a funny thing happened after the game. Rather than the usual treatment—getting skewered publicly for a critical mistake at a terrible time—Eli was hailed as a near-conquering hero for standing toe-to-toe with the great Brady (32 of 42, 356 yards, two touchdowns). The Giants, just for making the 16–0 Patriots sweat and for putting in a full effort when they could have easily taken a half day, became the pride of New York.

And for the next week, the noise coming out of the locker room was all about the incredible confidence the Giants had built in that loss. If they could nearly beat the unbeatable Patriots, they said, they clearly could beat anyone in the NFC. And if Eli can nearly out-duel Brady and have so much success against one of the NFL's best defenses, well surely the quarterback who had yet to win a playoff game was capable of leading the Giants on an extended playoff run.

Of course, that was just a lot of brave talk and it would have amounted to nothing if other things weren't happening, too. The biggest appeared to be a change of philosophy by the Giants' offensive staff. Gone was the downfield passing attack, the constant searching for the home run, the mindless throwing into the wind that occurred two weeks earlier against the Redskins. They seemed to switch to a more managed attack that relied on short passes, leaned heavily on the running game, and freed Eli of the pressure to win the game on his own with one or two big throws.

The notion of a philosophical switch was one that Eli and the coaching staff would refute. Some suggested Eli was just doing a better job of checking down to more sensible targets. Regardless, it was clear something different was going on from the meeting rooms all the way down to the field. It was even more evident the next week, when Eli won his first career playoff game, going 20 of 27 for 185 yards and two touchdowns in a 24–14 win in Tampa Bay over the Buccaneers.

"Except for very few quarterbacks—Tom Brady, Peyton Manning, Donovan McNabb—you can't ask these guys to go out every week and try to win the game," Phil Simms said. "It's too hard mentally. It's too hard physically. There's got to be what I call 'weeks off' where you throw eighteen to twenty times and the game is won because you run the ball, you play really good defense, and it gives you a break mentally a little bit. It sort of lets you catch a second wind or whatever.

"When I watched Eli Manning this year I never got the feeling that he was getting those breaks. Every week was, 'All right Eli, fire one down there, let's make some plays.' And that's tough. You get tired. But the last couple of weeks, it's been tremendous. It's like everything has been very, very coordinated with the team.

"I think we should've seen more games like we've seen the last few weeks, not only from Eli Manning, but maybe from the Giants and the coaching [staff] during the season. It just seems like it's been easier for him. He had some more short throws. There wasn't always time to make a big throw down the field to Plaxico Burress. To me, that's the big thing. Eli Manning took no chances."

That's certainly the way it appeared, but the coaching staff, Eli, and his teammates all pointed to other factors for the "sudden" emergence of the NFL's newest star. One was the weather. The games at Chicago, Philadelphia, and Buffalo as well as the home game against Washington were all played in cold, windy conditions that weren't conducive to throwing the ball. Taking out the

Minnesota game, which was an inexcusable disaster, he hadn't played in a fair-weather game since they beat the Lions in Detroit at Ford Field—a dome. In those perfect conditions, Eli completed 28 of 39 passes for 283 yards and a touchdown in a 16–10 win.

"We hit a stretch of four or five games where we were playing in monsoons," Burress said. "The winds were blowing thirty and forty miles per hour. [Eli] was taking a lot of criticism during that time. But I guess everybody kind of forgot about that. I guess he walked into his room, hit a switch and then four weeks later he was all of a sudden a great quarterback. I think he has really been playing that way all season. But, we weren't able to do it with the weather we were playing in."

Something else happened, too, which indirectly affected the game plan. Eli's teammates, who had been shaky at many times throughout the season, were suddenly stepping up. The Giants led the NFL in dropped passes with forty-two during the season—a completely unexpected and ridiculous number. But all of a sudden the butter-fingered receivers and running backs were holding onto the ball. The offensive line, which struggled in the second half of the season, was suddenly coming together, too. It didn't hurt that Shockey's absence made the sidelines calmer. So while it may have looked like Eli was finally putting all of his pieces together on his own, his teammates and coaches knew the sudden success had something to do with the pieces around him, too.

"You're like most people, you're putting it all on Eli," Palmer said when a reporter asked about Eli's seemingly sudden emergence. "I think it's a situation where we've played better as a group offensively. We've been more consistent as a group. I don't think anyone has picked up on that. I couldn't sit here and say, 'Eli's doing this better or that better,' or 'He's not doing this as good.' I think he's the same guy, but I think we've become more consistent as an offensive group.

"I know this," Palmer added. "If you went back to our first game plan and you went to our last game plan, you'd see a lot of similar plays. You'd see that maybe there's a little tweak here or different formation there. But we're doing the same things. I think that's what good teams do."

That, of course, was what the Giants were starting to become. But for all the praise Eli was getting, it came with a feeling that the compliments were backhanded at best. The credit he was getting was not for leading the Giants to victory or for becoming an elite quarterback. What he was doing so well was simply "managing the game."

That was even true during his first-ever venture into the divisional round of the playoffs, when the Giants went to Dallas on that January day. To win this game, everyone thought, Eli simply needed to avoid the big mistakes and stay out of trouble so the running game and defense could lead the way.

And that's what he did—for the most part.

. . .

DAVID CUTCLIFFE WAS sitting in his office at Duke University, sifting through reports on recruits and preparing for his first season as the Blue Devils' head coach. His mind was on rebuilding a program that had just finished a 1–11 season that, incredibly, was an improvement over the 0–12 mark they had the year before. It was a huge job that demanded his full attention. But he couldn't stop himself from watching what was on his TV.

It was January 13 and Eli Manning, his star pupil from his days as head coach at Ole Miss, was leading the Giants against the Dallas Cowboys in the second round of the playoffs. Cutcliffe had probably seen more of Eli's throws than anyone. He studied his tapes from high school when he recruited him to Ole Miss. He coached him for four years. He even knew the family from his days coaching Peyton when he was the offensive coordinator at Tennessee. In the worst of times for Eli in the NFL, he'd break down the tapes with him—sometimes over the phone, sometimes in person—going over decisions, mechanics, schemes, defenses. Whatever Eli wanted to talk about. Whatever Cutcliffe felt he needed.

So he was watching with the eye of a scout, a coach, an analyst, and a friend and he knew for sure—better than anyone—that there was something different happening. This wasn't the Eli he had seen through most of his four NFL seasons.

It was the Eli he had been waiting to see all along.

"It looks like Eli, finally," Cutcliffe said. "And I'm just tickled to death. I was watching the game and I was just smiling from ear to ear. It just looked exactly like Eli looks.

"And I hadn't seen that in a while."

He had started to look like that three weeks earlier, but now things were really coming together. He had a swagger back that he hadn't really displayed since college. His throws were on target, with pinpoint accuracy. His receivers no longer needed to constantly bail him out. He looked like he knew he could make the throw—any throw. He looked like he wanted the ball in his hands.

"I think what you see is just total command of what he's doing," Cutcliffe said. "That happens at different times for different reasons, but I think it's certainly evident. He's very comfortable in the pocket and he's just got command of what's going on. The anticipation is back like it was. For whatever reason, it's clicking."

Everyone could see that late in the first half. It was 14–7 Cowboys when the Giants got the ball back at their own twenty-nine with just forty-seven seconds remaining. Back in New York, Accorsi had turned off the television—but left the tape running—and went to Mass. He's a superstitious man who believed somehow that good things were going to happen if he wasn't watching. Being in church saying a few prayers couldn't hurt.

During the collection, he snuck a peek at his Blackberry and couldn't believe what he saw: Halftime. Cowboys 14, Giants 14.

What he didn't know was that Eli had just led the Giants down the field almost single-handedly—with an assist from a stupid fifteen-yard facemask penalty on Cowboys cornerback Jacques Reeves. Eli had hit two rookie receivers—Steve Smith and tight end Kevin Boss—with big passes. Then he zipped a four-yard touchdown pass to Toomer with seven seconds to play.

The confidence that gave the Giants going into halftime was immeasurable. The belief and faith in their quarterback could suddenly be felt in the Texas air.

"I tell you what," said Giants co-owner John Mara, "that drive at the end of the second quarter and that drive in the second half, I mean that was all the quarterback."

"In my opinion, he put us in the Super Bowl with forty-six seconds left before halftime of the Dallas game," added Jerry Reese. "In my mind, that was the biggest drive of our season."

Eli would do it again at the end of the third quarter and beginning of the fourth when he rallied the Giants from a 17–14 deficit and led them to Brandon Jacobs's go-ahead touchdown run. When it was over, Eli's numbers weren't overwhelming—12 of 18 for 163 yards and two touchdowns. It was the defense that shut down Tony Romo and Terrell Owens and sealed the game with an end zone interception in the final seconds that got credit for the 21–17 win.

Eli? Great job. Great drive. Way to "manage the game" again.

"You know, they use that term in a derogatory way almost always," Simms said. "It means, 'Well, you asked him to manage the game … not to win it, just not to lose it.' OK, well, now how do you do that? I love that. I always loved that phrase as a quarterback."

Here's the thing about Eli, though. He didn't care.

"I think it's a compliment," Eli said. "As a quarterback, a lot of it is just managing a game, figuring out what kind of game it's got to be, what you have to do to put your team in a situation to win. A lot of it is just finding ways to win. It doesn't always have to be the same way. It's a matter of making the plays when they're there and putting your team in the right situations and the right plays."

Eli was doing that, all right, but there was still a sense of unease outside the Giants' locker room, as if everyone was holding their breath, bracing for the magic bubble to burst. The perfect setting for that was coming up, too, in the NFC championship game. Never mind that the thought of up-and-down Eli leading his team to the Super Bowl so soon seemed so ridiculous. Now, standing in his way, was the great Brett Favre, seemingly in the midst of a Cinderella season, trying to make one last run at a championship at age thirty-eight and, as it turned out, in the last year of his career.

Plus, the Giants were heading to Lambeau Field, where the Packers were nearly unbeatable in the playoffs. Sure, the Giants had won an NFL-record nine straight games away from home, but that bubble was overdue to burst, too. And on top of that, the forecast was calling for temperatures around zero with wind chills surpassing twenty below. Favre had a career record of 43–5 at Lambeau when the temperature was under thirty-four. Meanwhile, the coldest game Eli had ever played kicked off with a temperature of just twenty degrees.

There were some cold facts about Eli in cold weather, too: He got worse as the temperature dropped. His completion percentage in six games with a kickoff temperature under forty degrees was just 48.7. That included four touchdowns and seven interceptions.

When the game arrived—with an unfortunate kickoff time of 5:42 p.m. Central Time on January 20, the conditions were worse than imagined. The Giants prepared for the game by importing brand new heated benches, lining the inside of their helmets with sheepskin, and giving players a gel used by mountain climbers designed to warm up their skin. One big story leading into the game was whether Eli would wear gloves. Eventually, he decided to wear one on his left hand to help him control the ball.

It's amazing that the fingers on his right hand didn't fall off. It was painfully cold at kickoff—an actual temperature of minus-one and a wind chill of minus-twenty-three. Even without the wind, it actually hurt your hands and face to be outside, and when the wind blew it was as if someone was firing tiny ice chips at you out of a gun. If you could manage to take a deep breath, you could actually feel it in your lungs. If you tried to breathe through your nose, you could feel your nose hairs ice up.

Frostbite can occur within minutes in those conditions. It takes a lot less time for discomfort to set in.

But if Eli was ever bothered by the cold, even for a moment, nobody could tell.

"His ability to throw the football in those conditions … as his brother, obviously I'm proud," Peyton said. "But as a quarterback, I just can't tell you how much I appreciate the way he played."

Here's what Eli did in "Ice Bowl II"—the third-coldest game in NFL history, the second-coldest ever at Lambeau, and the coldest in the eighty-three-year history of the Giants: 21 of 40, 254 yards, no interceptions. He even led the Giants to an apparent victory three different times. The first time came with 6:53 left, but kicker Lawrence Tynes missed a forty-three-yard field goal attempt. The second time came with four seconds left, but Tynes missed again—this time from thirty-six—to send the game into overtime.

The third time came in overtime, though it was mostly the doing of Corey Webster—a former second-round pick who had struggled so much at cornerback that he lost his starting job in week two and wasn't even dressed for a couple of games during the regular season. He stepped in front of the final pass of Favre's storied career, picked it off, and set the Giants up at the Packers' thirty-four just fifty-six seconds into overtime. Eli took over, handed the ball off twice, threw an incomplete pass and then left the field for Tynes, who was about to either become one of the Giants' all-time biggest heroes, or a goat who would forever conjure up memories of Trey Junkin and Joe Pisarcik.

Hero, it was. Tynes's kick was long and straight and everyone knew it as soon as he connected. Tynes turned, pumped his right fist in the air and took off through the tunnel. Eli raised his arms and spent the next few minutes hugging everyone that came his way.

. . .

FIVE WEEKS EARLIER, Eli had been booed right out of Giants Stadium by fans who were still angry about his attitude after the Vikings debacle three weeks before that. Now he was on his way to Super Bowl XLII? He had just beaten Favre, a sure-fire Hall of Famer. The Giants had just become the first NFC team in history to reach the Super Bowl by winning three straight on the road. The last two came against Dallas and Green Bay—the two best teams in the NFC, and two teams that beat them way back in weeks one and two.

And Eli had been nothing short of remarkable since that meaningless finale against New England. He had completed 75 of his 117 passes—64.1 percent—for 850 yards, eight touchdowns and—yes, you heard this right—just one interception. None in the postseason.

Who was this guy, and where did he come from?

"He's had big games before where he's made great throws and great decisions, and he's had some inconsistencies, but the thing that always gave us hope is you saw him make plays, you saw there was talent," Mara said. "The question was getting it out of him with a little bit more consistency."

It was coming out consistently, all right. It happened so suddenly, so impressively, that even Peyton was left speechless—sort of.

"It's funny, I left Eli a voicemail after the Packers game," Peyton said. "He called me back and I just kind of told him, 'I think I'm officially retired from giving you advice.' In his fourth year he's led his team to the Super Bowl. He just went on the road in three of the toughest places to play and won and played excellent. He doesn't need to hear any advice from me."

Meanwhile, one of his top advisors was back in Durham, North Carolina, beaming with pride at the amazing run his prized pupil had just pulled off. Cutcliffe had seen it before, but not since January 2, 2004, when Eli was a senior and Ole Miss was taking on Oklahoma State in the Cotton Bowl. Cutcliffe recalled Eli "flat took that game over" completing 22 of 31 passes for 259 yards, throwing for two touchdowns and running for a third as the Rebels won 31–28—their first win in a traditional New Year's Day bowl since Archie Manning led them to a win over Arkansas in the Sugar Bowl in 1970.

What Cutcliffe was seeing in Eli now was "total command of the offense and what's going on." He could see his well-hidden competitive spirit bubbling to the surface. He could see through his stoic demeanor and read the determined look on his face.

Still, it was only a four-game stretch in what at that point was a sixty-two-start career. The undefeated Patriots and Super Bowl XLII still loomed large, as did so many questions. Was this remarkable turnaround real? Was this the real Eli finally taking his place on the stage? Or was it a mirage—fool's gold luring everyone down the path to a crushing disappointment?

"No," Cutcliffe said, without a trace of doubt in his voice. "You're seeing Eli."

Twenty: "We know what it takes to beat them"

THE MIRACLE KICK still seemed like it was in the air, suspended forever in time, sailing between the uprights and over the crossbar, as the celebration took place on the field below. Tynes, fist in the air, ran straight for the tunnel. On the sideline, Coughlin, with a dangerous-looking red face—from the cold, this time, not from anger—managed to avoid a frigid Gatorade shower that probably would have killed him. Everyone else was either on the ground in prayer or disbelief, or running on the field from hug to warm hug.

Meanwhile, 1,900 miles away, oddsmakers, armed with statistics and a knowledge of public perception, were about to establish the Giants as twelve-point underdogs in Super Bowl XLII. Perfect, the Giants thought. That's just what they wanted.

"What's a better feeling than when you can silence the world?" asked Antonio Pierce.

One thing was clear: The world was expecting a Patriots coronation. It was a nice run by the Giants, but the consensus was that it was about to end. The Patriots were an impressive machine, powered by the most prolific offense in NFL history. For the Giants, running through the NFC—clearly the weaker of the two conferences for most of the last decade—was one thing. Beating the 18–0 Patriots, the dynasty of this generation with three titles in the previous six years?

No chance.

After all, hadn't the Giants just lost to New England 38–35 in their season finale? At home? With the Patriots missing two-fifths of their starting offensive line? The Giants' defense had given Tom Brady and the Patriots its best shot that night. They sacked Brady once and hit him eight times and he still managed to throw for 356 yards. The Patriots scored on seven of their nine possessions (not including the two at the end of the two halves where Brady simply took a knee), which means the Giants' defense barely provided the resistance of a speed bump.

Yes, the Giants celebrated that game as a moral victory, and they were celebrated for playing so hard in an otherwise meaningless game. Sure, it was probably the flashpoint that sparked their miraculous postseason run. But here's the part that everyone kept forgetting—the part that only now, with the reality of their Super Bowl opponent staring them in the face, were people starting to remember.

The Giants lost that game.

That made what Eli Manning said after the NFC championship game all the more stunning. It was minutes after Tynes's kick finally came down, and he was standing on the makeshift podium in the loud and crazy visitors' locker room at Lambeau Field, wearing his NFC championship T-shirt and hat, being interviewed by Fox's Terry Bradshaw, a man with four Super Bowl rings of his own.

"Let me ask you quickly," Bradshaw said. "You played against New England in week seventeen of the season. That helps, does it not, in going to the Super Bowl?"

"I think so," Eli answered. "I think that was a big game for us. We came out there, we played them well. We fell at the end, but that got us going. That got us a little momentum. It got us playing pretty good football again.

"And you know, we know what it takes. We know how good they are. But we know what it takes to beat them."

We know what it takes to beat them? Really? Aren't they 18–0?

In fact, nobody had figured out what it took to beat the Patriots since Eli's brother, Peyton, knocked them out in the previous year's AFC championship game. But forget about that bothersome fact for a moment. Was that really Eli Manning—bland, boring, Eli—making a bold statement like that? The kid who never heard a question that he couldn't answer with "I just have to make good decisions"? The kid whose leadership attempts were so out of character, Tiki Barber had labeled them "comical"? The kid who knew more clichés and ways to avoid answering a question than Crash Davis and Nuke Laloosh in *Bull Durham*?

Perhaps that was Eli's way of planting his flag, letting the world—or maybe just his teammates—know that he'd arrived, and he wasn't coming just to be a footnote in "The Tom Brady Story." Maybe it was nothing as contrived as that. Maybe it was just confidence. After all he had shown a confidence on the field in the last month that he never had displayed before.

He was a new man now. He wasn't the monotone kid with the blank face that had frustrated fans and media during the bad times. He was smiling. He looked cocky. He looked brash. He was finally embracing the "We'll show you" mentality that had carried his teammates—particularly the defense—all season long. In that one sentence—*We know what it takes to beat them*—he had finally become the type of brazen quarterback New York could love.

Now all he had to do was back his words up. That was for later, though. First he had two weeks to enjoy his moment in the sun.

That was one of the lessons he learned from watching Peyton one year earlier. His brother—who always seemed to have more fun on the field than Eli did, anyway—seemed to enjoy every second of

Super Bowl XLI. As expected, the star of Madison Avenue was the darling of the national media that had descended upon Miami. Though he was managed well by the controlling public relations staff in Indianapolis, Peyton was an engaging, thoughtful, funny, quotable interviewee whenever he was allowed to speak. He usually was all that, of course, but at the Super Bowl he was even better. He clearly stepped up his game.

Eli's declaration made it clear he'd follow suit, but no one could have guessed how well he'd do. He opened up during the two weeks of hype, told stories about his family that he always seemed reluctant to share before, gave hints about his excitement, refused to hide his confidence. He smiled more readily. He was animated. He had fun in a role where he used to appear entirely uncomfortable.

It's always difficult—and perhaps unfair—to judge these things from the safety of the interview room. But it sure seemed like there was a word to describe what he was finally beginning to display to the public: charisma.

Credit Olivia with an assist on that one. While Peyton was trying to avoid giving his brother advice—instead trying to play the role of ticket broker for the Manning clan—Eli said that when the Giants' charter touched down in Phoenix, he had a text message waiting from his mother.

"She said to smile a lot during this press conference," Eli said a few hours later. "That was her advice."

Apparently he listened, because Mr. Lack of Personality became a charmer when the national media descended. The pained expression usually on his face during press conferences and media sessions had completely disappeared. He seemed relaxed and engaged, even on Media Day, the annual circus that takes place at the Super Bowl stadium on the Tuesday before the game. Each player, coach, and executive is required—some would say forced—to sit there and take questions from the media for a full hour. And in this case, the "media" includes kid reporters, comedians, and even a Brazilian TV reporter dressed (barely) as a bride shouting marriage proposals instead of questions.

Of course, when the actual media was able to cut through the nonsense, the questions were all familiar and, as the hour dragged on, they became repetitive. Given his past history, it figured to be a loathsome setting for Eli.

Instead, he seemed like he was having … fun?

His teammates were having fun, too. A lot of it. Too much, some people thought. While the Patriots went about their business quietly (for the most part) like they had so many times before, the Giants arrived in the Phoenix area like a meteor thundering from the sky. They arrived all dressed in black as a show of team unity. Some players said the fashion statement was designed to show the Giants were all about business this week. Others quietly said the inside joke was that they were dressed for a funeral—a funeral for the Patriots' dynasty.

The truth depended on who you asked, but there seemed to be no doubt the Giants believed the Patriots' dynasty was about to end. Jerry Reese said as much to the *Bergen Record* the previous week when he said, "Absolutely I think we can beat them." The very next day, co-owner Steve Tisch, the Hollywood producer who had already equated the Giants' run to a few of his movies, echoed Reese to the same paper when he promised that at the end of the game, "We'll have more points than they do."

The boast that made the most noise, though, came the Monday before the game, when the Giants were arriving at Giants Stadium to collect their things and board the bus that would take them to Newark Airport for their charter flight to Super Bowl XLII. A *New York Post* reporter asked Plaxico Burress—who had already made some unwanted headlines by saying he believed the Giants' receivers were at least as good as or possibly better than the Patriots' record-setting receiving corps—if he was ready to make history.

"You better believe it," Burress said.

He was then asked for a prediction—a question most players know better than to answer.

Burress said "23–17."

Yikes. Burress appeared to toss out the prediction casually and lightly—he later joked that he picked the numbers because 23 was his high school basketball number and 17 was the number he wore with the Giants. But he couldn't have been surprised when his picture appeared on the back page of the *Post* on Tuesday morning, hovering over a crystal ball with 23–17 inside. Even if he was, he certainly wasn't about to back down. Given dozens of chances to take it back—or even soften it—over the next few days, Burress refused. His teammates, while not as boastful, supported his words, too.

Meanwhile, Coughlin seethed. This was not his style. John Mara was clearly uncomfortable, too. "I'd like to keep it as quiet as possible," Mara said.

Too late. The gauntlet had been thrown … right into Eli's lap

But it didn't seem to affect the unflappable quarterback at all. In fact, he appeared for the first time to welcome the attention, the pressure, the comparisons to his brother, the questions—all those things that had haunted him for four years.

"After the NFC championship I said to Tom Coughlin, 'All that crap that Eli takes about his personality and his demeanor? All I'm telling you is that what he's about to go through for the next two weeks, his personality is never ever going to serve him better than it is right now,'" Pat Hanlon said. "Because there's a lot of bullshit that goes along with the Super Bowl. Thank goodness we've got a guy who runs our offense who's unfazed by this stuff."

Of course, seeing how unfazed and seemingly comfortable Eli was only invited more over-analysis. Was it just his true personality shining through? Was it a symbol of his newfound confidence? Or was it the kind of cat-got-your-tongue look some of the Giants had on their faces before the NFC championship game back in 2000 when, after a week of watching film they were convinced—absolutely convinced—that they were going to hammer the Minnesota Vikings, who had a dangerous and prolific offense of their own.

Of course, the Giants ended up winning that game 41–0—a result that shocked the world.

Was Eli expecting to shock the world, too?

. . .

THE GIANTS WERE an oddly relaxed team as the game got closer, considering how tightly wound their head coach usually was and the fact that most people thought they were just tilting at windmills. Maybe that was it, after all. Tisch thought the pressure of being 18–0 got to the Patriots. And the fact that no one gave the Giants a chance somehow liberated his team.

Behind the scenes, though, there was some real concern. Burress was already hobbling around on his sprained ankle, but early in the week at the team hotel he slipped in the shower and sprained the MCL in his left knee. The Giants didn't reveal the knee injury until later in the week and downplayed it when they finally made it public. But for a while, while they were holding out hope, they weren't really sure if he was going to be able to play.

"Oh, he was hurt. Big-time hurt," Gilbride said. "He almost didn't play. Oh God, we couldn't believe it. I said, 'You've got to be kidding.' He was finally starting to practice once a week, now all of a sudden he can't practice again, and he may not even play and it's not even his ankle? I said, 'Oh my God, we can't catch a break for anything.'"

Every time Gilbride asked Coughlin or the trainers, he got an uncertain answer about Burress's status. Every time he asked Burress, though, the receiver said, "Yeah, I'll play." Eli believed him, too. Besides, the quarterback was used to not seeing his best receiver on the practice field during the week. "We thought, 'We've gone through it before. He'll be there Sunday and make the plays he needs to make,'" Eli said. "He wasn't going to miss that game."

Despite that looming crisis, though, the mood was light when Coughlin opened his Saturday night meeting with a short highlight video of the Giants' postseason run. He left the motivational pep talk up to Lieutenant Colonel Greg Gadson, a veteran of the war in Iraq who had lost both his legs in an explosion. Gadson, a friend and former West Point teammate of receivers coach Mike Sullivan, first addressed the Giants back in week three, before their season-saving come-from-behind win and goal-line stand in Washington. He was back again, speaking to individual players and sitting on the sidelines, once the playoff run began.

When he was done with his talk about pride, poise, and team, Coughlin took the stage with a smile on his face and told his team that he sincerely hoped they were enjoying every moment of their wild playoff ride. He reflected—something he rarely does—on his memories of winning Super Bowl XXV with the Giants when he was an assistant coach. He told them how much he wanted them and their families to share that kind of joy—how he felt they deserved to experience it all.

It wasn't exactly General Patton addressing the troops or even Vince Lombardi giving a pep talk to the Packers, but it was a speech that pushed all the right buttons. The players left the meeting feeling good, feeling confident, and feeling more determined than ever.

That was obvious once the game began. So was their strategy, which appeared to be a carbon copy of the Bill Parcells–Bill Belichick master game plan from Super Bowl XXV, when they took the air out of the football and slowed down the prolific offense of the Buffalo Bills. Eli wasn't going to be asked to win this game on his own. He was going to manage it, slow it down, play conservative and mistake-free football, all while letting the Giants' devastating pass rush seize the day.

And he did. On the opening drive of the game, Eli methodically led the Giants on a sixteen-play, sixty-three-yard march that consumed 9:59 off the clock—the most time-consuming drive in Super Bowl history. He completed five of his seven passes, but for only thirty-eight yards. It was enough to put the Giants in range for Tynes to kick a thirty-two-yard field goal so the Giants could take a 3–0 lead.

After the Patriots answered with a touchdown, Eli had the Giants in scoring position again before making a mistake that brought up all sorts of bad memories. From the Patriots' fourteen on third-and-five, he threw a slightly off-target pass towards receiver Steve Smith, but it bounced off the rookie's hands and was picked off by Ellis Hobbs. It was the first interception thrown by Eli since the one to Hobbs in the regular-season finale. It was either just the end of a very impressive streak, or a sign that Eli's anticipated unraveling had begun.

Thankfully for Eli, the Giants' defense was just getting warmed up. They made it clear from the start they were going to make it difficult—if not impossible—for Brady to breathe. They were relentless in their pressure, coming from all angles. By the end of the first half Brady had already been sacked three times. After allowing that touchdown on the Patriots' first drive, the Giants had allowed only three first downs. And they ended the first half in style when defensive end Justin Tuck hammered Brady near midfield and forced a fumble that Osi Umenyiora recovered.

Eli was only 8 for 16 and had thrown for 85 yards at that point and the Giants were trailing 7–3, but it was considered a mission accomplished. The Giants were controlling the tempo. Eli was managing the game, as ordered, and staying equal with Brady (8 for 14, 82 yards). They stuck right to that script through a scoreless third quarter, too. And as the fourth quarter began, it was the lowest-scoring Super Bowl since the Steelers carried a 9–0 lead over the Vikings into the fourth quarter of Super Bowl IX.

But Eli was just getting warmed up. On the first offensive play of the fourth quarter, he brought some life to the Super Bowl with a forty-five-yard pass over the middle to rookie tight end Kevin Boss. He tacked on a seventeen-yard pass to Smith later in the drive, setting up a five-yard touchdown pass to David Tyree. All of a sudden, the impossible dream was a little closer to reality. The Giants were up 10–7 with 11:05 left in the game.

Eli had a chance to put it all away on the next drive, too, after the Giants' defense stopped the Patriots' record-setting offense for the sixth consecutive drive. The Giants were at their own thirty with 8:32 remaining when Eli scrambled out of trouble and suckered Hobbs—who was covering Burress—into thinking he was going to run. As Hobbs ran towards Eli, Burress was wide open at the Giants' forty-five with a clear path for at least another ten yards. But Burress hesitated and Eli, in an attempt to hit his receiver in stride, overthrew his 6-foot-5 target by what might as well have been a mile.

Up in the stands, a nervous Accorsi had spent much of the game bouncing between his seat and the spacious concourse inside University of Phoenix Stadium. But there was no peace in the back because too many people recognized him and wanted to chat. At his seat, though, there was no peace of mind.

Regardless, there was no way he was going to miss the fourth quarter, so he was sitting in his seat watching in horror as Eli's pass sailed high over Burress's head. And as if Accorsi didn't feel responsible enough for every mistake Eli ever made for the Giants, a fan sitting a few rows in front of him turned around and glared.

"Your quarterback just cost us the world championship," he said.

The disgruntled fan sounded like a prophet a few minutes later when Brady did exactly what Brady was expected to do. He got the ball back on the Patriots' twenty with 7:54 to play and took the 18–0 Pats on a march for the ages. Twelve plays, eighty yards in 5:12. Brady went 8 for 11 along the way, accounting for all but nine of the yards. On the final play, he found his number one receiver, Randy Moss, open in the end zone because Giants cornerback Corey Webster had fallen. The six-yard touchdown had given the Patriots a 14–10 lead with 2:42 to play.

And that was it. The storybook was ending the way everybody expected the Super Bowl to end. Brady, this generation's Montana, would win a Super Bowl the way Montana did nineteen years earlier, with a touchdown in the closing minutes. The Giants would get some much-deserved praise for a job done much better than anyone had expected and for fighting hard throughout an impossible uphill climb. They just ran into the perfect team, people would say. Nothing to be ashamed of. In any other year, the solid game plan and stellar performance from their defense would've been enough. But not this year. Not against the perfect Patriots and the greatest coach and quarterback of their generation.

It was so over, in fact, that the sixteen members of the media who were voting for the MVP began turning in their ballots (they start collecting them with five minutes to play, but voters can hold on to them as long as they like). Patriots receiver Wes Welker, with his

Super Bowl–record tying eleven catches for 103 yards, was going to be the winner. That last drive helped him steal the award from Tuck, who with two of the Giants' five sacks and two of their nine hits on the battered Brady was the most destructive member of a defense that had controlled the play all game long.

Eli, at the moment the Giants got the ball back on their own seventeen trailing 14–10 with 2:39 to play, was only 14 for 25 for 178 yards, one touchdown, and one interception. It was hardly a performance worth getting excited about.

It was hardly a sign of what was still to come.

Twenty-One: "He's got to do it now"

IT REALLY DID look like it was over. The Giants' whole magical, unexpected run was wonderful, but it was finished. Brady and Moss had their Disneyworld moment and there seemed to be no way that wouldn't be the story of Super Bowl XLII. The Patriots had their storybook finish and their perfect season. The Giants had their pride.

Sure, they had more than two and a half minutes remaining, but they had scored only ten points in the previous fifty-seven and a half minutes. Destiny seemed to take control of the Super Bowl, and it clearly didn't belong to them. They had spent nearly an hour trying to dismantle a dynasty and couldn't do it.

How were they supposed to do it now with just 159 seconds left?

Up in the stands, Accorsi had finished his nervous pacing in the concourse and had nestled back into his sideline seat next to his three children. A noted historian of the game, he recognized a moment when he saw one, and he knew this was the moment he had been waiting for all his life. He had just watched Brady pull an Elway on his team—and despite his retirement, the Giants were still mostly Accorsi's team. Only this time, Brady did what Elway never did.

He left time on the clock.

A lot of time, Accorsi thought. Maybe a lot. Well, probably not enough. His heart kept telling him that Eli had a chance to do it, even though he wasn't brimming with confidence. He wanted to believe but he didn't want to be cocky. Mostly he just sat there in his seat, trying to concentrate through the tears building in his eyes. His quarterback—his legacy—had to drive his team eighty-three yards in 2:39. Two whole minutes and thirty-nine seconds.

A lifetime in so many ways.

The commercial break seemed to last forever before Eli came jogging out onto the field with the same blank expression he had carried during every one of his previous NFL games. Calm. Deep thought. Whatever it was, even in the biggest moment of his football life, the look on his face hadn't changed.

Accorsi wasn't as calm. Everything he ever believed about the young quarterback he spent so many years trying to find was about to collide in one spectacular moment. For better or for worse. Accorsi described his feelings as "numb." The only specific moment he could remember, right before the drive began, was what he said to his son.

"You know what?" Accorsi said to Michael. "If he's what we thought he was going to be, he's got to do it now."

If? That might have been the first time Accorsi had ever used the word "if" when referring to Eli. The kid had already led the Giants back from fourth-quarter deficits nine times in his short career, including five times in the 2007 season, and once (in Dallas) during this remarkable playoff run. Accorsi had seen him do it before and wanted to believe he could do it again. But how could anyone be sure? All the scouting, all the coaching, all the preparation and study … and still there's no way to know how a quarterback is going to respond in a last-gasp, championship-on-the-line, ball-in-your-hands moment like this.

Of course, Accorsi had good reason to be bracing for another disappointment, since he had plenty of them churning in the back of his mind. There was the horrible day Elway was traded. Then there was the way Elway haunted Accorsi for years. There was the 1986 AFC championship game, when his Browns had a 20–13 lead with 5:32 remaining and pinned Elway and the Broncos back on their own two, only to watch Elway pull off a five-minute, ninety-eight-yard miracle that would forever be known as "The Drive." That tied the game and let the Broncos win it overtime, driving a stake through Accorsi's heart. Elway did it to him in the 1987 AFC championship game, too, when he spoiled Bernie Kosar's 356-yard day by leading Denver to the winning touchdown with 4:01 remaining—a loss cemented by an Earnest Byner fumble on the goal line. Two years later, Elway threw for an amazing 385 yards, stopping Accorsi one game short of the Super Bowl for the third time in four years. And when Accorsi finally did reach the Super Bowl in the 2000 season, he watched his quarterback—Kerry Collins—fall apart and lose to, of all people, Trent Dilfer.

Hadn't he been through enough?

• • •

How DID ELI respond to the moment? If you believe what he said after the game, he responded like he was playing in the backyard with his brothers and friends, back when they were just kids imagining they were in the Super Bowl. The funny thing was that Peyton and Eli had talked about being in this exact situation. They had discussed it earlier in the 2007 season, in fact. If you're going to have to rally, they said, it's better to be down by four points, when a field goal just won't do. The quarterback should have to win the game with a touchdown. It's all supposed to come down to him.

"What situation would you want to be in?" Eli said. "If you're down three, you might just settle for a field goal. You're better off down by four where you have to score to win the Super Bowl."

Happy hindsight? Perhaps. But according to his teammates, when he jogged out onto the field with a nervous Accorsi and Giants fan base watching, he got to the huddle and calmly said, "Let's go win this thing. Who's with me?" A corny moment, perhaps, but it got his teammates' attention. They could see the calm confidence in his eyes.

Meanwhile, back on the sidelines, Michael Strahan took one look at the long faces of a defense that had battered Brady and the Patriots all game long—but one that was poised to become just another one of their victims—and decided he needed to inject some confidence and some life.

So he began pacing up the sidelines, forcing his sullen teammates to look him in the eye and repeat after him. "The final score will be 17–14. Say it! … Say it!" He had imparted the same message to the offense moments earlier, as they waited on the sidelines for their final chance. He told them, "17–14 is the final, OK? 17–14, fellas. One touchdown, we are world champions. Believe it and it will happen."

"I kept telling them, 'Repeat it,'" Strahan said. "I was walking up the sidelines saying 'You say it. Repeat it. You have to believe it.'"

One by one they said it. One by one they tried to believe it. Maybe some of them even did. After all, the Giants were never supposed to get this far. They were supposed to be finished in Dallas. They nearly were finished in Green Bay. Both games finished with incredible plays by the defense, with a huge assist in frigid Green

Bay from the special teams. The miracles had been coming fast and furious for most of the last month.

Maybe, they thought, it was Eli's turn.

. . .

THE DRIVE STARTED slow, with a little hint of the greatness that was coming. A methodical march deep into enemy territory wouldn't be enough. Maybe this was the way Eli wanted it, but the task was enormous. It was end zone or bust. So far, in the game, they had only been there once.

Yet off the Giants went, starting with a non-descript, eleven-yard pass to Amani Toomer, which for a moment looked like it would be the only good thing that would happen to the Giants on that drive. Forty seconds later, on a third-and-ten, Eli connected with Toomer about a foot short of the first-down marker, bringing up a do-or-die fourth and one with just ninety-four seconds left on the clock.

Brandon Jacobs powered through the line of scrimmage on the next play and was so close to falling short that the Patriots began signaling that they had stopped the Giants and won the game. Fortunately for the Giants, the Patriots were wrong, which was only the first of many bits of good fortune the Giants were about to have. On the next play, a first down from their own thirty-nine, Eli was flushed out of the pocket by New England linebacker Adalius Thomas, who blew right by left tackle David Diehl. Eli took off for a five-yard gain, but when Thomas caught him from behind he knocked the ball right out of the quarterback's hands.

Eli kept control of the loose ball with his legs—though it seemed pretty clear from the replays that his knees were down before the ball popped out, so it never would have been ruled a fumble.

For the moment, it simply was a symbol of what looked to be a chaotic Giants' attack that was flirting with disaster and certainly didn't seem capable of putting together a game-winning drive.

More evidence of that was coming. On the next play, second-and-five from the Giants' forty-four, Eli, out of the shotgun, threw about twenty yards down the right sideline in the direction of Tyree. But Tyree inexplicably cut back up field, leaving Patriots cornerback Asante Samuel alone with the pass coming right toward him.

Samuel jumped. The ball was right there in his hands. Then it bounced off his fingertips and harmlessly away.

Samuel called it "the play that easily could've ended the game." Toomer said, "As soon as Asante dropped that pick, I was like, 'You know what? We have a shot.'"

Maybe he knew it, but few others did. Eli was uncharacteristically steaming after that play. Cameras caught him screaming and shaking his head in the direction of Tyree—a special teams star who had only caught seven passes all season long before this drive. It was now third-and-five. There were only seventy-five seconds left. The Giants were still fifty-six yards from the end zone and a field goal just wouldn't do.

Then it happened.

• • •

EVERY GREAT ATHLETE has a defining moment in his career—a game, a drive, a play that they're associated with forever. Sometimes it takes years to determine which moment can stand the test of time.

Sometimes it's obvious right away.

So there's Eli Manning, two plays removed from a near fumble and one play removed from what should have been a championship-clinching interception. It's third down, time is running out, and any bad play—a sack, a dropped pass, an interception, a fumble—probably means the Patriots will be the Super Bowl champs.

Eli was back in the shotgun again because the Patriots rush was getting through way too much, especially from his left. The Patriots seemed to be focused on downfield coverage and they rushed only four men, but it took no time for three of them to invade Eli's space. First it was Thomas, who blew by Diehl again and swatted at Eli with his right hand. Then Richard Seymour and Jarvis Green came up the middle, each getting hold of Eli's jersey and slightly pulling him back.

"You look at it and kind of wonder how close the refs were to blowing the whistle and stopping the play," Eli said a few weeks later.

How close? Close. Very, very close. So close, in fact, that referee Mike Carey, working his first Super Bowl, had his whistle ready as he sprinted closer to the play to get a better look. "My radar was definitely up," Carey said, and he prepared to blow the play dead because he was sure the Patriots were, at the very least, about to have Eli "in the grasp." In fact, he was sure that moment was "imminent."

Carey had a better view of what happened next than anyone in the entire world. He was five yards behind Eli, with his eyes trained solely on him. And still, Carey couldn't believe what he saw.

"It was like a scene out of *Planet Earth* or *National Geographic*, where it's a lion jumping on the back of a wild horse," Carey said. "You could see him just desperately trying to pull out and somehow he did. Usually a quarterback goes straight ahead when that happens and just tries to get yardage. For some reason he turned around and ran back deeper in the pocket. Lucky for him that he did. He had a little safe haven."

"I saw Eli break a tackle," added center Shaun O'Hara. "I don't think he's ever done that before in his life."

Eli first pushed forward and amazingly escaped the grasp of Seymour—who appeared to have his arms around the quarterback before he was yanked away by his neck by O'Hara—and Green, who grabbed Eli's shoulder pads with his left hand and leaped onto his back and hit him in the head with his right. Eli then stumbled back in the direction of Carey and found some open space back at the thirty-three. Three more Patriots were still coming at him, yet he had the calmness and the presence of mind to set his feet, square his shoulders, and throw.

Up in the coach's booth, Chris Palmer wasn't surprised. He would recall, the next day, those long, hard days under the hot sun in Albany when he ran the quarterbacks through some goofy little drills. He recalled a drill where one quarterback would hold the ball and another would hold him from behind, "and they'd fool around and try to pull the ball out of each other's hands."

Eli's partner in the drill almost every time was backup quarterback Jared Lorenzen, who at nearly 300 pounds was pretty comparable in size to—though likely not as strong as—Thomas (270), Seymour (310), and Green (285). If nothing else, Eli had experience pulling away when a whole lot of dead weight was trying to anchor him down.

Palmer also recalled another, more famous drill that had delighted the crowds at the University at Albany—the one where his quarterbacks spun around some obstacles and then tossed at a target twenty yards away.

"I think ownership looked over at me when we were throwing at the dots and spinning around and thought, 'What the freak is this guy doing?'" Palmer said.

The object of the drill was to bring order to chaos, to teach the quarterbacks how to quickly refocus on a target even when they're dizzy and not sure what direction they're facing. And boy, did that pay off. Eli, in the space of about one second had to regain his composure and spot Tyree, who had settled in position thirty-two yards down the field.

"People have asked me, how did I get out of that jam I was in?" Eli said. "I really don't know. They just never pulled me down."

· · ·

THE DEBATE WILL probably last forever: Which was more amazing? The escape or the catch? One doesn't exist without the other. If neither had happened, the Giants wouldn't have been Super Bowl champs.

The pass had a little wobble to it and didn't exactly hit Tyree in stride. The play—"Phantom" was what the Giants called it—broke down almost immediately. Tyree was supposed to run a post and turn inside, but he was forced to break off his route because of the pressure Eli was under. By the time Eli let the pass go, Tyree looked like he was playing center field. He saw Eli in trouble and thought, "Oh, no." So he cut off his route, tried to follow his quarterback and settle into some open space so he'd have a place to throw the ball.

Once Eli threw it, Tyree watched the flight of the ball, settled himself in its path, and began to size it up like he was Mickey Mantle backing toward the outfield wall. He began calmly inching toward his right, getting ready to time his jump. Of course, it wasn't a wall he was about to hit, it was Patriots safety Rodney Harrison, who was coming from Tyree's right and timing his jump, too. Harrison—with a well-earned reputation for being one of the dirtiest players in the NFL—attacked Tyree with a tomahawk chop with his right hand that hit the ball, Tyree's left hand, right arm, and right shoulder all in one ferocious smack. When Tyree's left hand was knocked off the ball, the ball began to sneak out, but his right hand managed to pin the ball against his helmet. He got his left hand back on the ball as he fell backwards, being bent awkwardly over Harrison's knee. He held on and held it off the ground, even as Harrison tried to wrestle it away.

It was a play that Strahan later said "took a few years off my life." It shocked his fellow receivers, too, because two days earlier in practice Tyree was dropping every pass that Eli sent his way. It was the biggest catch of the game. Some would later call it the biggest, best, and most important play in Super Bowl history.

For Tyree, it was only his eighth catch of the entire year. He called the experience "supernatural." Teammate Barry Cofield, a defensive tackle who had a great view of it from the sidelines, called it "the greatest play I've ever seen."

"Some things just don't make sense," Tyree said. "I guess you could put that catch up there with those."

"You know what? I really never, ever get cocky," Accorsi said. "George Young taught me that. But when he flushed out of there—and I still don't know how he got out of there—I thought, 'They're not stopping us now.'"

No, they weren't. The Giants were twenty-four yards away from the biggest upset since Super Bowl III and they had momentum, confidence, and still fifty-nine seconds to play with. Plays like that don't usually happen in losing efforts. The Giants knew it. Surely the Patriots knew it, too.

Of course, they still had to score to win, and the Patriots weren't quite ready to give up on their perfect season that easily. On the next play, from the New England twenty-four, Eli was pressured again—the fourth straight play the pass rush got through. And this time there was no escape and Thomas blew by Diehl again and sacked Eli for a loss of a yard. He threw an incomplete pass in Tyree's direction on the next play, setting up a third-and-eleven from the Patriots' twenty-five.

Then the magic returned. Eli found Steve Smith on the sidelines—the same rookie receiver who had deflected a pass into the waiting arms of Hobbs back in the second quarter. This time Smith caught the pass at the eighteen and even managed to scamper up the sidelines, all the way to the thirteen for a huge first down before he was hammered out of bounds.

Then came the play the Giants had been waiting for the entire night.

• • •

IN THE GIANTS' loss to the Patriots in the regular-season finale, Gilbride kept calling for a pass to Burress, where the receiver would cut inside and should have been wide open when the Patriots were in man-to-man coverage. But every time he called it, Hobbs was there to defend it. It was driving Gilbride crazy and he couldn't figure out what was happening until he looked at the film.

"When I looked, I said, 'That son of a bitch. He's cheating,'" Gilbride recalled. Hobbs was turning his shoulders and leaning towards the inside so he was ready when Burress cut in. Gilbride went back and looked at the other Patriots' games from the 2007 season and damned if Hobbs didn't do that every single time.

"He was guessing," Gilbride said. "If it was a slant, he was going to make a play, but if it was a fade he was dead."

So Gilbride made an easy adjustment to the play. He told Eli and Burress that if he called the same play during the Super Bowl, Burress would fake to the inside and then cut to a fade toward the corner of the end zone. There would be no change in formation or change of signals, so the Patriots would think they knew what was coming. And if the Patriots blitzed in a situation like that and left Hobbs alone on Burress, the quarterback and the receiver would know what to do.

Gilbride actually called it on each of the final three plays of the game, but on the first two the Patriots didn't blitz, so Eli checked down to one of his other receivers. But with thirty-nine seconds left, with the Giants on the thirteen-yard line, the Patriots made a tactical mistake that few observers could believe. They called for what the Giants termed "a blitz zero," sending just about every available defender at the quarterback. Gilbride had already called for Jacobs to stay in and help protect because Diehl was getting abused by Thomas. So Eli would be safe, and now Hobbs would be alone on Burress, undoubtedly expecting the receiver to cut inside.

All it took at the line of scrimmage was one look from Eli in Burress's direction and both of them knew what was coming next. Eli took the snap, skipped back two steps, and floated a ball towards the corner of the end zone, where Burress had completely fooled Hobbs with his fake cut to the inside and managed to get open by five yards.

It seemed so fitting, completing the Super Bowl–winning touchdown pass to his number one receiver, one of Eli's biggest supporters, and of course the man who had guaranteed victory earlier in the week. It would go down in the books as a thirteen-yard touchdown that made the score 17–14.

Amazingly, it was only Burress's second catch of the night.

Of course, there were still thirty-five nail-biting seconds left on the clock, and all the Patriots needed was a field goal to tie. When Brady finally got the ball back after the kickoff there were twenty-nine seconds left—"an eternity" is how Troy Aikman described it on the Fox broadcast. The Pats were at their own twenty-six, a mere forty yards from the outer edge of placekicker Stephen Gostkowski's field goal range.

"If we had thirty-five seconds I'd think we had no shot," Accorsi said. "If they had thirty-five seconds, I'd think we had no shot to stop them. Boy, that first pass, when I saw that ball go sixty-five yards in the air with Moss running down there? They only needed a field goal to tie. If he catches that, it's tied."

Actually, the first pass was way, way off, landing somewhere in the no man's land between receivers Wes Welker and Jabar Gaffney. The closest man to it was Giants rookie corner Aaron Ross, but the ball was just out of his reach.

You think the Giants were a little bit nervous, though? Even after that horrible Brady pass, Fox cameras caught John Mara nervously fidgeting in the owners' box, his right hand reached across his chest, apparently searching for something in his left shirt pocket.

"Yeah, I had this little medal that this nun sent me," Mara said. "She used to be our grade school principal in Rye [New York] and she moved down to New Orleans. She sent me a great letter with this little medal of the Blessed Virgin. She said, 'I guarantee you that this will bring you luck.'"

Luck? You're supposed to make your own luck, and Mara's Giants were doing just that. On second down, rookie Jay Alford—a bit player whose biggest job this season had been long-snapping on field goals—blew by guard Russ Hochstein, who was filling in for injured starter Stephen Neal, and laid a vicious sack on Brady way back at the sixteen. It was the Giants' fifth sack of the game, maybe their most ferocious, and one final symbol of the pass rush that had battered Brady all game long.

Now it was third and twenty. Brady rolled out, set himself up at the thirteen and uncorked a brilliant, near-perfect pass that traveled an amazing sixty-seven yards in the air. It was going to land right in the hands of Moss, too, before Corey Webster—the same Corey Webster who surrendered the would-be game-winning touchdown catch to Moss one drive earlier—knocked it away with the tips of the fingers on his left hand.

One last play and the result was the same: another Hail Mary by Brady that was a little too deep for Moss and was knocked away by safety Gibril Wilson. And that was it. Game over. Dynasty over. Eli and the Giants had done what so few ever imagined they could do.

For a moment there was chaos. Coughlin was drenched from his Gatorade shower, and Bill Belichick jogged across the field to offer his congratulations. Then the Patriots coach took off for the locker room even though there was still one second left on the clock. Fans were celebrating. Players were celebrating. The field was a sea of people with referees and security guards trying to clear them as fast as they could.

Meanwhile, there was Eli on the field, too, calm and cool as ever, conducting business as usual, trying to get everyone off the field and his teammates into a huddle so he could call one last play.

If he smiled before the final gun, the cameras didn't catch it, even as his teammates were donning their championship shirts and hats on the sideline. He called the play, took the snap, took a knee, and—exactly three years, nine months, and ten days after his rights were traded to the New York Giants—the newly crowned Super Bowl champion turned and walked away from the line of scrimmage with his right hand pumping the football in the air.

. . .

A FEW MINUTES later, standing on top of a podium in the middle of the field with confetti swirling all around him, Mara—with the medallion of the Blessed Virgin still in his pocket—called what he just saw, "The greatest victory in the history of this franchise, without question."

For an eighty-three-year-old franchise that already had two Super Bowl trophies on display in its lobby—plus four NFL titles between 1927 and 1956—the statement was shocking and bold.

"I was thinking about that afterwards," Mara said, "wondering whether my emotions got the best of me at the time. But when you think about it, the '86 one was big because it was our first one. But there were so many unique circumstances this year. And look at who we beat: A team everybody thought was going 19–0 and was going to be called the greatest team of all time. And to come from where we came from. I just can't imagine any win in our history being bigger than that."

The Giants had certainly come out of nowhere, but no one had made a bigger climb than the man who was named the Super Bowl MVP—putting his name down in history with the likes of Brady, Elway, Montana, Simms, Bradshaw, and of course his older brother Peyton. Just ten weeks after being dubbed Eli the Terrible in big, bold, back-page type, he became only the second quarterback in Super Bowl history to throw two fourth-quarter touchdown passes, joining Montana, who did it in Super Bowl XXIII. That was the year Montana knocked off the Cincinnati Bengals with a ten-yard touchdown pass to John Taylor with thirty-four seconds left. Eli Manning and Joe Montana—the only two quarterbacks in forty-two years of Super Bowls to win it with a touchdown in the final minute of the game.

"The way he handled himself in that two-minute drill at the end, that's what it's all about," said Peyton, who had been caught on camera so many times screaming and pumping his fist up in his luxury box that he said he had "tons" of messages on his voicemail from friends telling him to calm down. It's a good bet that during that final drive he was far more nervous than his little brother, too. "I promise you he was just as calm in that two-minute drill as he was in week four in the first quarter," Peyton said. "That's the best characteristic he has and it's a great trait in quarterbacks."

Imagine that. That calmness, that blank expression, that unbothered demeanor that had ruffled so many feathers in New York for so many years, turned out to be exactly what was needed. And the city that wanted to disown him was suddenly, unconditionally, and perhaps even irrevocably in love.

"He's not Peyton Manning's little brother," Strahan said. "He's not Eli who slumps. None of that. Eli Manning is the world champion. I hope everybody remembers that, respects that, and understands that, because this team goes nowhere without him. Eli Manning has taken us to the Super Bowl and Eli Manning has won it for us."

When he did, there was a brief and unwanted moment of redemption up in the stands, where tears were now dripping all over Accorsi's face. That disgruntled fan who just a few minutes earlier had stared down Accorsi and angrily told him, "Your quarterback just cost us the world championship" was now climbing over the seats, heading in Accorsi's direction.

"When the game was over," Accorsi said, "he tried to kiss me on the lips."

Twenty-Two: "Winning a championship is bigger than that"

THE SUPER BOWL had been over for a month, now, and Accorsi was well into his annual spring training tour. In the hotel after the game he had run into Yankees general manager Brian Cashman and told him, "You know what? Now that this happened, I'm going to concentrate on the Yankees pitching staff." He wasn't kidding, either. He had nothing to worry about in football anymore. The last thread in the tapestry of his career had finally been woven into place. The ghost of Elway had been scared away. His legacy was secured.

Of course, there are always doubters, and there probably always will be when it comes to Eli Manning. "Listen," John Mara said. "If he comes out and throws three picks in his first game next year, he'll get booed. That's just the way it is around here." It's like that everywhere, it seemed, with Eli. Nothing would ever be enough.

Accorsi learned that one night in West Palm Beach, Florida when he sat down for dinner in a private room at Ruth's Chris Steak House with his good friend, PGA golfer Billy Andrade, and St. Louis Cardinals manager Tony La Russa. Andrade, a Patriots fan who grew up in Rhode Island, was Accorsi's guest in the stands at Super Bowl XLII. La Russa knew a few things about championships, having won two World Series titles of his own.

"You know," La Russa said to Accorsi that night, "if Eli doesn't win another title he's just going to be forgotten."

"No he won't," Accorsi countered. "Because Namath wasn't."

"In perspective, this was almost as historic as Super Bowl III," Accorsi said. "Against the Patriots' undefeated season, the way he did it. I said, 'You know, in all fairness, there are pure football people who have ultimate respect for Namath, and his field generalship was very important in that game. But he didn't take the team down the field with 2:39 to go like Eli did. Super Bowl III was won by Matt Snell and Emerson Boozer and Weeb Ewbank and their defense and a lot of other things. I don't think Namath threw a pass over twelve yards.'"

"So I said to La Russa, 'OK, I'm going to make a statement right now. You're probably going to make me sign it on a napkin. I won't be surprised if Eli wins more championships than his brother.'"

Accorsi did put that guarantee in writing, right there on a napkin, and he handed it over to La Russa. Once again, his name and reputation were staked on the shoulders of the young quarterback he had searched for all his life. And it was more than a moment of bravado. One month later, sitting at a restaurant on the east side of Manhattan, Accorsi was willing to guarantee it again.

"I'm not so sure he won't win more championships than Peyton," Accorsi said. "First of all, he's younger. And we may have the better team over the next ten years. So I think he will."

• • •

THERE WERE FOUR words that everybody kept waiting to hear from Eli Manning in the minutes, hours, days, weeks and months after his greatest triumph. But no matter how many times the question was asked, and no matter how tempted he might have been, he never once looked at the fans that booed him or the media that questioned him and said, "I told you so."

Well, maybe once. Sort of. It was two days after the Super Bowl and he had just taken a ride on a float next to Coughlin and Strahan down the Canyon of Heroes, holding the Vince Lombardi Trophy and waving to a crowd of a million people. It was the 177th ticker tape parade in New York history and the first ever for the Giants. This kid that New York seemed to take some perverse pleasure in bashing was now literally following in the footsteps of John Glenn, Neil Armstrong, Dwight Eisenhower, Harry Truman, John F. Kennedy, and Charles Lindbergh, along with kings, queens, countless Olympic athletes, soldiers, eight great Yankees teams, world leaders, and popes.

After that ride the team returned to Giants Stadium for the second part of their celebration in front of another 20,000 or so delirious fans. They were chanting "M-V-P" in Eli's direction, so his coaches and teammates encouraged him to step up to the microphone and say a few words.

"I know I speak for all of the Giants," Eli said, "when I say it's finally good to hear some cheers at Giants Stadium."

And there it was. Sort of. There was the one little "gotcha" moment he was willing to allow, the one hint that he might really be thinking, "I told you so." It was the only hint anyone was ever going to get that Eli had heard every discouraging word and was reveling in the way he proved everybody wrong.

Of course, he denied that was ever the case.

"That was just because we hadn't won at home much during the season," Eli said. "We heard some boos and had a bad home record. It was nice to get that winning feeling at home for a change."

He would hear plenty of cheers in the months after Super Bowl XLII, where fans who once booed him now bought him dinner and drinks and gave him a standing ovation whenever he walked into a room. His life had become a whirlwind of non-football activity, too. He had appearances to make, clothing stores to open, and products to endorse. He was approached about possibly becoming an underwear model. Publishers offered him book deals. He filmed a clip for a charity episode of *American Idol*. There was the traditional Disneyland parade for the Super Bowl MVP down Main Street, U.S.A. There were commercials to make—without his brother, even—and many others coming, as experts estimated his endorsement income could swell to $10 million or more per year. And oh, by the way, there was also his wedding to his longtime girlfriend, Abby McGrew.

And there were two trips to the White House, too, including one where he got a twenty-five-minute audience with President Bush in the Oval Office, thanks to Eli's position on the President's Council on Physical Fitness and Sports. On the other trip, Eli was joined by his teammates on the South Lawn, flanked by the vice president and cheered by members of Congress. He was the one who presented President Bush with a signed Super Bowl ball.

"It's good to be up here with the Super Bowl MVP, Eli Manning," the president said. "We have a few things in common. Eli has a father and a brother in the same business he's in, (and) sometimes the press are skeptical."

Yes, even the commander in chief knew that Eli had been feeling the heat in New York. Everyone knew it. It had become an inescapable part of who everyone believed Eli was. That's why so many read so much into what Mara called "a pretty telling comment" that day on the Giants Stadium stage.

"I really don't honestly believe he feels, 'Screw you. I told you,'" Gilbride said. "I don't think that's in his makeup. I don't think he has the need to express that. Now, as a human being, he has to feel, 'I felt all along I could do this. I worked very hard for this to happen. I know there are a lot of you out there who did not necessarily feel that way.' I know he feels very good about the fact he was able to prove to people they were wrong. By his outward behavior you might not be able to sense that, but there's a burning desire to compete and prove that he's good.

"So I think that comment gave you a little feel. It's nice to know that you did it and know that you proved all the non-believers wrong."

Ask Eli about that, thought, and there's not a trace of a need for vindication in his voice or in his face. He has no need to stare down his legions of doubters, to say it out loud. If it's tempting at all, he won't admit it. If he found it ironic that fans who once booed him were now cheering him in restaurants and paying for his meals, he wouldn't say it. This was not a time for insults or chest-thumping, or saying, "Look, I was right."

That's not what winning the Super Bowl is all about.

"Winning a championship is bigger than that," Eli said. "It's not a payback or a 'Look at me now' situation. It's a great thing for yourself, but also for your teammates, your ownership, everybody. It's too big of a thing, too important of a thing to give a remark or a comeback. If it was something minor you could do it, but this is more important than that."

• • •

Accorsi felt the same way. On the morning after the Super Bowl, while most of the members of the Giants organization were packing for their trip home and shaking off their hangovers from a wild victory party, their former general manager was in the lobby

271

of the Sheraton Wild Horse Pass resort—the secluded hotel in the middle of the desert in Chandler, Arizona, that had housed the Giants all week. He was surrounded by a group of familiar New York sportswriters asking him to tell the story of his quarterback one more time. And during that half hour of part conversation, part interview, part trip down Memory Lane, he was asked the same question over and over again:

Do you feel vindicated now that your quarterback has won it all?

"I'm not saying that," Accorsi said. "That's for you guys to say that. I hate that word, you know?"

He meant it, too. He had taken plenty of abuse over the last four years. He had been ridiculed for paying so much for such a seemingly overrated quarterback. He was portrayed as obsessed and blinded by the Manning name. He was painted as a man whose career-long search for the next Unitas, the next Elway, caused him to reach too far for a quarterback who was going to destroy his legacy. But he didn't care then, and he didn't care now. Yes, he was proven right. Yes, his hand-picked quarterback had just won the Super Bowl at the tender age of twenty-seven.

What did you want him to do? Take a bow?

"I have a thick skin," Accorsi said. "To me, it's part of the job. So I don't get into that. I'm thrilled for him. He took more than I did. Sure, it's a great moment. But I don't have any vindictive feelings whatsoever. It was too great a moment to even think about that. And I'm not trying to be a phony. I don't live my life that way. I'm so happy, that I don't need that to make me any happier. I don't care. I'm not going to pile on."

Two months later, as he sat at that east side restaurant, his thoughts on that hadn't changed.

"The joy you feel is enough," Accorsi said. "You don't need a bonus of making other people look bad. What do you care?"

The joy Accorsi felt was everywhere he looked. It was in that napkin on which he made his brash guarantee that Eli would outdo Peyton in the end. It was in his memories of that frigid night in Oxford, Mississippi—the night where he first saw the greatness for himself. It was in the scouting report he later typed out, the one where he talked about the "magic" Eli had; the one where he compared him to Unitas and Montana; the one written in bold capital letters where he wrote, "I honestly give this guy a chance to be better than his brother."

"That's not a ridiculous statement anymore," Accorsi said. "If you look at what he's achieved, he's achieved everything faster. And I love his brother, don't get me wrong."

Accorsi's joy was right there on his voicemail, too—one special message among hundreds he received in the days after Super Bowl XLII. At first, he didn't recognize the voice of Jason Garrett, the Dallas Cowboys offensive coordinator and a backup quarterback on Accorsi's Giants from 2000–03.

His message was only one sentence long:

"Can the quarterback take his team down the field, with the championship on the line, and into the end zone?"

Accorsi couldn't help but smile. Finally, after nearly four decades of searching, he found one who could.

• • •

ELI DIDN'T GET much sleep on Super Sunday night. He described the hours after the game as "chaos" as he went around the locker room and then the hotel, trying to find and congratulate every teammate and coach he could. And when he went back to his hotel room, he couldn't help himself, really. He had to turn on the TV and watch, just to make sure it was real. He watched himself leading his team down the field and into the end zone with the championship on the line over and over and over again. And when he finally had seen it enough times, he laid in his bed with his eyes wide open, going over the whole Super Bowl again in his head.

The next morning he was whisked downtown to the Phoenix Convention Center where he was presented with his MVP trophy and a brand new car. He was asked to relive his moment of glory one more time, and to consider how his life was different now that he had fulfilled the unreasonable expectations that had always hovered over his head.

"I'm a Super Bowl champion," he said. "That's the difference. It doesn't change my attitude, my personality, or even my goals for next season. It's still the same."

In truth, though, everything had changed. He was a championship quarterback now, and would be forever. He had done it five years faster and at a younger age than his Hall of Fame–bound brother. Only twenty-seven quarterbacks had ever won a Super Bowl. Only seventeen had ever been named the Super Bowl MVP. He was all of a sudden the newest member of one of the most exclusive clubs on the planet. Things were bound to change.

Not everything, of course. A little more than a month after it was over, he was back at Giants Stadium, meeting with Palmer to discuss his goals for 2008. By Eli's count, he had met six of his eight individual goals in 2007, but now he had a much longer list. "I had to cut it off after a while," he said. "I said, 'I can't keep writing anymore.'" He considered his championship season nothing more than one month of good football. He wanted to do better than that.

"Some people might look at it and say, 'He's won a championship,'" Eli said. "But I guess it really doesn't matter what other people think. I still think I need to become a better quarterback."

"Yeah," Palmer added. "That sounds like Eli to me."

Of course, it was hard to blame him. Playing in the ultimate what-have-you-done-for-me-lately town, Eli knew his Super Bowl honeymoon would be short. As Mara said, a fresh set of boos was always right around the corner. It wasn't necessarily a long walk from Eli the Champion to Eli the Terrible again. And now the expectations were higher. Eli was no longer a struggling young quarterback. He had arrived.

So what could he do for an encore? Win back-to-back championships? Start a dynasty? Beat his brother in what suddenly seemed like an inevitable all-Manning Super Bowl? He fulfilled one set of expectations. Now it was time for another. Even his own brother, who had been so bothered by the pressure that was once heaped upon Eli's young shoulders, wasn't wary of turning the pressure up.

"I have to say that I feel strongly that this will not be the last Super Bowl that he will play in," Peyton said. "I just think he has what it takes to lead his team to championships. I've always thought he has that. I just don't think this will be the last one for him, I really don't."

What did Eli think about that? As usual there was no way to tell from the expression on his face or even the tone of his words. With people suddenly predicting multiple championships all around him, he was as completely and maddeningly unaffected as ever. If there was one thing he had grown accustomed to during his four years in New York, it was living in the shadow of unreal expectations.

After all, wasn't winning a Super Bowl championship exactly what he was drafted to do?

"I don't think I ever felt that way," Eli said. "From my point of view my goal was to win games for the Giants and become the best quarterback I could be. Obviously you want to win a championship. That's always the goal. But I don't think that has to put a mark on your career. Some great quarterbacks have never won a championship. It's not because they're not great quarterbacks or they didn't do everything they were supposed to do."

Of course, even Eli knows the truly great ones find a way when the game, the season, or the championship is on the line and he needs to get his team into the end zone one last time.

"If you're down and you've got a two-minute drive, you want a quarterback who feels confident and thinks it's a position he wants to be in," Eli said. "You want a quarterback who thinks this is where he's going to prove he's the right guy and that he can win the big game when it counts, when it matters."

Finally, after all those years, that's one thing Eli Manning doesn't have to prove anymore.

Twenty-Three: He is elite. Period.

THE HONEYMOON DIDN'T last very long after that first championship. In New York, it rarely does. It only took Eli Manning
through most of the season after Super Bowl XLII when he had
the Giants looking like the best team in football. They were 10-1
at one point in 2008, and looking like a budding dynasty. Then
Plaxico Burress shot himself in the leg at a nightclub in Manhattan
and the whole thing fell apart.

It wasn't Manning's fault, of course, but it wasn't long before the
lingering image wasn't of his miraculous charge to a Super Bowl
championship, but of how he couldn't pull his powerful team back
from the abyss after Burress was gone. What New York seemed to
remember was that the 2008 Giants were the No. 1 seed in the
NFC, and then opened the playoffs by losing at home to the rival
Philadelphia Eagles. The magic of 2007 had already started to fade
away.

The next two years didn't turn out much better—his team
missed the playoffs twice, collapsing at the end of both seasons—
and suddenly Manning seemed to be right back where he started,
caught somewhere between good and great, but not really being
accepted as either. Maybe it was naïve to think that one championship would settle all doubts and turn a legion of doubters into
believers. Maybe it was too idealistic to think the Super Bowl XLII
championship would catapult him to the upper echelon of quarter-

backs. Four years after that remarkable night in Glendale, Arizona, he still seemed to be absolutely nowhere at times. The gaudy championship ring on his finger had become more like a flash of his potential. A tease.

He had become a better quarterback over the years, though. No one doubted that. Since his Super Bowl MVP performance, his numbers had gone up significantly. He became a 4,000-yard passer. He would complete more than 60 percent of his passes in each of the next four seasons. He was clearly a better player. Most people placed him squarely in the top ten.

Still, he was no Peyton. He was no Tom Brady, or Drew Brees, or Ben Roethlisberger, who at the end of the 2008 season had won his second Super Bowl ring. He wasn't even Green Bay's Aaron Rodgers, the new kid on the block who jumped Eli's place in line with his own remarkable run to a title in 2010.

Eli remained inconsistent and erratic. For every two good things he did, he managed to do something bad. The proof was in his 2010 season, when he had impressive numbers—a career-best completion percentage of 62.9, 4,002 yards, and a career-high in touchdown passes (31)—but he also failed to lead his ten-win team to the playoffs, and led the league in interceptions with twenty-five.

By now, Eli Manning had completed seven NFL seasons. There was no more waiting for him to come of age. He was of age. The general consensus was that this was the Eli we'd always see. Good, but not great. Top ten, but not elite.

And as the Super Bowl XLII championship faded into the distance, more and more people chose to remember how the Giants' defense and its incredible pass rush were really responsible for that run.

Maybe that's why everyone was so stunned on August 16, 2011, when Eli made one of his regular weekly appearances on ESPN

Radio's *The Michael Kay Show* in New York. At first, it was hardly even noticed. Given his penchant for milquetoast answers, it was hardly a must-listen segment. Eli had mastered the art of answering questions without creating news.

So no one was expecting a direct or headline-making answer when Kay said to him, "I'll ask you straight out: Is Eli Manning an 'elite' quarterback? Are you a top five, top ten quarterback?"

But Eli did not back down. Without a moment of hesitation, he stepped way out of his usual bland character and said, "Yeah, I think I am."

Then Kay pushed him even further. He asked Eli, coming off a year filled with those twenty-five interceptions, if he considered himself to be in the same class as Tom Brady—a future Hall of Famer with three Super Bowl rings, two Super Bowl MVP trophies, two MVP trophies, and six trips to the Pro Bowl.

Manning's response was stunning: "I consider myself in that class."

"And Tom Brady is a great quarterback," Manning said. "He's a great player and what you've seen with him is he's gotten better every year. He started off and was winning championships and I think he's a better quarterback now than what he was, in all honesty, when he was winning those championships.

"It's funny. You say, 'Well, he won championships.' But I think now he's grown up and gotten better every year and that's what I'm trying to do. I kind of hope these next seven years of my quarterback days are my best."

In the months that followed, everything Manning did would be measured up against those words. A debate raged in New York City and around the country about whether he really was what he thought he was—whether he was really "elite." Manning would be asked about his words constantly and his response was always the same: "What was I supposed to say?"

"I thought I gave an honest answer," Manning said months later. "I didn't regret it at the time or think anything of it at the time. Obviously it's been made into a big deal, but I can't always control that."

Except that he always has. The Manning image has been carefully crafted and protected across generations. He knew there were a million less-controversial ways to answer those questions, and in the past he would've taken any other one.

Manning had always shown his teammates a uniquely quiet confidence, especially in the face of difficult situations. But for the first time, for whatever reason, he was willing to show them something else.

He showed them swagger.

"It means a lot," said safety Antrel Rolle, one of Manning's most-outspoken teammates. "It lets me know what kind of guy we have leading this team. Eli is the leader of this team, without a doubt. He is an elite quarterback. I don't think that needs any further discussion. I think he's definitely proven himself. I think he's proven himself before this year, to be honest with you. But being a part of this league, you have to go through your ups and downs, your criticism, speculation of what people may think, what they might not think. But when it's all said and done you have to know yourself. You just have to believe within yourself. And that's what he does."

Manning may have believed, but his numbers had sprouted doubters—particularly those twenty-five interceptions, which included at least eight catchable passes that deflected off of his own receivers' hands. In that same radio interview, Manning defiantly insisted that those numbers were an aberration.

"I'm not a twenty-five-interception quarterback, I know that," Manning said. "That's going to get fixed and it should be a good year."

Unfortunately for Eli, the 2011 season didn't start out that way. He didn't throw a touchdown pass in the Giants' regular-season opener and was badly out-played by Rex Grossman—no one's idea of an "elite" quarterback, by any measure. Then, in week two, the Giants beat the St. Louis Rams, but Eli was still out-played by Sam Bradford, one of the many young quarterbacks seemingly getting ready to jump over him on the charts. Two weeks into the season and Eli was good, but not great. He was exactly what he had always been.

No one was surprised, either, because of the way the season had begun with the offense disintegrating around him. The first thing the Giants had done after the five-month-long NFL lockout ended was cut veteran offensive linemen Shaun O'Hara and Rich Seubert. Then they let Pro Bowl receiver Steve Smith sign with the Eagles and tight end Kevin Boss sign with the Raiders. They even flirted with a reunion with Burress, fresh out of the prison sentence he served for that infamous nightclub shooting, but the Giants let him sign with the Jets instead.

Yes, Manning still had emerging star receiver Hakeem Nicks at his disposal, and Mario Manningham was more than a solid secondary target. But he was suddenly stuck behind a patchwork offensive line; his starting tight end, Jake Ballard, was a player who made the NFL out of Ohio State for his blocking ability; and his third receiver was an undrafted kid out of UMass who had one big preseason game on his resume—Victor Cruz.

Manning knew a secret, though. During the final days of the lockout, in the hopes that football would soon return, the quarterback had arranged six hour-long workouts, mostly in the rain, at Hoboken High School in New Jersey. He invited most of his receivers, running backs, and tight ends, but only a few showed up.

One of them was Cruz, the kid from Paterson, New Jersey, who was there almost every day. And as Manning said, "We got close."

The closeness paid off in a week three game in Philadelphia, when Cruz had to fill in for the injured Manningham. His break-out play came on a short pass where Cruz bounced off Eagles safety Kurt Coleman and then made cornerback Nnamdi Asomugha miss. When the two defensive backs collided behind him, Cruz flew down the sidelines for a 74-yard touchdown.

He ended up with three catches for 110 yards and two touch-downs, and just like that, a new dynamic duo was born. Cruz, who later admitted that his goal heading into the season was just "to make a catch in a game that mattered," finished the season with eighty-two catches in regular-season games that mattered for a franchise-record 1,536 yards and nine touchdowns. Ballard, the blocking tight end who had never had an NFL catch either, caught thirty-eight passes for 604 yards and would've had more if he hadn't injured his knee in week fourteen.

Manning was doing something great quarterbacks are supposed to do—he was making his teammates better. He didn't complain that he was backed by what was statistically the worst rushing attack in the NFL, or a defense that was collapsing under the weight of a mountain of injuries (including the loss of two starters—middle linebacker Jonathan Goff and cornerback Terrell Thomas—during the preseason) and ranked just twenty-seventh in the NFL. He did what those other "elite" quarterbacks had always done—the one thing no one accused him of doing during the run to Super Bowl XLII: He put the team on his back and carried them to the finish line.

And for a long time, it really was all him. Five times in the regular season, Manning led the Giants back from a fourth-quarter deficit to a victory. Once, in a remarkable 24–20 win over the New England Patriots in Foxborough, Massachusetts, on November 6, he actually had to come back late in the game twice.

He nearly led them to other comebacks, too, like when the Giants fell to the undefeated Green Bay Packers, 38–35, on December 4, on a Mason Crosby field goal with no time remaining. Or three weeks earlier in San Francisco, when he had a final, game-tying touchdown pass deflected at the line of scrimmage in the final seconds, sealing a 27–20 loss to the 49ers.

Manning was backing up his brash words, and then some. He was putting on an aerial show no one could have anticipated. He completed 61 percent of his passes and shattered the Giants' single-season mark with 4,933 passing yards. He had twenty-nine touchdowns, too, and dropped his interceptions all the way down to sixteen.

The book on the Giants was simple: When Eli was on, they had a chance. When he wasn't, they were in trouble. Just like the analysts always said about Brady, Peyton, and Brees, Eli was the team. And yes, when they were struggling at 7–7 after an ugly home loss to the Washington Redskins in week fifteen—a game in which an erratic Eli briefly resurfaced to throw three interceptions—everyone knew he'd need help if they were going to make another unlikely run to a championship.

But this time it was clear he wouldn't just be along for the ride.

Actually, that was never a fair description of what happened in 2007, according to players and coaches from that team. They swear that the younger Manning was never just being carried to a title by his teammates. He may not have had the flashy stats back then, and the offense might have been simplified so he could manage the game better during the playoffs, but his coaches always said he never got enough credit for what he did during that entire miraculous run.

"I don't think people realize what he did for the offense back then," said Chris Palmer, who was Eli's quarterbacks coach back then and is now the offensive coordinator of the Tennessee Titans. "That was the year where we were running the ball pretty well. He always did a tremendous job of getting the line into the right blocking scheme and the right angles, which wasn't apparent to the normal fans. He would check into the right plays. He would run plays away from the blitzes.

"I think this year the fact that he threw the ball fifty-eight times in San Francisco (in the NFC Championship game), makes the average fan say 'Whoa! Wait, he did carry the team.' But I think he's doing the same thing that he did back in '07."

Perhaps that's true, but this time around he did it on another level. In a winner-take-all season finale against the Dallas Cowboys, he helped the Giants clinch the NFC East and a playoff spot by completing 72.7 percent of his passes (24 of 33) for 346 yards and three touchdowns. In four postseason games, he had nine touchdown passes and just one interception, and his lowest passing total was 277 yards.

And each performance seemed to be more impressive than the last. He returned to Green Bay, the site of the 2007 NFC Championship game, for the divisional playoffs against a Packers team that had won twenty-one of its last twenty-two games. Against Rodgers, the reigning Super Bowl MVP and soon to be the NFL's MVP, Manning was the better quarterback, completing 21 of 33 passes for 330 yards and three touchdowns. Rodgers completed 26 of 46 for 264 yards and two touchdowns and struggled to connect with open receivers throughout the entire game.

One week later, in a driving rain and on a muddy field in San Francisco, Eli took a beating in the NFC Championship game. He was sacked six times, hit countless more, and still stood in there to hit 32 of those 58 passes for 316 yards and two touchdowns. He played a strong game in ridiculous conditions—not unlike his performance in frigid Green Bay in the NFC Championship game four years earlier—and he kept the Giants alive until the 49ers made the key mistake that turned the game. It came in overtime, on a fumbled punt return by Kyle Williams, who was starting in place of the injured Ted Ginn Jr., which set up a game-winning, overtime field goal by Lawrence Tynes.

For Tynes, it was his second NFC Championship-winning overtime field goal in four years. But the Giants knew it was Eli Manning's toughness that really won them that game.

"When people talk about toughness, they talk about linebackers or a fullback—they don't think of the quarterback," said offensive coordinator Kevin Gilbride. "But the willingness to stand in there and focus on your job, which is delivering the pass, and knowing that you're going to get hit is a different kind of courage. And Eli definitely possesses it."

"A lot of people question, just because of the facial expressions that he may make, how much fight does he have? How tough is he?" Rolle added. "Let's put it this way: If he can handle and withstand what he did going up against the 49ers and their front seven, you can't question his toughness."

There was still one more question for Eli to answer, though, because—wouldn't you know it?—after all this time, Tom Brady was the last man standing in his way. They were facing each other again, truly in a class by themselves, getting ready to play Super Bowl XLVI in Indianapolis—Peyton's hometown, just to add to the juicy storyline. A season that had mirrored 2007 for the Giants in so many eerie ways was about to end with the eeriest similarity of all: A rematch of one of the greatest Super Bowls ever played.

Eli stood toe-to-toe with Brady for most of the game, just like he had done four years earlier. He set a Super Bowl record by completing nine straight passes to open the game. Then, Brady would set his own Super Bowl record later by completing sixteen straight. They would battle back and forth, just like they did in Super Bowl XLII, until Manning found his team trailing 17–9 in the third quarter and then 17–15 when the fourth quarter began.

Then history repeated itself in the most incredible fashion imaginable. One more time, Eli Manning—already with six fourth-quarter comebacks during the season and twenty-one in his career—found himself jogging out onto the field, just like he did in Super Bowl XLII, with the ball in his hands and the game on the line. He had the ball deep in his own territory—this time at the twelve-yard line—with 3:46 to play.

Time for one last championship-winning drive.

It started with some magic, too. Patriots coach Bill Belichick huddled his defense on the sidelines and told them, "This is still a Cruz and Nicks game. I know we're right on them. It's tight, but those are still the guys. Make them go to Manningham."

And so he did. On the first play of the drive, Eli fired a pass deep down the left sidelines that Manningham caught just before he tapped both his feet barely in bounds. The Patriots challenged the thirty-eight-yard reception, but the replay was clear, and as Cruz watched it from midfield, he gave voice to the sequence: "Catch… right…left…Yes!"

That was the drive-saving, David Tyree-like moment, and from there it seemed all too easy. The only difference this time was that the drive didn't end with the joy the Giants experienced in Super Bowl XLII, when Burress caught the game-winning touchdown pass with just thirty-five seconds remaining. This time, the game-winner was an awkward moment, when Ahmad Bradshaw literally fell into the end zone when he was trying not to score.

The Giants had hoped to take their time and kick a game-winning field goal, but when Bradshaw's momentum carried him across the goal line, the Giants feared they had left too much time on the clock. There were fifty-seven seconds this time—twenty-two more than Brady had four years earlier. But Brady couldn't get the Patriots beyond the 50 yard line, leaving him with one last desperation Hail Mary pass.

It hung in the air for what seemed like forever. Some players closed their eyes on the bench. John Mara, the Giants' co-owner, was in his box, rubbing the same little medal of the Blessed Virgin that he was rubbing four years earlier—the one that had been sent to him by the nun he knew from Rye, New York. He tried to breathe, but he couldn't.

"That would've been a horrible way to lose the game," he said.

Then Giants safety Kenny Phillips leaped into the air and batted the Hail Mary pass harmlessly out of the way.

Then came the celebration...again. The confetti...again. Players running around the field looking for someone to hug...again. It was another championship they never saw coming, and one nearly as miraculous as the first.

"To get one Super Bowl win in the manner that we got it four years ago usually lasts a whole career," said Giants co-owner John Mara. "But to get two of these? It is beyond description. It really is."

The question now is this: What will this mean for the legacy of Eli Manning? After that first Super Bowl championship, Ernie Accorsi, the former Giants general manager who brought Eli to the Giants back in 2004, swore that someday the quarterback he waited his entire career for would eventually end up with more championships than his Hall of Fame-bound brother. And with Peyton's career in limbo at age thirty-five after recent neck surgeries, and Eli feeling healthy and four years younger, Accorsi might already be right.

Two rings have also always been a quarterback's ticket into the Pro Football Hall of Fame. Only Jim Plunkett finished his career with two championships and didn't end up with a bust in Canton. The second ring might have vaulted Eli beyond the "elite" level.

It might be enough to make him a football immortal.

Whatever the final judgment is on his career, though, it will certainly be hard for anyone to question Eli Manning now. He's just won his second Super Bowl and his second Super Bowl MVP, and both have come against arguably the greatest team and quarterback of this generation.

How could any of his doubters argue with that?

"I don't think that's the story," Manning said after the game. "I think the story is the New York Giants are World Champions. That's what I'm proud of. That's all that matters. The only important thing is for this organization—the Giants, these guys that are on this team, the coaches—[to have] an opportunity to say, 'We are the World Champions.' That's the story."

Maybe it really will be that simple from now on, though it rarely ever has been for Eli Manning. One Super Bowl championship wasn't enough to convince his critics. Surely, he still has some doubters after two.

None of them are in the Giants organization, though, where Accorsi's big draft day trade is hailed as one of the greatest moments the franchise has ever had. It was the moment that led to two of the four Vince Lombardi Trophies that now sit in a glass case in their lobby. Eli Manning is on his way to becoming the greatest quarterback in Giants history, and no one in the organization would dispute that.

So let others wonder if Eli is "elite" or if he belongs in the "top five" of his generation.

The Giants have him forever ranked higher than that.

"He's never, ever been anything less than top one to me," said Tom Coughlin. "And that's all I care about. He is elite. Period."

Acknowledgments

WE USED TO joke in the press room at Giants Stadium about who Ernie Accorsi would mention first in his annual pre-draft press conference—John Elway, Bernie Kosar, Bert Jones, or Johnny Unitas. He'd certainly never mention the name of a player in the upcoming draft, but he had a knack for relating almost every question to a story about old times—and old quarterbacks—in the NFL.

I don't want Ernie to think that all we did was laugh. I listened and absorbed every old story, and it was from those tales that I got the original idea for this book. I'm forever grateful for that, as I am for his brilliantly written foreword and for his willingness to interrupt his retirement to tell me a little more.

Every person quoted in this book deserves to be thanked, along with many other sources that aren't named. I'm particularly grateful to a couple of former Giants quarterbacks and Sirius radio colleagues—Jim Miller and Tim Hasselbeck—for sharing their thoughts and insights of what they saw in Eli up close and behind the scenes. John Mara deserves my gratitude, too, for giving me a peek inside his organization on many different occasions during Eli Manning's career.

When the Super Bowl ended and this book became a reality, it became a mad dash for the finish line. As I researched the details of Eli's four-year career I leaned heavily on the reporting of my colleagues at the New York *Daily News*—Rich Cimini, Hank Gola, Gary Myers, and Ohm Youngmisuk. There's not a finer group of football writers anywhere in the country. The Giants' great public relations staff—including Pat Hanlon, Peter John-Baptiste, and Avis Roper—was also a huge help in quickly getting me the information and interviews I needed. Getting me access to their assistant coaches and team executives while they were busy preparing for the NFL draft was quite a coup.

I owe some thanks, too, to Eli Manning and his entire family, who have been nothing but a pleasure to cover for the last four years. At times, I was one of his critics and his interrogators, not that it ever seemed to matter to him. I even wrote the game story that got the back page headline "Eli the Terrible." None of that ever stopped him from being a willing and polite interview subject for me. I've spent countless hours with him over the course of his career, and he's a true professional who rarely ever leaves before the last question is asked and answered. Clearly the apple didn't fall far from the tree. His father, Archie, and brothers, Peyton and Cooper, are the same way.

Thanks also to my agent, Shari Wenk, who never gave up on a project that started three years ago, and helped push it (and me) along even during those days when the quarterback I wanted to write about hardly seemed worthy of a book. And thanks to the good people at Skyhorse Publishing—particularly my editor, Mark Weinstein, and publisher, Tony Lyons—for believing in this project even before Eli won his Super Bowl ring.

Finally, on a much more personal note, writing this book has been the culmination of a lifelong goal, and it never would have happened without the love and support of my mother Carole, my father Ralph Sr., and my sister Janice. There aren't enough pages here for me to thank them enough.

And no one deserves more thanks than by beautiful wife, Kara, and my wonderful daughter, Alexandra, for the way they stood by me and supported me, especially during the sprint to the finish. Thank you both for helping make my dreams come true—and I don't just mean this book.

About the Author

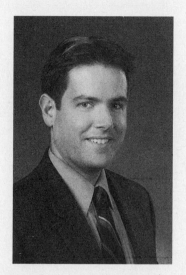

RALPH VACCHIANO IS an award-winning sportswriter for the New York *Daily News*, where he has worked since 1997. The Giants' Super Bowl championship–winning 2007 season was his eleventh covering the team (seventh at the *Daily News*) and his thirteenth covering the NFL. He's also a regular host on Sirius NFL radio, where he co-hosts *Press Pass*. And he's a regular panelist on SportsNet New York's *Daily News Live*.

Born in Brooklyn, New York, and raised on Long Island, he graduated from Syracuse University in 1991 and began his professional career covering the Buffalo Bills for the *Niagara Gazette* in Niagara Falls, New York. After two seasons there, he spent four years covering the Giants and the NFL for the *North Jersey Herald*

& News in Passaic, New Jersey. In 1997 he was hired by the *Daily News* to cover hockey—first the New York Islanders, then the New Jersey Devils—before returning to football in 2001.

He lives with his wife, Kara, and his daughter, Alexandra, in West Caldwell, New Jersey.